Day by Day with Saint Augustine

Day by Day
with Saint Augustine

Donald X. Burt, O.S.A.

LITURGICAL PRESS
Collegeville, Minnesota

www.litpress.org

Cover design by Joachim Rhoades, O.S.B. *Saint Augustine* by Antonello da Messina (?1430–1479). Photo credit: Scala / Art Resource, NY.

Library of Congress Cataloging-in-Publication Data

Burt, Donald X.
    Day by day with Saint Augustine / Donald X. Burt.
      p. cm.
    Cover title: Day by day with Saint Augustine.
    Summary: "A series of reflections for each day of the year based on thoughts from St. Augustine and the author's consideration of them; reflections include: the ever-moving life of the individual, the search for God, the mystery of oneself, the glory and troubles of being human, sin, immortality, love, the search for peace, etc."— Provided by publisher.
    Includes bibliographical references and index.
    ISBN-13: 978-0-8146-1519-5 (pbk. : alk. paper)
    ISBN-10: 0-8146-1519-8 (pbk. : alk. paper)
      1. Devotional calendars—Catholic Church. 2. Catholic Church—Prayer-books and devotions—English. 3. Spiritual life—Catholic Church. 4. Augustine, Saint, Bishop of Hippo. I. Title. II. Title: Day by day with Saint Augustine.

BX2170.C56B87 2006
242'.2—dc22

                              2005006661

Contents

Introduction

The pages that follow contain reflections from Saint Augustine on the troubles and travails of this life and the wonder of the life to come as described in the teachings of Jesus Christ. He is a fitting commentator on both aspects of human life.

Augustine was born in the fourth century in North Africa of a dedicated Christian mother and a happily pagan father. He grew into an adult with little or no faith in anything. He had an eleven-year relationship with a good woman, and by her had a child. Eventually he sent her away when she seemed to be an obstacle to his career. He was a teacher who had trouble controlling his students and eventually gave up that profession to become a speech-writer at the Imperial Court. After years of wandering, he rediscovered Christ in his early thirties and was baptized. For the next forty years he served the church in North Africa as a parish priest, bishop, and confidant of the humble and the powerful. He preached to his parish congregation every day for forty years. Finally, as he lay dying, he could hear pagan hordes pounding on the gates of his beloved city.

There was little in the human experience that he did not himself experience and comment on. I am convinced that his words have as much meaning today as they had in the fifth century. The selections are far from a word-for-word translation of his writing, but I believe they are faithful to the sense of the original text. If they disturb some, please blame me and not him.

The following sources were especially useful in writing this book: *Sermons*, The Works of Saint Augustine, trans. Edmund Hill (New Rochelle, N.Y.: New City Press); *Exposition of the Psalms*, The Works of Saint Augustine, trans. Maria Boulding (New Rochelle, N.Y.: New City Press); *Tractates on the Gospel of*

John 112–24: Tractates on the First Epistle of John, trans. John W. Wettig (Washington, D.C.: Catholic University of America Press); and various other excellent translations of Augustine done over the years in the Fathers of the Church series.

Donald X. Burt, O.S.A.

January 1

A Flowing Life

As a torrent gathers together from the rains and then overflows, roaring down the slope as it hastens to finish its course, so too does our life rush away just now. The human race is collected together from hidden sources and begins to flow on, traveling through death to new hidden places. This fleeting state that is now our life roars and passes away.

Commentary on Psalm 109, 20

On New Year's Day Augustine's analogy for life as a flowing river seems quite appropriate. Whether my life just now is bad or good, one thing is certain: I am moving on. Experience tells me that I am rushing towards death. For a good period of his early life Augustine believed that death was the end. But then he rediscovered the Christ he had known as a child and flew with him to the heights of time and peeked into eternity. Looking down from his lofty perch on the arm of God, he saw his earthly life as it truly was, a river rushing not simply towards death but through death into an eternal life beyond. The consoling message of our faith is that indeed we are rushing through life but our destiny is not death. It is resurrection.

January 2

We Are Our Times

"The times are troubled! The times are bad!" This is what we humans say. But we are our times. If only we would live properly, our times would be good. Such as *we* are, such are our times.

Sermon 80, 8

The constant challenge of human life is to survive the times of our lives. We are immortal. We shall live forever whether we want to or not; but to truly survive our times now means to value our present times. It also means that we must endure our bad times with as much hope and joy as we can. We develop such endurance through the message of our faith that Jesus Christ still walks through this world, as mixed up and as troublesome as it may sometimes be. No matter how good or bad our times may be now, the most important fact is that we humans are on the move with Jesus. We are no longer stuck in one place. We are on the move again towards that place where finally and forever we shall be at home with our flesh and blood, Jesus Christ the Lord.

January 3

Hold on to Christ

The river of worldly affairs sweeps us along but Jesus our Lord stands like a strong tree on the banks of the rushing waters. In a manner of speaking, he chose to "plant" himself close by the river of our passing times. True, we are still tossed about in the whirling waters but we have now a place on land to anchor our hope.

Commentary on the Epistle of John, 2.10

The paradox of our lives is that we are constantly in motion while seeking to be still. As soon as we think we have finally found a stable life, everything changes. We do everything we can to stay well only to get sick. We do everything we can to hold onto our loved ones only to have them leave us in death. We do everything we can to hold onto that great job or great career through which we have made our mark on the world, only to be told one day that we are redundant. Such change is part of life, but it would be pleasant to find something on which we could "anchor" our hopes. Augustine suggests that Christ is that unchanging reality. If we listen carefully, we can hear Christ whispering to us, "I am here and I will never leave you in time or eternity!"

January 4

My Love Is My Weight

A "weight" in a body is not necessarily a tendency to seek the lowest level but rather to seek its proper place. Thus, fire rises upward; a stone falls downward. They are moved by their weights to seek their proper place. In my case, my "weight" is my love. By my love I am drawn wherever I go.

Confessions, 13.9.10

All of us, as creatures with bodies, are subject to the law of gravity. Tripping on a stone, we have no choice but to fall down. But since we are also spiritual beings we are able to have some control over the direction of our life. Love is the force that moves us this way or that (our spiritual "gravity," if you will). When we perceive something that seems "good for us," we are drawn towards it, by our emerging love. All things that exist in nature are "good" because they reflect the goodness of their Creator, but unfortunately this does not mean that they are "good for us." We sometimes choose the wrong "good." Indeed, most of the mess in our lives comes from loves that have gone awry. It follows that the challenge of life, by God's grace, is to choose only those "goods" the possession of which will bring us closer to our eternal destiny in our proper place in the arms of God.

January 5

Love and Do Whatever You Will

The love of God consists in keeping these commandments: "You must love God with your whole heart and
soul and mind. You must love your neighbor as yourself"
(Matthew 22:37). If you love properly, it is impossible to
do anything evil. Love . . . and then do whatever you
will. From the root of love only good can grow.

Commentary on the Epistle of John, 10.7.1

Some critics in Augustine's day were upset by his words
"Love and do what you will." In their mind he seemed to be
saying, "If only you do something out of love, then whatever
you do cannot be evil." Of course this is not what Augustine
meant. What he was saying was that, if we love in such a way
that the two great commandments—love of God and love of
neighbor—are fulfilled, then our actions cannot help but be
good. He also was saying good acts that come from evil intentions are not in fact good. God wants us to act out of love as a
means of observing his two great commandments of love. If
we could do that then our salvation would be assured.

January 6

Reaching for the Stars

The life of a good Christian is driven by desire for the
holy. In this life none of us see what we long for but the
very act of desire prepares us so that when God finally
comes we are able to see and be completely satisfied.

Commentary on the Epistle of John, 4.6

The burden and blessing of being human is that we are born with a longing to be more than we are, to fly far above this earth and reach the stars. Deep down, all of us desire to escape the narrow confines of our life and soar to something better. In light of this, Augustine says that, in our restless search for a joyful life, we finally realize that we must go beyond ourselves in order to find such happiness (*Sermon 399*, 6). The hopeful message of the Christian Faith is that, although our dream of reaching the stars in this life may never be fulfilled, we have the power, by the grace of God, to reach the stars that lie just beyond the borders of this life. In the meantime the brilliance of God shines on us even here.

January 7

Let Me Know Myself; Let Me Know You

O unchanging God, this is my prayer: let me know myself and let me know you.

Soliloquies, 2.1.1

Soon after his baptism, in his early thirties, Augustine asked himself what he most needed to know in order to achieve heaven. His answer was, "I need to know who I am; I need to know who God is." He was convinced that if he could discover the truth about himself and God, then the path to heaven would become clear. He recognized that one must know many things to get through life; but, most importantly, he recognized the ultimate truth of knowing oneself and God. Indeed, it is in our knowledge of God that we come to know ourselves, and become perfected. Each of us, however, comes to know God in a unique way, in ways that are uniquely fitted to one's own self. Augustine spent most of his life delving into the mystery of his self and God, and the knowledge he gained, spare as it might be, was for him more precious than anything else he knew.

January 8

The Mystery of My "Self"

O Lord, only you know what I am. Even though Paul said, "No man knows what he is in himself except through his own spirit" (1 Corinthians 2:11), there is much that my spirit does not know about my true "self."

Confessions, 10.5.7

Augustine's prayer "Let me know myself!" is a difficult wish to fulfill. There is a darkness inside each of us that cannot easily be penetrated. As Augustine admitted, "To some extent I may be able to discover what I am today but what I shall be tomorrow I do not know" (*Sermon 179,* 10). Once I begin the journey to find myself, I understand the truth to his observation that within the self there is an abyss deeper than any sea (*Commentary on Psalm 41,* 14; *Commentary on Psalm 76,* 18). Like Augustine, I discover that the place within the depths of my self has facets and passages beyond my wildest dreams (*Confessions,* 10.17.26). Such a self is difficult to know. Still, despite the distress it may cause, my search for self must be done. Unless I am able to find the true "me," there is little in me to be loved by others. Without some honest discovery of my self, there will be no "me" to be loved. I will be an empty shell of no importance.

We Are "Cracked"

Many people promise themselves that they will live a holy life but they fail because they have been put into the furnace and have come out *cracked!*

Commentary on Psalm 99, 11

The humbling fact about being human is that we are all like pots that have been kept in the oven too long. We have come into the world "cracked" in one way or another and, despite our occasional delusions of grandeur, we remain cracked pots. These cracks show themselves primarily in our confused mind and weak will. As Augustine told his listeners,

> Either you don't know what you should do or, if you do know, you discover that you are too weak to do it. Such confusion and weakness is the root of every evil that we humans do.
>
> *Sermon 182, 6*

At the same time, there are good reasons for hope. Jesus is not only our Lord God, he is also our doctor. He comes not to condemn us but to heal us. As Augustine says:

> The important thing is not to give up while the healing is going on. Remember that Jesus loved you when there was little lovely about you at all. Can you imagine what he will do for you when you are finally healed, considering that he died for you when you were still warped and ugly?
>
> *Sermon 142, 2-7*

January 10

The Value of Being Human

> Considering that as God planned the universe not even one leaf on a tree is wasteful, it is not possible that any human being be without importance.
>
> *On Freedom of the Will, 3.23.66*

Considering how we are sometimes ignored as we go through life, it is sometimes hard to believe that we are worth anything at all. When people look through us and beyond us as we talk to them, we may come to believe that we are of no account because no one seems to take account of us. In such situations all we can do is to try to get beyond the humiliation and reach out in faith. It was because of his Christian Faith that Augustine (in the name of the human race) could humbly brag:

> We are made in the image of God and that same God who made us human became human himself for our sake. The blood of God's only Son was poured out for us so that all of us might become God's children.
>
> *Commentary on Psalm 32/2, #4*

Granted that all humans are reflections of God, why am *I* so important, considering that there are so many others more gifted and virtuous people? The answer is that I am unique. I must be important to God because otherwise I would not have been called into existence. Small as I may be, and cracked as I am, without me the universe would be lacking that special color of God's presence that my unimpressive life provides. On days when I feel dull and unimportant, I think of that and am consoled.

January 11

The Search for God

Late have I loved you, O Beauty ever ancient yet ever new, late have I loved you! You were here inside me all the time as I was running around outside looking for you.

Confessions, 10.27

There is no handbook on how to find God. All we can do is establish the conditions for finding him. First of all, we must be free of earthly interests that rob us of time and energy needed for our search. We need to try to reserve some quiet time in our busy lives because, more often than not, God speaks to us in the way he spoke to the prophet Elijah (1 Kings 19:11-13)—in a gentle breeze, rather than a violent wind. If there is too much noise in our lives, we will not hear his words. As Augustine discovered, we need not travel to some foreign land to find the Lord. If we wait patiently, he will come to us and speak to us in the midst of our ordinary days. We are nailed in the place given to us by the Providence of God, nailed to that special cross that is our life. All we can do is wait in place and turn our head in his direction. We must try to imitate Dismas on his Calvary cross, turning his head towards the suffering Jesus with a prayer that he might be taken with him into eternity.

January 12

What Is God Like?

Certainly it is a great bliss to have a little knowledge about God; but to completely understand him, to comprehend him, is altogether impossible.

Sermon 117, 5

In our attempt to discover something about our God, there are two sorts of questions that can be asked. One question is, "what is the nature of God?" Augustine responds that it is easier to say what God is not, than what he is (*Commentary on Psalm 85*, 12). In answer to the second question, "What is God like?", we have the advantage of looking at the life of the God/ man, Jesus, and listening to the stories he told about God, especially the story of the Prodigal Son (Luke 15:11-32). The consoling message of the story is that God is a father who will throw a party for a returning child who had foolishly wandered far away, and he is also a father who can patiently endure a sulking child who stays at home. We do not know what happened to the two boys after the party was over. But there is one thing we do know about the father in the story and, by inference, our God: he will always be ready to take back any of his children who return asking forgiveness.

January 13

Knowing God through Jesus

The most important reason for Christ's coming was that people might know how much God loves them and, once knowing the depth of God's love, they might begin to burn with love for this God who loved them first. Following Christ's commandments to love and his example, they might then come to love their neighbor. Indeed, Jesus Christ, by loving even those who were wandering far from him, has become a neighbor to all of us.

On Catechizing the Uninstructed, 4.8

All of us seek something to believe in, something that will make sense of our lives. This is the force that drives many to search for God. But, to be honest, it is hard to know much about a God who is a spirit far above us. As a young man, before his conversion to Christianity, Augustine was inconsolable after the death of a dear friend. He sadly admitted that his dead friend was more real to him that this "God" about whom others spoke. The mystery of God was lessened when he came to believe in Jesus Christ as God incarnate walking the paths of this earth. His discovery that Jesus was not only a human being to be revered, but a God to be worshipped and followed, gave him the direction he so desperately sought in life. Through his passionate search for answers, Augustine discovered Jesus-God and through that discovery he discovered hope.

January 14

The Nature of Faith

To have Faith means only this: to think with assent.

Predestination of the Saints, 2.5

Augustine's cryptic definition of faith points to a truth that becomes quite evident when you begin to think about it. Faith is both a "thinking" and a "choosing" but the driving force in coming to believe requires an act of the will. Put simply, to believe in something we must choose to believe. This is so because every act of faith involves a "leap into darkness." To believe means to embrace something that we have never directly experienced ourselves, something that we come to know only through the testimony of others. The act of faith does not rest on evidence of the event so much as evidence supporting the reliability of the witness who tells us about the event. However faith still involves thinking. It is not an ecstatic movement of the emotions, a good feeling for no good reason. Faith is an exercise of the mind, a judgment that this indeed is so. Although the content of faith—the *what* we know—resides in the mind, the act of faith—the *that* we know—is an act of the will whereby we choose to believe. However, we do not choose anything unless we desire it. In matters of God and our eternal salvation it is only through the grace of God that this desire grows in us and moves us to believe.

January 15

The Reasonableness of Faith

Without faith we would not know about foreign lands and cities. We would not know facts about the past. We would not know what is happening now without the news of the world that is daily brought to us by those who report it. Without believing others we would not even know where we were born or who our parents were. Obviously it would be absurd to deny that we know such things because we learned them by believing in others.

The Trinity, 15.12.21

To those who proclaim, "I will not accept any fact that I have not experienced myself," Augustine responds that this is simply nonsense. Most of our day-to-day knowledge comes to us through faith. Except for a few direct experiences (which in themselves might be questionable) and a few basic truths from mathematics and philosophy, all of my knowledge rests on faith in the testimony of others. Others must tell me about those many lands I have never seen. Doctors must tell me what is wrong with me when I get sick. Trustworthy prophets are my only source for knowledge about a future that I have yet to live. Faith in supernatural truths—the existence of God who loves me; the existence of the heaven he prepares for me—are certainly more important matters than the pedestrian things I must believe in order to get through the day. But such faith in the supernatural is no more unreasonable than my faith in the ordinary truths of life that I accept without question. They are just harder to believe because they seem too good to be true.

January 16

The Need for Grace to Believe

> We who have Faith have Faith only through the grace of God. It is a gift of God and we should not take pride in having it. Do you suppose that God chose us because we were good? God does not choose "good" people; he chooses people he wishes to make good.
>
> *Sermon 229F, 1*

All humans will be saved through Jesus Christ and, for those called to be Christians, there must be knowledge of Christ and Christianity. Such knowledge of Christ and his teachings will not make one believe in Christ but it is evident that one cannot believe in someone without first knowing something about them. Augustine was convinced that the force pushing some to believe in Jesus Christ and Christianity is the grace of God. This gift of faith is given by God working inside the individual, by making the individual delight in belief and by providing an environment in which belief is possible (*On the Spirit and the Letter*, 34.60). Sadly, not all humans have come to know Christ and we do not know how the grace of God works in them. God wills that all humans be saved and therefore he must have hidden ways of drawing even the apparent "unbeliever" towards him. All humans have been redeemed; how the grace of God brings any of us salvation remains a mystery.

January 17

Faith and Reason

Intelligam ut credo (I understand in order to believe) (*Letter 102, 38*). . . . *Credo ut intelligam* (I believe in order to understand) (*On Freedom of the Will, 2.2.6*).

It is true that many times Augustine seems to emphasize faith over reason but this is only because the truths revealed by faith are more important for our eternal destiny. How, except through faith, could we know that someday we will rise from our dead body and soul to a never-ending life? Although we might be able to come to some knowledge of God by examining nature, as Augustine believed we could, how could our unaided reason reveal to us that this God loves us, became human and died for our sake, and now lives not only in heaven, but deep inside each one of us? Still, it is true that in some sense reason comes first. This is the meaning of Augustine's saying "I understand in order to believe." It is only because we are beings of reason, beings with minds, that we can come to faith. Moreover, before we can believe in Christ, we must first "know about" Christ through our natural powers of knowing. The natural goal of our belief in such things as a loving God is that someday we will not need to believe in him because then we will see him. Our time of faith is meant to be an intermediate stage in our eternal life. The goal of faith is vision! This is the meaning of Augustine's second statement, "I believe in order to understand." In heaven we will not need faith because at last we will see!

January 18

Science and Wisdom

It would be foolish to believe that a man who has faith in you, O God, but who does not know the track of the Great Bear constellation, is worse off than the man who measures the sky and counts the stars and weighs the elements but neglects you who give to all things their size, their number, and their weight.

Confessions, 5.4.7

Augustine believed that both *science*, the knowledge whereby we use the things of this earth well, and *wisdom*, whereby we are able to contemplate eternal verities, are both important in our lives (*The Trinity*, 12.14.22). Without science we could not achieve the skills to live decent lives and to regulate this world in a way that leads to eternal blessedness (*The Trinity*, 12.14.21). Wisdom allows us to subordinate created things to the Creator, to see nature as the work of the Divine Artist (*Sermon 252*, 10). The purpose of this life is to achieve the eternal happiness of seeing God face to face in heaven. In the meantime, science helps us live in this world, but it has little worth if it does not lead to some sort of wisdom whereby we are able to discover the eternal truths hidden in and regulating the sweep of earthly affairs.

January 19

Preparation for Receiving Faith

How will you be able to lift up your heart to God? Does your heart not need first to be healed before you can come to see God? Are you not revealing your pride when you cry out "First let me see and then I will be healed"?

Commentary on Psalm 39, 21

Augustine believed that personal purification is necessary before conversion can be possible. We need "space" in our lives before God can pour into us the gift of faith in the supernatural (*Sermon 173, 2*). Even before the Fall of Adam and Eve, faithfulness to the will of God was not an easy task. After sin, it became even more difficult. Now there are obstacles in knowing the truth and choosing the good. Our eyes are covered by cataracts of the spirit which make even the most brilliant truths seem cloudy and gray. Our unaided wills are now too weak to focus attention on eternal truths for any length of time. Because of our condition, we cannot give ourselves faith. But we can prepare to receive faith by leading a decent life, by trying to purify ourselves of selfishness and laziness. This healing process takes place when we listen and live by what our conscience tells us.

January 20

The Burden that Comes with Faith

The living a life of faith is often hard labor. Who ever said this was not the case? It is often a struggle, but this is the work for which heaven is the payment. If you want to be paid, do not be lazy in your work. After all, if you had hired a workman, you would not count out his pay before you had put him to work. You would say to him "Do the work, then you will get paid." He would not dare to say to you, "Pay me now and then I will do the work." This is the way God deals with us.

Sermon 38, 4

To be a devoted Christian is never easy. Faith is easy when it is just talk. It is when we act on it that it becomes hard labor. Our faith is constantly challenged by temptations to do such things as fake our work, take a bribe, or have an illicit affair. To fight against such temptations is hard work but it must be done if faith is to be more than just a word. Faith may also become a burden when suddenly the society in which we live looks down on us, makes fun of us, or dismisses us as irrelevant because of our belief. Sometimes the sarcasm of a late-night talk-show host or a newspaper columnist can cut very deeply.

January 21

Faith and Good Works

If, as St. Paul says, Faith profits us nothing without Charity (1 Corinthians 13:2) and Charity must always be active wherever it is found, then Faith itself leads to good works by choosing to love. How then is it possible for anyone to be justified by Faith apart from works?

Commentary on Psalm 31/2, 6

The relationship between faith and love is evident both in the way we know things and choose things: you cannot love that which you do not know. But what we know often requires some faith. On the supernatural level this is even more evident. As Augustine observes, "We are told to love God and neighbor but how can this happen without Faith? How can you love God if you don't believe in God?" (*Sermon 90, 9*). Moreover, good works flow from the love that faith engenders. Faith, which reveals God, and the good that is other human beings, will lead us to love. This love takes the form of prayer and charity. The natural effect of faith is love which expresses itself in good works. Saying "I believe" will not lead to our eternal salvation. Without good works love is sterile and the faith that we claim to possess is dead (*Commentary on the Letter of John, 10.1.2*).

January 22

Charity without Faith

Although people without Faith may claim to perform good works, their apparent praiseworthy works do not bring them closer to salvation. No one should think that actions performed without Faith merit heaven. Where there is no Faith, there are no good actions either. It is the intention that makes an action good and intention is directed by Faith.

Commentary on Psalm 31/2, 4

Augustine believed that loving was more important than knowing. Knowing a lot of things (even about God) will not get us into heaven; only loving rightly will do that. But loving rightly requires that we are going in the right direction. By pointing us in the right direction, faith tells us what and how we should love. It is for this reason that Augustine says that, just as faith without good works is dead, so love without faith will do little to save us. God gives us the theological virtues of faith, hope, and charity to keep us on the right track. The charity that gives us the assurance of salvation is the love of the God revealed in Scripture and tradition.

January 23

Faith and Hope

Faith does not waver if it is supported by hope. Take away hope, and faith falters. If you want to go somewhere, will you even begin walking if you have no hope of reaching your destination? Furthermore, if you have no love for anything, what is the point of believing and hoping? You cannot hope for something you do not love. Love kindles hope and hope can only exist through love.

Sermon 359A, 5

Hope is the conviction that somehow or other the future will be better than the present. The theological virtue of hope assures of an eternal happiness after death. Like faith and charity, hope comes to us only by the grace of God. As Augustine says in the quote above, it is intertwined with faith and love. Faith in the revealed God gives us a sense of security, a knowledge that things will work out. At the same time faith depends on hope because it hard to have faith in a hopeless situation. Augustine once remarked, "No one loses Faith except by throwing it away" (*Commentary on Psalm 55*, 19). Faith is easy to lose when we have lost hope; we lose hope when we have lost what we love. Therefore, if we are to pray for anything in our lives we should pray that God will give us the grace of hoping. If we at least hope, there is a chance that other good things will follow.

January 24

The Value of Hope

Hope is a necessity for us in these days of exile from heaven. It is our consolation on the journey. When a traveler gets tired of walking along the dusty road, he puts up with fatigue because he hopes to arrive home. Rob him of any hope of arriving and immediately his strength for walking is broken. So too, the hope for heaven which we have now is an important factor easing the pain of our just exile and sometimes harsh journey.

Sermon 158, 8

As we go through the trials and tribulations of this life, hoping against hope that someday things will be better, we may be tempted to ask ourselves and God, "Why does it have to be this way? Why did you not give us everything we wanted in the beginning so that there would be no need to live in hope?" Of course the story of Eden shows that, even in paradise, we always want more. Of course we do not live in paradise, but we are moving toward a heavenly paradise. As the passage above suggests, if we have hope, we at least keep moving. Moreover, "God, by postponing the realization of our hope, expands our desire. By desire our mind is stretched and by such stretching it is able to hold even more" (*Commentary on the First Epistle of John* 4.6). The "more" that our expanded spirit holds is the grace of God supporting us through the continuing trials of this life and strengthening our hope for the heaven promised in the next.

January 25

Reasons for Hoping

The great God has made us humans the loveliest ornaments of the earth. Oh, it is true that we must someday die, but in our present life God has given us some marvelous gifts that enhance our pilgrimage through time. Most important of all, we have the promise from our lovely Lord that if we use well the good things he has given us here, we shall receive a fantastic life later on. Beyond death we shall receive peace and all the healing grace and final glory that go with it. Best of all, we shall know that this great gift of peace will be everlasting. Our joy will never end.

City of God, 19.13

Augustine's Christian faith convinced him that there were very good reasons for hope in this sometimes mixed up world. Here are three of his many reasons: though bad things happen, the present world has much good in it; God supports us in times of difficulty; we need not fear death because God offers the grace to persevere as well as forgiveness for our shortcomings. In sum, as Christians our hope is based on the promises that Jesus Christ awaits us in an eternal heaven, and is with us now in our current struggles.

January 26

Foolish Hope

> Some delude themselves because of God's mercy. They say: "I still have a little time left to live how I like. Why shouldn't I live how I like as much as I like and then turn to God later? After all, God has promised to pardon me." I respond, "True, but he has not promised that you are going to be alive tomorrow."
>
> *Sermon 339, 7*

Hope can be foolish. For example, there is no use hoping that someone will love us when we know that they love another. There is no use hoping that someday we will get a particular job when it is far beyond our capabilities. There is no use hoping that we will never die. Certainly as Christians we have great reason to hope in our future happiness because of the promises of Christ. But it would be terribly foolish to believe that we are guaranteed salvation no matter what we do. God will not go against our free choice to walk away from him. It is also foolish to believe that we can put repentance off to a later date. We know that God will pardon any sin as long as we repent in this life; however he has made the day of our death unknown (*Commentary on the Gospel of John*, 33.8.4).

21

January 27

The Darkness of Despair

> Despair can kill the soul and sometimes it infects people. They begin to think of the terrible lives they have led and become convinced that forgiveness is impossible. They die in despair, saying to themselves "There is no hope for me now. Clearly the dreadful things I have done cannot possibly be forgiven. So why try to change my lust-filled life?"
>
> *Sermon 87, 10*

At one point in his early life, Augustine seems to have been overcome by the despair reflected in the passage above (see *Confessions,* 6.6.9–10). Not only did he believe that his life was hopelessly confused, he could not believe in a God of forgiveness. He was at a low point in his life. Paradoxically, he was a young and healthy man of great promise. Some years later, recalling those terrible days, he cried out to God, "Where were you, the God I had known as a boy? I walked in darkness and seemed to be sliding ever deeper into an abyss. I plunged into the depths of a sea of confusion. I lost hope and despaired of ever finding any secure truth" (*Confessions,* 6.1.1)

By the grace of God Augustine was eventually able to overcome his despair through persistent prayer, even in his darkest moments. He proved by his life the truth he would later put into words: "Those who can cry out from the abyss are not in the very depths of the abyss. Their very cry lifts them up" (*Commentary on Psalm 39, 3*).

January 28

The Good Old Days

We complain that our days are gloomy. Our grandparents and their grandparents probably did the same thing. People are never completely pleased with the days they live through but they frequently think that the days of their ancestors were quite pleasant. Those ancestors were pleased with past days they had never experienced, which is why they thought them pleasant. . . . It is only the present that the heart feels so acutely. Practically every year when we experience the changing weather we say "It's never been so cold." "It's never been so hot." Comparison with a "better" past is always in our minds.

Sermon 25, 1

While there is much that is wrong in today's world, it is important that we resist the temptation to romanticize the past. To be sure, our past may have been filled with loved ones who are now gone. But those times can never return and, if you think about them seriously, you realize that they may have been no better than the present. The past is often not "what was" but "what we would have liked it to have been." As Augustine told his listeners, "From the time of Adam right up to the present there existed the same 'toil and sweat,' the same 'thorns and thistles'" (*Sermon 346C, 1*).

January 29

The Danger of Great Expectations

When we are infants we look forward to childhood; in childhood we look forward to adolescence; in adolescence we look forward to being an adult in the prime of life; when we are in our prime we look ahead to middle age; in middle age we await the coming of old age. But when we are old we realize that there is to be no new age in this life.

Letter 213, 1

We are born with great expectations about the future. When we discover that those expectations are difficult to fulfill, we are overcome with sadness. The laughter of our infant days is followed by the tears of an imperfect life, one that necessarily falls short of our idea of happiness. We enter each episode of our life with an ability to wonder, a desire for excitement, to discover what is new. Then either it falls short of our expectations or it is so wonderful that we develop a foolish expectation that it will never end. Of course it must end and to try to hold onto what is past can empty our present of all its glory. All ages have the glory of being a vessel of God. This is the only great expectation that is assured fulfillment because all we need do is to move on to the next age and open our hearts to the God who is waiting to join us.

January 30

In Memory I Find My Self

In the immense palace of my memory the sky and earth and sea are present before me, together with all the remembered creatures I saw in them. Indeed, in my memory I discover my self. When I bring my "self" to mind I am able to see when and where I did various deeds and how I felt when I did them.

Confessions, 10.8.14

The power of memory is a precious gift. It brings us the joy of past sunsets, ocean air, the fragrance of gardens long since withered. In my memory I can rejoice in past victories, but avoid the disasters. In my memory I can remember past sins long since repented and temptations long since survived. It is in my memory that I discover my true self, the experiences, hopes and fears, joys and sorrows that have created my self. Only memory can bring such fullness. My present is but a flitting moment, gone before it can be captured. My future does not yet exist. Only my past is the stable reality which can be captured and held still for contemplation. The sadness of those who lose all memory is that they lose themselves. They may be somewhat aware of their present but all knowledge of their own self has disappeared. We don't know if this terrible affliction will touch any one of us, but this we know: God will still be with us. He will remember us even when we forget ourselves.

January 31

The Folly of Fooling Myself

The whole thrust of the command to "know myself" comes down to this: I should not ascribe to my self those qualities which in fact are not present and I should accept in my self those qualities which in fact are present.

The Trinity, 10.16

In the search for one's true self, Augustine makes an interesting distinction between what we *think* we are and what we *know* we are. We often create bloated and glorious pictures of ourselves, fabrications based on what we would like to be. At the same time, sometimes hidden deep within ourselves, there are those facts about ourselves that we indeed know but try to avoid because they are unpleasant or humbling. This creative remembering of a self that never was is an innocent diversion as long as it does not stand in the way of seeing my self for what I am now. Like it or not, I am a continuum, and to know the true me depends upon an honest reading of my past. Facing my self honestly, I can be thankful for the folly that might have been while regretting the stupidity that sometimes was.

February 1

The Sea and the Sponge

I imagined creation as a vast body made up of many parts and I pictured you, O God, as enveloping this mass on all sides and penetrating it in every part. It was as though water was everywhere, nothing but an immense, infinite ocean, and somewhere within it a sponge filled through and through with the ocean's water. And I said to myself, "Here is how God encloses all creation in himself and fills it with his presence."

Confessions, 7.5.7

Augustine was convinced of the intimate relationship between God and his creation even before he had a clear idea of either. After his conversion he was still convinced that God was present in the world, but in a different way than he originally thought. In his pre-Christian days he saw God only as a power pulsating in every part of the world. After his conversion he learned from Christ that God was in the world, not simply as a blind power, but as a loving person who knew and loved every part of his creation. As a young man snorkeling in the warm waters off Miami, I knew that if I were in danger, the ocean would not rescue me. Thank God that the God who is around me and in me is not like that! It is a good thing because sometimes I still swim foolishly beyond my depth.

February 2

Bringing Christ to Our World

The mother Mary bore Jesus in her womb; let us bear him in our hearts. The virgin became pregnant through the incarnation of Christ; let our hearts be filled with his presence through our faith in him. Let our souls be a fertile field in which God can grow and flourish.

Sermon 189, 3

Our task as Christians is to bring Christ to the world each day. To do that we must allow Christ to live in us. Mary testified to that second life living in her long before the wombed Christ could be perceived directly by others. The Baptist felt the presence of Jesus still hidden in Mary and he jumped for joy in Elizabeth's womb. If we can make Jesus live in us as he lived in Mary, then we too can bring Jesus into our world. He will leap from us just as he once leaped from the womb of Mary. We do not need great talent to proclaim God's word. We need great hearts. God needs human beings who are willing to say "yes" to his call and to be firm in their yes. Mary said "yes!" to God in her youth and she stayed faithful to that yes throughout her days on earth. As a result, God worked through her more powerfully than through any other human being.

February 3

The Teacher Within

There is a great mystery, my friends, in my attempts to teach you. The sound of my words may strike your ears but the real teacher is inside you. You really do not *learn* anything from another human being. Oh, I can *suggest*

27

some truths through the sound of my voice, but if the Divine Teacher is not in you, the sounds I make are empty. It is the Divine Master within who teaches you. It is Christ who teaches you and if you do not hear his words sounding within, any words blaring from outside are useless clatter.

Commentary on the Epistle of John, 3.13.2

Augustine believed that Christ dwells within each one of us where he teaches us through our conscience. Just as the sounds of the voice of a teacher resounding outside touch the delicate membrane of our ear, causing it to vibrate and carry the message inside, so the whisper of God pierces the even more slender membrane in the depths of our soul. The touch of God's voice deep inside causes our soul to resonate in tandem and suddenly we "know" the truth about ourselves and God that he wants to reveal to us. These truths are sometimes difficult to accept but they are also terribly important. I can be saved (Thank God!) without knowing too much geometry; but I cannot be saved and thereby see God if I avoid the truths that the God within is whispering to me deep inside.

February 4

The Need for Quiet

Let us leave a little room for reflection in our lives, room too for silence. Let us look within ourselves and see whether there is some delightful hidden place inside where we can be free of noise and argument. Let us hear the Word of God in stillness and perhaps we will then come to understand it.

Sermon 52, 22

The problem we have living in this hurly-burly world is that there seems to be no quiet place where we can listen to the Divine Teacher speaking softly inside the depths of our soul. Day after day we are on the move, tossed here and there by the currents of our lives, grasping at this or that so that we might be secure, and always failing because everything we grasp at is as transient as we are. Far from special "words" soothing the discordant disruption of our days, there seem to be too many words in our lives. It seems we are surrounded by noise, shouting voices screaming endlessly about what God is like, what God hates, who is evil and who is good. Augustine's prayer for relief from noise is a good prayer for all of us still struggling for the serenity of eternity in the midst of noise: "Speak here inside me Lord, because only you always tell me the truth. I shall leave all the noisy world outside and retire to my own little room deep inside my heart and there I will sing my love song to you" (*Confessions*, 12.16).

February 5

Blindness

What a great gift is given when a doctor cures the blindness of a person who cannot see! What payment can match the gift of sight restored? The cured blind person may give the doctor gold piled upon gold, but the doctor gave the power to see light! If you ever wished to remind the newly seeing person that in giving gold he truly gave nothing, just put them in a room without light and tell them to look for the colors of all that gold!

Commentary on Psalm 26/2, 8

As we travel through life sometimes we seem to be floating in the dark. We would like to see for certain where we are going. But we cannot because we are blind. In such dark periods all we can do is to put up with them and wait for the light to come. The fact that we cannot see is no sign that Jesus-God is not present. In the gospel story Jesus was with the blind Bartimeus even before he cured him. So too, every life is guided by the providence of a God who loves both those who can see him clearly and those who are still blind to his presence. As we wait for the light, it is best to heed Augustine's advice to try to reach out to others who are going through their own darkness. In trying to serve others who, like ourselves cannot see, we are in fact serving the unseen Lord who knows our love. We give him the gift of our blindness and ask him to make good use of it.

February 6

Illnesses of the Spirit

> There is no one who claims that there is no God who is not infected by carnal desire or a lust for earthly power or the delightful madness of some showy spectacle. They love such temporal things and seek their happiness in them. They pursue the earthy objects of their desire wherever they lead and fear anyone who seems to have the power to take them away.
>
> *On True Religion 38, 69*

To pursue our journey towards union with God, we must first overcome the illnesses of the spirit which stand in the way. The first of these is the sickness of *pride,* a disease of the brain whereby we develop the insane conviction that we are in charge of the universe. The second is a form of heart failure, a *despair* that makes us give up on ourselves and on the grace of God. The third is the *cancer of malignant earthiness,* an over-attachment to the people and things of this world. Afflicted by these illnesses, we cry out with Augustine, "How mixed up I get, Jesus! My soul still seems convinced that it can be happy without you and in its solitary room it turns this way and that on its chosen bed only to feel more and more uncomfortable. Come Lord Jesus! And bring me peace!" (*Confessions*, 6.16).

February 7

Earthly Attachment

> In this life there are two loves in conflict: the love of this world and the love of God. Whichever one wins out draws the lover like gravity in its direction. It is not through feet or wings but by desire that we come to God. And it is not by some physical bond or iron chain that we are bound to earth. We are bound simply by our desire for the things of earth.
>
> *Sermon 344, 1*

We are not born infected with pride or despair or lust or avarice but we are born with "earthly attachment." Like young animals, we are born deeply involved in and pleasured by the material things around us. In the beginning, our joys and sorrows are naturally limited to the pleasures and needs of the body. Babies must reach out for the food and drink and physical comfort they need to survive. However, to continue such a life of earthy, lusty desire eventually becomes a matter of choice and some never seem to make that choice. They never develop the detachment from earthly goods because they cannot see God. As Augustine observes, "God comes to the hearts of men like a farmer seeking land to possess. If he finds it covered with woods, he roots out all the trees. Once he has a clear field, he plants it with the tree of divine love. What are the woods that stood in the way? Nothing else than the excessive love of this world" (*Commentary on the Epistle of John*, 2.8).

February 8

Concupiscence of the Flesh

Craving for pleasures of the flesh causes many evils. It is the root of adultery and fornication, dissipation and drunkenness. It makes the spirit become the slave of the body. How in the world can you live an upright life when inside you are so "upside-down"?

Sermon 313a, 2

In Augustine's usage the word concupiscence is neutral; it means simply "desire." Even though the phrase "concupiscence of the flesh" has a negative connotation, it refers not to a dysfunctional body but to a disorder in the will (*Against Julian the Heretic,* 3.9.18). It is entirely natural for our bodies to seek those goods necessary to preserve life on earth. Our troubles come from the "cracked" machinery (our mind and free will) through which we desire and pursue such things. No matter how virtuous we pretend to be our body remains like a young horse prancing here and there following any and all delights that tempt it to wander from the right path. We must train our bodily appetites as we might train young colts, using reins that are neither too slack nor too firm in order to channel their natural vigor towards the good (*Confessions,* 10.31.47).

February 9

Vain Curiosity

What vulgarity is caused by our sometimes shameless curiosity! This is what has been called "concupiscence of the eyes" and it manifests itself in our eager craving for frivolous shows and spectacles.

Sermon 313a, 3

Like the people of his day, we sometimes are overcome by curiosity about what is happening around us. As he said to his parish congregation, "We truly are hopeless creatures. The less we concentrate on our own faults, the more interested we become in the faults of others" (*Sermon 19*, 2-3). Augustine used the phrase "concupiscence of the eyes" to describe our excessive curiosity in public spectacle and individual perversion. There is nothing inherently evil in being interested in the lives of others, in playing at games, at enjoying entertainment. Indeed, one who loses all interest in this world is not acting in a healthy fashion. The danger of "concupiscence of the eyes" is that it diverts our attention from doing the good that we must do. The trouble is that it is an enticing temptation because this world is indeed an interesting place. And so we should learn to see the world as a reflection of the wonders of God.

February 10

Worldly Ambition

The world continues to grab at us, enticing us with its charms. We like lots of money, we like splendid honors, we like the power to dominate others. We like all these things, but let's keep in mind the words of the apostle: "We brought nothing into this world, neither can we take anything out" (1 Timothy 6:7). Honor should be looking for you, not you for it.

Sermon 39, 2

Worldly ambition or "pride of life" means more than the simple desire to make our mark in this world. As the phrase is used in Scripture and by Augustine, it stands for the malignant desire to be important on earth and to be prepared to use any means to get there. Such passion is malignant in a number of ways. It is malignant because, when we choose wealth or fame or power on earth as our only goal, we turn our back on God. It is malignant in its willingness to sacrifice morality and other people in pursuit of its selfish ends. Pride promotes the belief that our accomplishments are purely through our own efforts. As Augustine wisely observes, "It is truly foolish because our eternal value comes, not from what we do, but from what we are and what we love" (*Sermon 313A, 2*). Unfortunately, in a world that seems to value doing over being it is sometimes hard to be convinced of this consoling truth.

February 11

Praise

What a belch is to the satisfied stomach, that's what praise is to the satisfied heart.

Sermon 255, 5

Whether praise is good or bad depends mightily on what causes it. Augustine's somewhat crude analogy above refers to how we will feel when we are completely satisfied in the arms of God. His point is that when the heart is full, it expresses its fullness joyfully in praise just as a healthy belch is sometimes the after-effects of a fine meal. If we receive praise from some who are truly moved by the decency of our lives, it is a good praise in that it reflects the fullness of their hearts, a fullness to which we have somehow contributed (*Letter 231, 4*). However, Augustine adds that it is difficult for us to know whether we are free of the inordinate desire for praise (*Confessions, 10.37.60*). "We are constantly tempted to look around to see if anyone appreciates us. We can take a vow of poverty to combat greed. We can vow celibacy to control our lust. But how can we give up praise when praise comes from others and not ourselves? And even if we could, we might then seek praise because of our saintliness. In short, we have become humble and are proud of it" (*Confessions*, 10.38.63).

February 12

Using One's Talents

Lord, you frighten me! You demand from me what you gave me. You gave me my talents because you want to profit from them. You don't want them hidden away in some secret place. You don't want to get back only what you gave me. You want more. You want back all your money, every coin that bears your image—i.e., every human soul that ever existed.

Sermon 125, 8

Being too ambitious and desiring too much praise from others does not excuse us from using the talents we have to make the world a better place. As indicated in the passage above, Augustine took seriously the story of the servant who hid away the wealth given him by the master for investment (Luke 19:11ff). He felt compelled to use his talents to try to bring others closer to God by his preaching and writing. Few of us have talents equal to those of Augustine, but all of us have talents that are unique to us. We have the talent to love those we meet every day. At the very least we have the talent to not make people's lives more difficult than they are. In exercising even that modest talent we are doing our part to make Christ's love a reality in a world which desperately needs it.

February 13

Joyful Work

It is a mistake to think that humans were placed in paradise as slaves to servile work. Rather they were given the commission to "cultivate and guard" the land so that they could experience the special pleasure that comes from doing a work befitting human dignity.

A Literal Meaning of Genesis, 8.9.18

Augustine died at seventy-six years of age, having worked most days of his life. He seemed to agree with the sentiments of the ancient writer: "To eat and drink and enjoy the fruit of one's labor is for every human being a gift of God. Indeed, there is nothing better for humans than to rejoice in their work" (Ecclesiastes 3:12-13; 3:22). Humans were put into paradise and told to work not as a punishment but so they could experience the joy of creation, bringing to life something that was not there before. Augustine praised farming but he certainly did not mean to suggest that the work of the mind was less important or less valuable (*City of God,* 22.24). Indeed, as he says, "Any work that is done without fault or deception is a good work" (*The Work of Monks,* 12.14). Still, our primary work is to cultivate the reflection of God that is present in us. It is a difficult task, one that prompted Augustine to cry out, "My work is myself. I have become for myself a land of difficulty and too much sweat" (*Confessions,* 10.16.25).

February 14

Frustrating Work

If you are upset at having to set aside some great work that you consider more important than the task you are now forced to do, you ought to reflect that it is uncertain what is indeed more important. If something happens to disturb your plans, you should get on with doing it lest you be broken.

On Catechizing the Uninstructed, 14.20

Augustine speaks of the frustration of being called away from what you really want to do in order to do what you must do. For him the frustration came as bishop in being forced to give up his quiet reflection on Scripture to sit in judgment over the endless squabbles in his congregation. For many ordinary humans the dream of being a great artist, athlete, or rock-star is squashed by the need to make a living. Because of the need to support themselves and their families, many are forced to work at jobs that are boring at best and degrading at worst. The mystic, Simone Weil, believed that those who are forced to do repetitive work in factories and offices are subjected to a form of modern slavery. All such unfortunates can do is to try to follow Augustine's advice "to bend lest you be broken." Hopefully anyone submerged in such work can find some consolation in remembering those loved ones for whom the work is done and by the assurance that any work decently done is honored by God, if by no one else.

February 15

Obsessed with Work

> The promise of eternity when "The Lord will tell us to lay
> back and rest so that he might wait on us" is not as attrac-
> tive as it should be for those who are now working them-
> selves to the bone. They do not understand that, although
> such eternal rest comes only by working for it, the time
> for work will eventually be over for all of us.
>
> *Sermon 104, 7*

The effect of frustration at work may be debilitating but it is
not as dangerous as work obsession. When we are frustrated,
we are not tempted to make our work the sole reason for living. When we are obsessed, we are unable to see anything else
beyond our work. Augustine was not immune to such obsession. In his younger years he had a passion to win at all costs,
sometimes cheating at his childhood games because "I was
overcome by a vain desire for pre-eminence" (*Confessions,*
1.19.30). He later observed that such childish "gamesmanship"
often continues in our adult years but then we dignify it by
calling it "business" (*Confessions,* 1.9.15). Moreover, in time
many adults become defined exclusively by their work, making retirement unimaginable. Many of my confreres held onto
their jobs "tooth and claw" until finally having died on the job.

February 16

The Pain of Losing a Job

> John, on meeting Jesus, said "He must increase, and I
> must diminish" (John 3:30). This prediction was symbol-
> ized by the day of their birth and the way they died. John

was born during the summer solstice when daylight begins to diminish; Jesus was born during the winter solstice when daylight gradually increases. And, in their dying, John was "diminished" by a head while Jesus was "increased" by a cross.

83 Various Questions, 58.1

John the Baptist is the patron saint of those who have lost a job. His virtue was that he was both realistic and humble. He was realistic in knowing that he had done his work and it was over. He was humble in knowing that the one who took his place would certainly do the job better. Of course, when we lose a job our replacement is far less awe-inspiring. But, as it was for John, when we lose a long-held job we must approach our lives differently. Even though we were not obsessed with our job, we had gotten used to it. It gave a reason to get up in the morning. When all this is taken away, a gap opens in our lives which demands to be filled in some way. Some fill the gap with apathy and resignation, while others reach out to others. The latter give their loved ones the memory of someone who could bear the disappointments of life bravely.

February 17

Pass the Salt

This present world (which we call "Babylon") has its lovers. They hope for peace on earth and find all their joy in earthly peace and do not go beyond it. But, dear friends, take note of what these "rivers of Babylon" are. They are all things that humans love on earth, things which quickly flow away.

Commentary on Psalm 136, 2

One of the gentle jokes we have in our community is that when sitting at lunch and hearing that a confrere has died, someone is bound to say, "Old John is dead. Pass the salt." We are sad to be sure that "Old John" has "passed," but at the same time our getting on with life (symbolized by the request to "pass the salt") represents a healthy attitude. It acknowledges that we and all our accomplishments are rushing away on the "river of Babylon," the flowing river of change. It warns us that we should not take our accomplishments too seriously. Books go out of print. Inventions are superseded by even greater inventions. Our accomplishments are like rising smoke, becoming thinner as they disappear into the heavens (*Commentary on Psalm 36/3*, 14). Apart from our worldly achievements, we remain human beings (*City of God*, 5.17). But we are human beings in whom God dwells, holding us close as we rush down the river of time to the eternal sea where finally we will rest.

February 18

Holy Indifference

Jesus chose to endure with us all the pains of being human to teach us that we should not seek our happiness in earthly goods nor be afraid of becoming unhappy when we must give them up.

On Catechizing the Uninstructed, 40

When Jesus told us to be detached from this world, he was not telling us that we must give up everything that gives us joy—things like good health, being in love, possessions, or fulfilling our ambitions. His command to love God above all and our neighbor as ourselves suggests that there is nothing wrong in taking care of ourselves. The problem is that we can become so attached to the good things in life that we cannot detach ourselves from them when they stand in the way of our eternal destiny. We need to maintain a "holy indifference" whereby we subordinate all persons, objects, and conditions of life to our pursuit of God so that if and when we lose them we are able to say with Job, "The Lord has given, the Lord has taken away; as it pleased the Lord, so has it happened; may the name of the Lord be blessed" (Job 1:21). This indeed is holy indifference because it is an indifference that will eventually make us holy.

February 19

The Need for Contemplation

No person should spend so much time in contemplation that they ignore the needs of the neighbor. No person should spend so much time absorbed in action that they dispense with contemplation of God.

City of God, 19.19

The life of every Christian should be a healthy mixture of contemplation and action. By contemplation we fill ourselves up with God. By action we pour this God out on the world around us. Contemplation is necessary because of a truth repeated again and again by Augustine: "If you are seeking a place where holiness dwells, seek it within yourself" (*Commentary on the Gospel of John,* 15.25). He was convinced that there is no place, guru, thing, or event outside of oneself that will bring us to God. Our self is like the center of a circle from which we can see in some unified way the universe that surrounds us. To the extent that we rush away from that center to the multiple places and events at the circumference, we lose the ability to find the unity that is God. God is at our very center and only by returning to that center can we see ourselves and the universe through his eyes. Only by returning to our "self" can we find the God who will help us "put it all together" (*On Order,* 1.2.3).

February 20

Grasping at Straws

Nobody can bring yesterday back; tomorrow is already treading on the heels of today, pushing to "get it over with." We should worry more about living a good life now so that we can get to that heavenly land where we will not need to worry about "getting over with" anything.

Sermon 124, 4

Sometimes we are tempted to ignore the reality described by Augustine's words. Our hearts become sticky like a hummingbird's tongue. We flit about in our present trying to find sweet nourishment, something to love and call our own. Clutching some blossoming twig or person, we hope it will hold us in place so that we can enjoy its delight forever, resisting the persistent pull of time that moves us on. This is not to say we should not take time off to enjoy a particular moment or thing. Even the strongest ship must "lay to" every once in a while to take on supplies and get its bearings. The danger comes when we refuse to let go of our delightful twigs, refuse to move forward with our lives. Faith tells us that something awaits us after death. Time is a river rushing towards eternity. It is time for us to join it and see what world waits us beyond rising mists ahead.

February 21

Charity: The Most Important Virtue

Nothing is more excellent than the God-given gift of charity. This alone is what separates those who will be saved from those who will be lost. Other good gifts are given through the Spirit but what use are they without charity? A man may not have the gift of tongues or prophecy, nor have great knowledge, nor have given away all his property to the poor (perhaps because he has nothing to give or because of family obligations), but charity will still bring him to heaven.

The Trinity, 15.5.32

The theological virtue of charity, along with faith and hope, is one of the foundation virtues that are at the center of a good life. It is the gift of being able to "enjoy [love] God for his own sake and to enjoy [love] ourselves and our neighbor for the sake of God" (*On Christian Instruction,* 3/10/16). It is the most important virtue because it is only through love that we are moved to reach out to God and be with him for eternity. As Augustine told his friends, "We run to God not with our feet but with our affection" (*Commentary on the Gospel of John,* 26.8.2). It follows that the most important thing to pray for is the gift of charity—the grace to love God, ourselves, and our fellow human beings as we should.

February 22

Trials on the Road to Perfection

There are two reasons why we sin: either we do not see what ought to be done or we do not do what we now know must be done. The first of these causes is ignorance; the second is weakness. We must fight against them but to conquer them we need divine aid—the grace to see what should be done and the grace to make our delight in doing it stronger than our delight in those things which make us sin knowingly with our eyes wide open.

Enchiridion on Faith, Hope, and Charity, 22.81

In his *Commentary on Psalm 106* (4–7) Augustine lists four trials on the road to perfection. The first is *not knowing* what we are meant to do. The second trial is actually *doing* that which we know must be done. The third trial is, after long years of doing the right thing, managing the *boredom* of living a moral life day in and day out. If we successfully overcome such boredom, we may face the fourth trial—people impressed with our goodness will say, "Old John (or Mary) really have their lives in order. Let's put them in charge!" We need God's grace to overcome the pride that results from our overcoming the other trials. We need God's grace to persevere through the tedium of the "same-old." Finally, we need the grace of humility to recognize that we cannot live a good life without these and many other graces of God.

February 23

God-given Love

When you (Julian) come to list the various gifts by which God helps us, you never mention "by giving love." Despite this, John says "Love is from God" (1 John 4:7). It is by reason of this love, which is given to the human heart by the Holy Spirit that John will say "He gave them the power to become sons of God" (John 1:12).

Incomplete Work Against Julian, 3.106

Augustine believed that virtue is not knowledge; rather it is a love caused by a delight that is given by God. We become believers by coming to delight in what we believe. We become doers of the good by coming to delight in doing good. Just as illumination is needed to recognize God's will, so too delight is needed to desire to do what we now see and understand. The way to greater holiness is to have one's delight in "the things of heaven" overcome the earthly delights of the here and now. The grace of charity allows us to delight in God so that we desire him. We will be saved if, in the end, we have that love for God and the delight in heavenly things that impels us to choose the "path of righteousness" revealed by God's law. With such love and delight, "doing good" will become easy. Indeed, doing anything else would be truly unthinkable (*On Nature and Grace,* 57.67).

February 24

Grace and Freedom

Show a green branch to a sheep and you will attract it. Show a child some chestnuts and you will attract it. It is drawn by its love, by its desire. Since all of us are drawn by what pleases us, are we to say that Christ cannot draw a person to Him? What indeed do we hunger for more than wisdom, righteousness, truth, eternity?

Commentary on the Gospel of John, 26.6.5

It is only through the grace of God that we are able to love as we should and thereby stay on the path to heaven. The grace of God works inside us by giving the delight that draws us to the things of God. Like the sheep and the child in the passage above, we are not *pushed* to love; we are *drawn* to love. But if the delight that draws us to the good comes from God, is our choosing still free? It would seem so. God's intervention uses only those factors natural to the act of choosing—knowledge, delight, and love. His action is no more invasive than the acts of a clever teacher who invites a student to understand, delight in, and finally love a foreign discipline. When we act for the good under the influence of grace, we are still exercising our ability to choose (*On the Spirit and the Letter,* 32.53).

February 25

Give Thanks for Sins Avoided

To those who pride themselves on not committing adultery, God says: "You were not an adulterer because I protected you. In some circumstances you had no ready companion. I brought it about that there was no companion. At other times, the time and place were not suitable. I brought it about that this was so. When a companion was present and the time and place were suitable, I was the one who terrified you lest you consent." Recognize therefore the grace of the God to whom you are in debt even for the sins you *did not* commit.

Sermon 99, 6

Though most of us are not determined to act in one way or another by our environment, a good or bad environment can have a major effect on how we choose. God sometimes assists our goodness by eliminating that which draws us to sin. In other words, sometimes we have been good because evil options were not available to us. Sometimes our untoward intentions were interrupted. Perhaps a desire to avenge an enemy was cooled by his or her absence. Augustine's point is that we should thank God not only for helping us to live virtuous lives but also thank him for protecting us from vices that, given the chance, we could not resist.

February 26

Bored with Being Good

Consider what may happen when you finally overcome evil and live honorably among others. You may then be attacked by a new trial, the trial of boredom with the tedium of the good life. Sin no longer attracts you but now God's word gives you no pleasure. You are glad to have escaped the dangers of ignorance and concupiscence but you are now in danger of being killed by weariness and boredom.

Commentary on Psalm 106, 6

It is said that when wandering nomad tribes meet on the roads of Afghanistan, they greet each other with the words, *Staru Mashai!* (may you not become weary). It is a fitting prayer for one who has been on the road for a long, long time. We are all pilgrim people on the road to a distant place that is our true home. But there is a deep-boned tiredness that may come with days and years of traveling. Though heaven is a worthy destination, there is the chance that we may run out of steam. To conquer this "noon-day devil" we must find a restful time to recover our energies and to pray for the strength from God to continue. Though we may be too tired to hear the words, I have no doubt that God looks down on us as we try to continue our journey and whispers, "May you not grow weary!"

February 27

Heaven's Song

When people celebrate on earth, they usually provide some kind of music which adds to the pleasure of the guests. When passers-by happen to hear it, we ask them what is going on. And they tell us that it's some kind of party. Well, in God's home there is an everlasting party. The choirs of angels keep eternal festival because the eternally present face of God brings a joy that is never diminished. The sweet strains of that celebration sometimes drift into the ears of those who still walk on earth and draw them towards the refreshing springs that eternally flow in heaven.

Commentary on Psalm 41, 9

Sometimes, as we make our weary way through life, we are lifted up by hearing the sounds of a distant party. It is almost as though we were hearing faint heavenly songs. This hint of heaven may happen in the midst of the ordinary events. Sometimes it may come as we sit quietly on a beach watching the sunset. It may come in the embrace of a loved one, or a look into the eyes of our newborn daughter. However it comes, we suddenly believe again in life—the joys of this life and the good things that await us in the life to come. It is a precious time because for a moment we have experienced heaven. We have heard the melodies of the eternal party that we will join someday. Hearing the distant song makes it easier for us as we wait to join the party and the good times that will then be ours.

February 28

Loving the Hidden God

How should we prepare ourselves for loving God? By loving each other! You may say to me, "I have not seen God." Can you say to me, "I have not seen other human beings?" Love each other! If you love the human whom you see, you will love God too for you will experience love itself, the love that is the God who dwells within each of us.

Commentary on the Epistle of John, 5.7.2

There is no doubt about the two commandments that point out the path to heaven. I must love God above all and I must love my neighbor as myself. But how can I love a God whom I do not see? How can we truly love this God who is still hidden and will likely remain hidden until death? The answer given by John and Augustine is to turn our love towards those whom we can see, those with whom we share humanity. If we are able to love others with a pure love, not dictated by our own self-love, then we are at least beginning to love God through them. The apostle John wrote to his followers: "We must love one another because love is a gift of God. True, no one has ever seen God but if we love one another, God lives in us. If you say you love God, you must also love your neighbor" (1 John 4:7-21).

March 1

The Season of Lent

The days before Easter signify the life that we live now with all its trials and troubles. The days after Easter signify the happy days that lie beyond death. What we commemorate before Easter is what we experience in this life, what we celebrate after Easter points to something we do not yet possess.

Commentary on Psalm 148, 1–2

The season of Lent is important as a preparation for the days of death and resurrection that lie ahead for us. It is a time for coming to terms with the truth Augustine preached:

Your entire life and all the things you use during life should seem to you as a hotel might seem to a traveler. It should certainly not be treated as a place for settling down. You may have covered part of your journey but there is still some traveling to do. (*Commentary on Psalm* 34/1, 6)

Lent reminds us that we are on the move and that someday we must exit this life. It is a time of repentance, purification, self-examination, and reconciliation with others. It should be an exciting time because it reminds us that our present life is but the preamble to the grand life that awaits us beyond death. We are rushing to resurrection and the prospect should fill us with joy.

March 2

The Inn of the Samaritan

The present condition of the human race is symbolized by that man described in Scripture (Luke 10:30-37) who was robbed by bandits and left lying half-dead in a ditch. He was ignored by the passing crowd until a passing Samaritan stopped and took care of him. His rescuer was a Samaritan, a foreigner far removed from him in nationality who became a neighbor by showing mercy. Our Lord Jesus wants us to understand that the Good Samaritan in the story represents himself.

Sermon 171, 2

Augustine believed our situation is like that of the poor fellow in the story of the Good Samaritan. We too were on our way to heaven but then became terribly injured, falling helplessly into the pit created by our sins. Jesus-God looked down and took pity. He emptied himself and came down into our pit and lifted us up on his own body. He then placed us in this wayside inn, a place for healing where we are destined to be for the rest of our earthly lives. Though there are times of pain and trial, there are good times too. Above all this healing place is a place of hope because Jesus has promised that someday he will return to take us the rest of the way home. Our task now is to recognize our woundedness and do our best to cleanse ourselves of anything that can stand in the way of continuing our trip with Jesus when he comes for us.

Humility: The Way to Christ

The way to Christ is first through humility, second through humility, third through humility. If humility does not precede and accompany and follow every good work we do, if it is not before us to focus on, if it is not beside us to lean upon, if it is not behind us to fence us in, pride will wrench from our hand any good deed we do at the very moment we do it.

Letter 118, 3.32

In many ways humility is more fundamental to a good life than even the so-called theological virtues. To receive faith we must first be humble enough to know that we don't know everything. To have charity towards God and neighbor we must first be humble enough to know that we are less than God and no better than other humans. To have hope we must have the humility to know that the impossible task of salvation does not depend solely on us. To be humble does not mean that we deny our own value; it means that we know exactly who we are (*Commentary on the Gospel of John*, 25.16.2). Thus, if we praise ourselves, it should be because God works through our gifts to accomplish his purpose in the world (*Commentary on Psalm 144*, 7).

March 4

The Lord's Donkey

Those who do not want to be praised in the Lord are not gentle beasts of burden; they are savage, rough, arrogant and proud. The Lord wants gentle, compliant animals for

his use. Do not fear that you may stumble or fall head-
long. A donkey's colt you may be, but you are carrying
Christ. Remember that Christ entered Jerusalem on the
gentle and meek foal of a donkey. That humble beast is
now saying to you: "Do not hope to be praised in yourself; let him who rides you be praised."

Commentary on Psalm 33/2, 5

Augustine's point in the passage above is that we should be
humble about the good we do. It is only by the grace of God
that we accomplish any good. We carry the Lord Jesus Christ
and it is he who sets us in the right direction by giving us delight in doing good, gently slapping us with the reins when we
are tempted to wander off the path. We are like that little donkey
that carried Jesus into Jerusalem. As we try to bring him into
the cities where we dwell, we would be terribly mistaken if we
think that we deserved all the credit for the good things that
happen. If that Jerusalem-donkey had somehow come to believe that all the praise was for him, he would have proven that
he was indeed a jackass. And so will we if we claim that our
success in bringing Christ to our world is our doing more than
his.

March 5

The Reality of Sin

A wicked will is the cause of all evil. If the will were in
accord with its nature, it would never act against it and
thereby be wicked. It follows that the root of evil is just
this: "Not being in accord with nature."

On Freedom of the Will, 3.17.167

At the beginning of Lent it is good to start with the reflection that sin is real. No one doubts that there is much suffering in the world. Augustine's words about his own time are just as true today: "Humans are injured, laid waste and oppressed. By whom is this done? Certainly not by lions or serpents or scorpions. It is done by other humans" (*Sermon 311*, 8.8). But is this sin? In the passage above Augustine repeats the common idea that sin is an act which is not in accord with one's nature, which we do in many ways: thinking and acting as though we were God, not treating others with respect or as equals, or living a profligate life style. But are these actions sins? The answer is yes if we know what we are doing and freely choose to do it. The message of Christianity is that sometimes we choose to sin (*Commentary on Psalm 31*, 16). The question remaining is what we will do about it.

March 6

Augustine Steals Some Pears

Here is how I remember the incident. My delight in stealing came not from *what* I stole but from the fact *that* I stole. Still, I doubt that I would have enjoyed doing it alone. Friendship sometimes causes us to sin just for the fun of it. Someone cries "Come on, let's do it" and we are ashamed to be ashamed of doing it!

Confessions, 2.9

The incident that prompted the reflection above occurred when Augustine was in his teens. In the dead of night, he and some friends sneaked into a neighbor's yard and stole some pears. This they did and then ran away laughing, destroying the stolen fruit as they ran. Augustine gives two reasons for why we sometimes sin. The first reason is because we like it. Sadly, it seems the level of excitement in being good cannot compete with the excitement of being bad, especially when we can be bad with others. When we are lonely in our virtue sometimes we are tempted to find company in vice. Betraying our spouse, cheating in business, tearing down the good name of others, drinking ourselves into oblivion—all these destructive behaviors seem easier to do in the midst of others who are doing the same. Unfortunately our salvation depends on what we do and the excuse that "everybody was doing it with us" will carry little weight on the day of judgment.

March 7

Perverting Choices

Our infancy shows how ignorant we are when we begin life and our adolescence demonstrates how full of folly and wild desires we are. In fact, if anyone were left to live as they pleased and do what they desired, they would likely go through the whole list of disorders, including the lechery previously discussed and perhaps add a few other depravities that I forgot to mention.

City of God, 22.22.1

What I call a "perverting choice" is a choice that, once made, changes our life for the worst. Such a choice was made by Judas when he chose to deny Christ. The consequent guilt was too much for him and he hanged himself in despair. For us the list of possible perverting choices seems endless because we are easily attracted by pleasurable action even though it carries the threat of ruining our own lives and the lives of those who care about us. And so we drive drunk and run over a child. We must pray that God protect us from making such choices. If we have already made such a choice then all we can do is to pray for God's forgiveness and the forgiveness of the victims of our choice. We know God will forgive even the worst offense but it is not as certain that those who loved and respected us will ever be able to forgive or forget what we have done.

March 8

Baptizing a Drunk

You know that there are quite a few drunkards. Suppose you are one of them and you decide to be baptized. You have heard with dread that drunkenness is on the list of evils which bar people from getting into heaven (1 Corinthians 6:9-10), and so you get baptized that all your past drunkenness might be forgiven. But you still have the habit. You must fight not to get drunk again. The lust for a drink still wells up in you laying siege to your senses. The urge to drink would like to shatter the walls that protect you and drag you away as its prisoner again. The habit is still fighting and you must continue to fight back.

Sermon 151, 4

Augustine's warning above is very simple: if you baptize a drunk, all you get is a baptized drunk. Because we are all "cracked-pots" trying to preserve the spirit of God within, we retain our weakness even while living a virtuous life. No matter how long we live we will never outgrow the wounds of a clouded mind and a weakened will. Therefore we cannot take too much comfort in disreputable acts that have been forgiven. Their residue still is present in us. Even after repentance there remains a habit of recklessness that could easily break out again. We must pray that we will not fall anew into our old, disruptive habit.

March 9

Cleaning out the Bilges

You have guarded against great sins like adultery or murder. You do not steal other people's goods. You do not blaspheme. You do not give false testimony. All these are mountainous sins. But what about the small ones? You have gotten rid of the mountain; take care lest you be buried by the sand.

Commentary on Psalm 39, 22

Lent is a good time for repentance and renewal. The fact that we are taking Lent seriously suggests that we have conquered the great sins in our life. We are sailing along successfully on the road to heaven. Now is the time to clean up the ship lest we be sunk by seeping "bilge-water," little sins that, over time, slow up or stop our progress. Such sins include laziness, unkind gossip, greed, gluttony, hurt feelings leading to anger, slacking off our responsibilities. As Augustine warned his listeners: "Not even slight sins are to be treated lightly. They are nothing very big of course, but they do pile up. Look, sea water seeps little by little through the seams of a ship and it can eventually fill the bilges. If it isn't pumped out by good works it will sink the ship" (*Sermon 77B*, 7). Every day is an opportunity for avoiding serious sin, but the days of Lent are an especially good time for removing our "bilge-water" through prayer, penance, and kindness to others.

March 10

King David's Confession

Let us lead good lives and while we lead good lives let us not think that we are without sin. Living a life that is praiseworthy includes begging pardon for things that are blameworthy. This is the example that David gave us when he confessed his sins to God. He was his own prosecutor and judge and so he was able to ask to be spared. Sin is punished either by man repenting or by God judging. What is repentance but being angry with oneself? Give your heart a shaking by repentance and this will be a sacrifice to God.

Sermon 19, 2

For Augustine, King David in the Old Testament was both an example of the "crackedness" of human beings and the power of grace that brings them to repent. Though a chosen one of God, David was overcome with a lust that drove him to do a terrible thing: having a husband killed so that he could marry his wife. It is to his credit that, when finally confronted by God through the prophet Nathan, he did not deny his awful sin nor did he try to excuse himself. He humbly confessed, "I have sinned against the Lord" (2 Samuel 12:13) and heard the consoling words, "The Lord has forgiven you." He still had to suffer and do penance for his sin, but at least his friendship with God could be restored. The same is true with our friendship if we can confess our sins to God.

March 11

The Threat of a "Second Death"

If only there were just a "first death," a death which re-
leases the spirit from the body! We should fear more a
"second death where the soul is not pulled *from* the body
but is tormented *with* the body. Don't be afraid of the momentary "first death"; be afraid of the "second death"
that is forever. There is no worse death than a death that
never dies.

Sermon 335B, 5

Augustine frequently warned his friends of a "second death"
more dreadful than the inevitable "first death" they feared so
much. "First death" happens to the body when the soul departs;
"second death" happens to the soul when God departs (*City of
God*, 13.2). If God leaves us at the last judgment we will endure
an eternal suffering that cannot be imagined. The reason for
our anguish is that we have been made with a hunger for God
that can be satisfied only by union. To have that hunger eternally unsatisfied and to know that it is our fault will cause a
pain and sorrow that tears us apart. However, the good news is
that we can avoid a "second death." By the grace of God we
may be able to avoid a sin that could kill us for all eternity.
And, even if we commit such an appalling sin, there is always
a chance to say "I'm sorry!" and thereby have God forgive us.

March 12

The Sad Necessity for Hell

To lose the kingdom of God, to be an exile from heaven, to
be separated from Divine Life, to lose the abundant

sweetness of union with God, would cause an agony of such eternal proportions that no earthly tortures, even if they were endless, can be compared with it.

Enchiridion on Faith, Hope, and Charity, 29.112

One of the frightening results of the creation of immortal beings with free will is that it made "hell" a sad necessity. Once granted that human beings have free choice, it becomes possible for humans to reject God by lack of repentance for grave sins. Hell is not an intense form of Purgatory, a place for cleansing those who have been dirtied by sin. It is more like an asylum for the incurably insane, those who have knowingly and freely turned their backs on God and walked away. Those in hell can never ascend to the "City of God" because of their crippled condition, a condition that they brought upon themselves with full knowledge of what they were doing. The consoling teaching of Christianity is that life does not end with death, that there are two final destination points: heaven and hell. The good news is that where we finally end up is within our control.

March 13

The Possibility of My Salvation

We are on our way to Jesus-God and the Jesus who shares our humanity is the way through which we are going. If we are going to him and *through* him, why should any of us fear becoming lost?

Sermon 123, 3

The words of Augustine are indeed encouraging, but at the same time how can I be sure that I will stay on the "way" outlined by Christ in his life and teaching? How sure can I be that I will fulfill his two great commandments of love of God and neighbor well enough to get into heaven? I know I have been redeemed but I do not know if, in the end, I will be saved. Like Augustine, "I may be able to know to some extent what I am today, but what I shall be tomorrow I do not know" (*Sermon 179,* 10). The good news is that I need not be *perfect* to be saved, just repentant. Scripture tells us that the saved will include not only great saints, but also many who barely survived life's challenges—those who ". . . washed their robes and made them white in the blood of the Lamb" (Revelation 7:14). With God's help I hope to be among that happy, cleansed band, moving from this land of grace-assisted living to that heavenly land of unmerited loving.

March 14

Lent: A Time for Frugality

Gluttony and Drunkenness are to be avoided even at other times; but during these days of Lent even permissible meals should be restricted. Let your fasting be accompanied by frugality. There is nothing wrong in refreshing and supporting your body in its fast but this should be done through any ordinary food that is readily available, not by elaborate and exotic dishes.

Sermon 207, 2

Augustine's point is that there is little use in giving up tunafish for Lent if we have caviar for lunch. It is easy to fool ourselves in our Lenten fast. When the old rules of fasting were in place, we were allowed three meals but only one of them could be a full meal. The other two added together could not equal the quantity of the main meal. Some of my confreres solved the problem by eating as much as they could at the one main meal, which more than compensated for the fast meals. We may have been fasting but we were far from Augustine's ideal of frugality. We missed the point of the Lenten fast that we should train ourselves to use the earthly goods that we truly need, rather than consuming what we want. Without frugality we may be over-weight due to a life of over-consumption when the Lord comes to take us home.

March 15

A Prayer for Prayer

O God, I ask for the grace to pray. You are too good to allow anyone to be lost who is really trying to find you. Indeed, you are so good that I know that you will give me the grace to try and find you. Wash me free of all my silly earthly desires so that I may be clear-eyed enough to see you.

Soliloquies, 1.6

Prayer is usually defined as "raising the heart and mind to God." It is often easier said than done. Still, that we desire to pray is a very good beginning. Our desire for God, perhaps for a God who seems far distant and hidden, is itself a prayer (*Commentary on Psalm 37*, 13–14). The trouble in trying to "raise our minds and hearts" to the heavens is that our "crackedness" functions like gravity. Gravity is always an obstacle to flying; flying with weakened wings is all the more a challenge. If only we could overcome for a moment the distractions of this world, then we might receive the grace to pray. Even without saying too much, our attention and our love would gradually become fixed on God. Our love would then become "our weight" drawing us towards the heavens. We will have "raised our heart and mind" to God.

March 16

***

Anger Management

If we are continually frustrated in doing what we like to do, we become angry. Anger is the impassioned urge to overcome anything that stands in the way of what we want to do. Thus, we are angry at other humans when they oppose us. We slash and break the pen we write with, the dice we gamble with, the brush we paint with and in general with anything that causes us frustration.

Letter 9, 4

There is no question that in this turbulent world there are many situations which cause us to become angry (*Sermon 211*, 1). There is "road rage," "phone rage," "supermarket rage," and, worst of all, "life rage"— anger with the condition of our life. We get angry with God, our spouses, children, and in general anyone who gets in our way. We even get angry with ourselves because of our wasted lives and our sins (*Commentary on Psalm 33/2*, 19). This last anger can be therapeutic, however, if it leads to repentance. Still, even good anger needs to be controlled and unwarranted anger needs to be eliminated. As vinegar corrodes the vessel that contains it, anger corrodes the heart if left to fester too long (*Letter 210*, 2). If left unattended, anger will poison our body, our soul, and the places where we live out our lives (*Letter 9*, 4).

March 17

***

Hatred: The Death of the Soul

If anger lasts too long, it may become hatred. Anger inflames the eye, but hatred blinds it. If love is life, hatred is death. Perhaps you ran into people who were furious with you. What lasting harm could they do you? In their rage they threaten to kill the body, but by hating them you have killed the soul. They have killed the body of another in anger; in hating them you have killed your own soul.

Commentary on Psalm 54, 7

The real danger of anger is that it may lead to hatred. Anger is just an emotional reaction to frustration. Anger is momentary and does not threaten to kill us. Hatred, on the other hand, is death-dealing because it destroys the love that is the life of the soul. It is through loving that we are able to lead a truly human life. By being filled with love we can enjoy eternal life in heaven. Love is the opposite of hate. Love draws us towards the beloved, makes us value them for the good that they are, makes us want to be united to them. Hatred makes us revile those we hate, makes us distance ourselves from them, indeed makes us wish that they did not exist at all. Especially in the season of Lent we should strive to control our angers and eliminate our hatreds. Anger may upset our stomach but hatred can kill us for all eternity.

March 18

Fasting from Anger

What can I say about the work of mercy where your wealth is not given away but where something is let go from your heart? I'm talking about the anger you store up against someone. What could be sillier than to avoid an external enemy and retain a much worse one in the depths of your heart? That is precisely what you do if you don't very quickly get rid of your anger. If anger has boldly and shamelessly lived in your breast up to these holy days, at least now let it beat a retreat from there so that your prayers may proceed without anxiety and not stammer or grow dumb under the piercing guilt of an angry conscience.

Lent is a special season for prayer, fasting, and almsgiving. Through prayer we try to raise our spirits to the heavens. Through fasting and almsgiving we try to control our passion for "good living" and acquisitiveness. Augustine believed that the most important part of fasting and almsgiving is not the material things that we give up or give away. Fasting from anger and hatred is more important than giving up desserts. We should give financial support to those in need but it is more important to give forgiveness to those who have injured us, to ask forgiveness from those we have injured. These are "alms" that even the poorest of the poor can give to each other. Admittedly, it takes great humility and charity to give such spiritual "alms" but it must be done for our prayer to be effective. These are the "wings" on which our prayer is raised to the heavens (*Sermon 206*, 3).

March 19

Forgiveness

When your enemies come to you and ask your pardon for the evil they have done to you, you must forgive them immediately. If you don't, then you are not merely erasing the Lord's Prayer from your heart (where you say "forgive us as we forgive"); you are erasing yourself from God's book.

Sermon 56, 16

The movie *Love Story* made famous the phrase "love means to never need to say 'I'm sorry'!" I submit that the principle is charming but inaccurate. In this world of "cracked people" we must always be prepared to say "I'm sorry." The world is made livable because, by the grace of God, we are able to forgive others for injuring us, and able to ask the forgiveness of those we have injured. All of us are in a place for healing, a hospice, where bruised pilgrims rest and recuperate for the road ahead. We must accept that each one of us is wounded and give each other the opportunity and the time to heal. It is hard to forgive when someone has in one way or another nailed our body and spirit to a cross. But eventually we must repeat the words of Christ on his Cross: "Forgive them Father for they know not what they do" (Luke 23:34).

March 20

Looking Ahead

As you look ahead in life you begin to realize that all of us are going to die someday. In your infancy you look forward to being a child. When you are a child you look forward to being a teenager. As a teen you look forward to being a young adult. In your days of young adulthood you look forward to being middle-aged. When you reach middle-age you look forward to old age. But when you finally get old you realize that there is nothing more to look forward to in this life. There is no age after old age.

Letter 213, 1

Towards the end of Lent it is natural for us to begin to look ahead to the terrible events that will conclude it: the death and burial of our Lord Jesus Christ. To be sure, we will someday have our Easter when we will rise again as Jesus rose; but first we must go through our own Good Friday of dying and our own Holy Saturday of resting in the tomb. Now is the time to think about the days between death and resurrection. It is somewhat frightening that, as I live out my days in this inn for travelers, my future must involve dying, but it is only by going through death that I will be able to rise again on my own day of resurrection.

March 21

The Race towards Death

Life is nothing but a race towards death, a race in which no one can stand still or slow down, even for a moment. Those who live many years and those who live only a few days run with equal speed. Just as a long journey does not mean that travelers slow their steps, so on the way to death those who take more time proceed no more slowly than those who seem to reach the goal more quickly.

City of God, 13.10

Faith tells us that we are racing towards eternity. Experience tells us that the race must go through the door of death. On most days we do not think about it. As children we looked forward to growing up. In school we anticipate exciting careers. In the midst of our career, we looked forward to retirement. The thought of death as our destiny does not usually occur to us until we get sick or old. In the end, the only difference between living a short or long life is the number of memories and the amount of good or evil we accomplished. We are indeed moving towards eternal life, but just now we are racing towards the death that is the door . . . and sometimes we get very scared.

March 22

Dying to Live

When one age approaches, another is dying. When child-hood comes, infancy dies. When old age comes, youth dies. When death comes, every age dies. When you wish for a particular number of "ages" in life, you are wishing for an equal number of deaths of those ages.

Commentary on Psalm 127, 15

The reality of my life is that the present moment is flying by. I am constantly "dying" to the past so that I might "live" the new age that awaits me. Augustine believed that we never lose our past ages (infancy, childhood, etc.); we merely build on top of them. To die to our age allows us to receive the full stature God has planned for us. To refuse to move on is to condemn ourselves to a spiritual "dwarfism," refusing to be as big and tall as we were meant to be. Moreover, to refuse to move on is to stand in the way of those coming behind us. Augustine speaks of a new-born child saying to its parents, "Well, I am here. Should you not be thinking about getting off the stage of life so that I can have the room to play my part?" (*Commentary on Psalm 127,* 15). Despite its challenges, refusing to die to our present stage in life only deprives us of the new life that God has prepared for us.

March 23

Fearing Death

It is amazing how the sweetness in this often distressing life is still so great that it causes us to have such a fear of dying. Even those who believe that they will pass through death to a life without death still wish that they could avoid going through the dying to get there.

Sermon 280, 3

Soon after his conversion Augustine admitted that he had three great fears: the fear of losing those he loved, the fear of pain, and the fear of death (*Soliloquies*, 1.9). Later on he dismissed the Stoic claim that they feared nothing by observing that someone without fear is probably already dead (*Sermon 348, 3*). I am afraid I would be a bad Stoic because even now in my "geezer-hood" I have a fear of dying, for at least I know this world, and have even come to enjoy it. It is natural to fear change, especially if your life is still interesting. Augustine observed, "the very fear of death is a daily winter" (*Sermon 38, 7*) . . . "and its cold blast can chill me even when I am in the midst of my waning summer days. I should not feel guilty about my fears (even Adam did not belittle death)" (*Sermon 335B, 1*). I must not let it freeze me in place and stop me from living out the warm days that remain.

March 24

Dealing with Death

We think of the dead when we carry them out to be buried. We say: "Poor fellow, only yesterday he was walking around!" But we think this way only as long as we are busy about the funeral. We bury the thought of death along with our dead friend. We put aside the thought that someday it will be our turn to die.

Sermon 361, 5

Nothing can be done about the fact that we will someday die. Augustine uses the analogy of an oil-lamp to make this point. The light can be kept burning only by supplying new oil.

However, the time will come for all lamps when the light dies forever because the wick has slowly been eaten away by time and use (*Sermon 362*, 11). We humans are like living lamps—we require nourishment in order to function. But this cannot go on forever. The vessel in which the vital activity is carried becomes corroded and worn out. The day will come when it can no longer support the flame of life, no matter how much oil is poured into it. Because death is inevitable, we ought to factor it into our lives and live accordingly (*Letter 10*, 2). Now is the time to heed Augustine's advice: "Anyone who lives a good life is not able to have a bad death" (*Sermon 249*, 2).

March 25

Helping the Dying

The consolation of friends did the most to give me strength in my sorrow. Signs of love coming from the hearts of friends shine through eyes and mouth and speech and thousands of gestures. They make one out of many, bringing hearts together like bundled kindling.

Confessions, 4.18.13

The passage above describes how Augustine was able to recover from the death of a friend. They show the support we need from others in living through tragedy. This is especially so when our time comes to die. Dying is always a solitary experience. Even without the tubes and tents of hospital technology, there is a wall between the living and the dying that prevents empathy. The best we can do is to be with the dying as they die. This is a great gift to the dying because death is a solitary event. People do not fear death so much as they fear dying without the care of others. To assist the dying is a great sign of love. It is also one of the most difficult tasks in life, one that must be prepared for with prayer and resolution. It is a great thing to be able to help someone exit this life in peace, but to do so we must be at peace ourselves, truly believing in the wonder of the beautiful life that exists just beyond death's door.

March 26

When a Loved One Dies

It is unavoidable that we should be sad when those we love leave us in death. Although we know that they are not leaving us forever, that they have but gone a little ahead of us, that we who remain will follow them, our nature still recoils from their death. Even though our hope in the divine promises brings some sort of healing, because we are human we still mourn their loss.

Sermon 172, 1

Few things are more difficult than the death of a friend. When they leave us in death they seem to take with them half our heart. We ask ourselves if it would have been better not to have loved, only to realize that our lives would have been the lesser for not having done so. We would have lived a "half-hearted" life. Love from others can help us move on with our life, but such love will never take the place of the beloved we have lost. The hole that their absence leaves in our lives will never be filled, but the incoming tide of new loves can enable us to float above the void. Nostalgia gradually takes over— that sweet gentle word for fond memories that can never return. Through such fond memories our grief may finally be soothed.

March 27

Piercing the Dome

The prospect of the future prompted Paul to cry "The dark times of this life cannot be compared to the glory that shall be revealed to us" (Romans 8:18). What in the world can this glory be? Nothing else than to truly see! . . . to be like the angels and see the light that is God.

Commentary on Psalm 36/2, 8

For some years now I have been wondering more and more about the experience of death. One image that sticks in my mind is that dying will be like piercing the dome. The image was suggested by the recent movie, *The Truman Show*, in which a man lived out his whole life in a huge dome created by a television network. He did not know until the very end that he was living in a fantasy world created for the amusement of the hidden audience. When he finally found the door to the real world beyond the dome, he rushed through it saying "Till I see you again, my friends, I can only say 'Good Night! Good Morning! Good Afternoon.'" I sometimes think that those would be great words to say at the moment of death as I "pierced the dome" of this life. Faith tells me that we live now on the edge of eternity. If only we could reach out far enough with our spirit, we would feel the smooth surface of the thin wall that separates our present, confined life from the brilliant, boundless eternity that awaits us once we have "pierced the dome" that separates us from heaven.

March 28

The Sleep of Death

What else is sleep but a daily death, a sleep which does not permanently remove us from our present moment, a sleep that does not last all that long? And what else is death but a long-lasting and very deep sleep, a sleep from which God will wake us up one day.

Sermon 221, 3

Augustine believed that death was very much like being asleep. As with our earthly sleep, in our death-sleep we will not be totally unconscious. We will begin to taste the full joy or despair that awaits us after the day of resurrection (cf. *Sermon 223C*). How can we be asleep and yet conscious? Perhaps the answer is suggested by the *dreaming sleep* that we experience in this life. Sometimes our dreams are steeds that carry us to pleasant places; at other times they are "nightmares" that leave terror in their wake. When God comes to wake us at the end of time it will be forever (*Commentary on the Gospel of John*, 49.10). The only important questions then will be whether we did our best to be faithful to him in life and whether we were sorry when we failed. If the answer to such questions is yes, we shall wake from our death-sleep and be very happy, experiencing an ecstasy which knows no fear and has no end (*Sermon 399*, 13).

March 29

Life after Death

I know that you just love being alive and that you don't ever want to die. You would like to remain alive while moving on to a life that is even better. That's what you would really like to happen and I think every human shares your wish. Indeed, this desire is so universal that it seems engraved on our human nature.

Sermon 344, 4

We are certain that someday we will die; we would like to be just as certain about what comes after life. Is there life after death? Unfortunately there is no decisive proof from reason for the existence of an afterlife. Both Plato and Augustine tried to offer such proofs but, though their logic was cogent, the arguments were far from convincing. Augustine in his later years even admitted that he could barely understand the argument he had offered as a young man (*Retractions,* 1.5.1). Regarding such matters as falling in love and life after death, I don't want logic. I want experience! But those with experience of death are not around to tell about it, so to believe in one's immortality requires a leap of faith. It is for this reason that my conviction about my immortality rests on my faith in the Jesus-God who tells me that I will live forever.

March 30

Resurrection

When you die your body will disappear for a while only to rejoin you at the end of time. This is going to happen whether you like it or not. You are not going to rise from the grave because you want to, nor will your not wanting it prevent it from happening. Even if you don't believe in your eventual resurrection, you will still rise from the grave "willy-nilly."

Sermon 344, 4

Augustine's words are consoling to me because I am one of those who, in order to be happy, needs assurance that after death I will continue to exist with my body. I want my body to be with me in my eternal afterlife, but the only way I can be sure of this is by believing in the promise of someone who has the power to do it. For the Christian that person is Jesus Christ, who gives us the hope that we too can rise one day to a blessed life. We know this will happen because he has shown us that he has the power over death and he has promised that he will use that power to bring us back whole and entire at the end of time. Our faith in the reality of Jesus and his rising from the dead is the foundation for our hope that someday the same thing will happen to us. We know that it will happen because this he has promised!

March 31

Passion Time

> The passion of our Lord and Savior Jesus Christ guarantees our future glory. It is a great thing that the Lord promises, but it is a much greater thing that he has already done for us. How can we weak human beings doubt that someday we will live with God when God has died for the sake of human beings?
>
> *Sermon 218C, 1*

The end of March points to the end of the Lenten Season, the two weeks that are the season of the Passion. It is paradoxical that Passion time ends with a week that we call "Holy Week" but it is fitting because it was God who did the suffering. The terrible suffering and sacrifice of Jesus-God in the last week of his life was holy because he was God's instrument in restoring holiness to the human race. By God's birth as a human being he proved that he wanted to be our friend; by Jesus-God's death on the cross he proved that he wanted to be our savior, saving us from the effects of original sin. Passion time is a time of sorrow and suffering but it also a time of glory because it proves how much God loves each one of us.

April 1

This Is My Body; This Is My Blood

I have promised those of you who have just been baptized a sermon to explain the sacrament of the Lord's table. That bread which you can see on the altar, sanctified by the Word of God, is the Body of Christ. That cup, or rather what the cup contains, sanctified by the Word of God, is the Blood of Christ. If you receive them worthily, you become what you receive. As the apostle says, "We, being many, are one loaf, one body" (1 Corinthians 10:17). That's how he explained the effect of the sacrament of the Lord's table on us; one loaf, one body is what we become, many though we may be.

Sermon 227

There were two major events that occurred during the last week of Jesus' life. On Thursday Jesus, through the institution of the Holy Eucharist, took steps to remain with his followers till the end of time. On Friday, through his death on the cross, he gave us the chance to be with him eternally. The wonderful mystery of the Eucharist is that through worthy reception, God lives in us and we join with him in a mystical union (*Sermon 228B, 3*). On Good Friday Jesus would climb the hill of Golgotha to his death, but he left behind great gifts: his many teachings, a few frightened Christians bound to him by love, and the great sacrament of his Body and Blood, the Holy Eucharist.

April 2

Judas

It was not the crime of Judas so much as his despair of pardon that brought him to total destruction. He killed himself in despair, suffocating himself with a noose. What he did to his body is what happened to his soul. Just as those who pull something tight round their throats kill themselves by driving from their lungs the earthy spirit of air, so too do those who despair of God's merciful kindness inwardly suffocate themselves and make it impossible for the Holy Spirit to remain in them.

Sermon 352, 8

The tragedy of Judas teaches an important lesson. No matter how close to Christ one is, there is always a chance of betrayal. Receiving the Holy Eucharist provides no absolute protection. If we are to believe the chronology set down in Scripture, Judas attended the last supper, received the Eucharist with the rest of the disciples, and then betrayed Jesus. Scripture reports that later Judas hanged himself in despair. Some have suggested that this merited condemnation; but if he was condemned, it was not because he betrayed Christ, nor because he received the Blessed Sacrament unworthily. It was because he came to believe that his sin was unforgivable. There is a lesson in this: as long as we do not give up on God's mercy there is always a chance for us to be saved through his loving grace.

April 3

Dismas

The Lord was crucified between two bandits. One of those bandits came to believe in Jesus. He said to his fellow robber (who had made fun of Jesus): "We are suffering these things for our evil deeds, but this man is the Holy One of God." Then he said to Jesus, "Lord, remember me when you come into your kingdom" (Luke 23:39-42). What Faith! He could see Jesus dying next to him and yet hoped that someday Jesus would reign over him. Dismas was a great man! He took the kingdom of heaven by storm. Where did he learn his great Faith? Jesus was dying by his side but he was already teaching him in the depths of his heart.

Sermon 328, 7

The story of Dismas, the "good thief," is one of the bright spots in the sad story of Good Friday. Dismas met Jesus for the first time on Calvary and, despite his own suffering, he reached out to him with love. He upbraided the other robber for taunting Jesus, saying, "Leave him alone! He has done nothing wrong!" Sometimes great love can lead to faith. As Augustine suggests above, this faith was given to Dismas by the God who was dying by his side but already living in his heart. The encouraging message of Dismas' salvation somehow softens the example of Judas' failure. Judas showed that it is never too late to reject Jesus; Dismas shows that it is never too late to embrace him.

April 4

Free among the Dead

How great was your love for us, O great Father, for you did not spare your own Son but gave him up to save us sinners! Jesus-God who alone was free among the dead (free to lay down his life and free to take it up again) became for us both victor and victim. He freed us from

slavery and made us your children. We might have despaired of ourselves if he had not come to dwell among
us.

Confessions, 10.43.69

It is a paradoxical image: to be free among the dead. For
most of us death seems to be the end of freedom. When we die
we do not consider ourselves free, merely dead. Jesus Christ
shows us that this is not true. He shows us that we too can be
free among the dead. By his death and resurrection he shows
us that death is not the end; it is the beginning of a new life free
from death. Because Christ died for our sins, we no longer
need to fear that terrible second death that Augustine writes
about, the death that comes to a living human being when they
are separated from God for all eternity. Jesus Christ, by dying
for our sins, freed us from sin so that, unfettered, we too can
run to God free among the dead.

April 5

Holy Saturday

We keep vigil on this night when the crucified Lord was
in his tomb; let us keep awake during the time in which
he slept for our sakes. We keep vigil the night when he
slept in the tomb in order to live by the death which he
suffered. We keep vigil over his temporal slumber, so that
he might watch over us during our death-slumber until
we rise again to that eternal day when we will remain
tirelessly awake forever.

Sermon 223B, 2

In Augustine's day the evening of Holy Saturday was spent
in an all-night vigil, remembering sadly what had happened
the day before and waiting joyously for what would happen

before daybreak. The original Holy Saturday must have had more sorrow than joy. Jesus was dead in the tomb and no one yet knew that he would soon rise again. The great virtue of the disciples was that they patiently waited. The lesson of that holy night is that, though it may appear that God has abandoned us, he has in fact not. Indeed, he is still here strengthening us to develop a faith strong enough to believe in a God whom we cannot see and who sometimes truly seems to be dead and gone.

April 6

The Consolation of Easter

Christ made himself an example of the life we live now by his labors, his temptations, his suffering, and his death. In his resurrection he demonstrates the life we will live after death. Without him all that we would have known about human life is that we are born and we die. We would not have known that anyone could rise from the dead and live forever. He took upon himself the human condition that we all knew and gave us a proof of the resurrected life that we did not know. This is why he has become our hope in distressful times.

Commentary on Psalm 60, 4

Good Friday for the disciples must have been an end—an end to their hopes, the end of Christ, and the end of them. This is the reason why Easter was so important for them and for us. Christ's return from the grave proved that it was possible for a human being to have a life beyond death. Christ proved by *his* resurrection that *our* resurrection was possible (*Commentary on Psalm 65, 6*). Easter showed that our earthly life is but a dot on a line that extends forever. The promise of resurrection, that someday we will enjoy a new life, may not solve our current problems but it can help us continue on. Now at least we have a promise of a better life, an eternal life of happiness, the enjoyment of which is within our control.

April 7

Easter Morning: The Chronology

All four evangelists were unable to keep quiet either about Jesus' passion or his resurrection. One dealt with this aspect, another with that, but all remained in perfect harmony with the truth. If I tried to show you how this could be, I'm afraid you would be overcome with boredom long before you began to understand the truth.

Sermon 240, 1

Rather than exaltation, those early hours of Easter Sunday were characterized by sorrow and disbelief. Jesus' resurrection remained yet unknown. But Mary Magdalene and other holy women were to discover the empty tomb early in the morning, only to rush back to Jerusalem to tell the apostles. Peter and John inspect the tomb for themselves, but see no sign of the risen Jesus. Mary Magdalene met Jesus himself just outside the tomb, at which time Jesus told her to return again to Jerusalem and tell the apostles that the report of the resurrection is indeed true, that she had actually seen him. Of course, Mary Magdalene was not believed by the disciples. In the depths of their despair, the disciples, huddled in their hidden room, could not believe in the resurrection. It seemed simply too good to be true.

April 8

"Don't Touch Me, Mary!"

What Christ was saying to Mary was this: "You think of me as a man. I am indeed a man; but don't let your faith stay at that level. Do not touch me, believing that I am only a man. When I have ascended to my Father, then come and touch me. Understand that I am equal to the Father and then touch me and you will be saved. Do not, by touching earth, lose heaven; do not, by remaining with me as human being, fail to believe I am God."

Sermon 244, 3

Mary Magdalene was the first human to actually see the risen Christ but she did not recognize him until he spoke her name. Overcome with joy, she must have made a rush towards him because Jesus warned her not to touch him. But why this warning? Augustine suggests that word *touching* here means *believing* and what Jesus said to Mary was that the time would come when she would be called upon to touch the "whole Christ" by faith. He could be touched physically as long as he roamed the earth, but only after his Ascension could he be believed in his fullness—in his resurrected humanity and divinity. But also, perhaps he feared that if she embraced him, she would be like Peter on the hill of the Transfiguration, asking to stay there forever. Imprisoned in the ecstasy of the present, she would no longer desire the eternity still in front of her.

April 9

On the Road to Emmaus

Jesus had foretold his resurrection but his death had erased the words from the memories of the disciples on the road to Emmaus. They were so shattered when they saw him crucified, that they forgot about his teaching. They did not expect him to rise again. They had forgotten what he had promised. He was indeed alive but he found the hearts of his disciples dead. As a result, when they saw him on the road they did not recognize him.

Sermon 235, 2

It was about nine o'clock on Easter morning when two disciples began their journey to Emmaus. They firmly believed that Jesus Christ was dead and so were unable to recognize him as we walked with them. Arriving at Emmaus in late afternoon, the disciples invited the stranger to eat with them and, as they broke bread together, they recognized him as their beloved Lord. As Augustine later observed, "What the disciples had lost through 'not believing' was restored through hospitality" (*Sermon 235,* 3). Through concern for a stranger they discovered Jesus Christ, at which time he began to live in them. They experienced the truth that, "It is a greater thing to have Christ in your heart than in your house" (*Sermon 232,* 7).

April 10

"I Am Not a Ghost!"

God became flesh and dwelt among us, taking up the *whole person* of a human being, body and soul. As God created the whole human person, so he redeemed the whole person. In the resurrected Christ there is a human mind and human intelligence, a soul giving life to the flesh, and a true and complete body. The only thing that we have that he did not have is sin.

Sermon 237, 4

On the evening of Easter Sunday, Jesus appeared to the disciples still hiding in the upper room in Jerusalem. By this time they had heard the stories of Mary Magdalene and the holy women and the Emmaus disciples; though they heard that Jesus was risen, they still had their doubts. Jesus' entrance through a locked door did little to dispel their fear that what had been seen was a ghost (Luke 24:37). Jesus showed them his wounds and ate with them, which allayed their fears. As Augustine comments, "He saw the wounds in their minds and sought to cure them by showing them the scars in his body" (*Sermon 237, 3*). As was the case on the road to Emmaus, eating led to believing. The disciples had entered the room grieving for a dead Christ. They left it as his Church carrying the message "Jesus lives!"

April 11

Doubting Thomas

By putting his hand into the body of Christ, Thomas perfected his faith. The fullness of faith is to believe that Christ is both man and God. This disciple was offered the scars of his Savior to touch and when he touched them he exclaimed "My Lord and My God!" He touched the man, he recognized God.

Sermon 258, 3

When Jesus appeared to the disciples on the evening of Easter, Thomas was not there. When he heard the news of the resurrection, he would not believe until he touched his body and felt his wounds and established for himself that this was the Jesus he had known and loved. Jesus knew this and thus insisted that this doubting apostle touch his scars with his fingers and put his hand into the wound in his side. The experience had a profound effect. Thomas's words, "My Lord and My God!," were more than a declaration that he now believed. It was a declaration that this friend was in fact the almighty God. Touching Jesus' scars allowed him to recognize his sin, and that of the whole human race. It changed Thomas's life forever.

April 12

Gone Fishing

In forming his church, Jesus did not begin with emperors or senators, but with fishermen. Had any persons of rank been the first to be chosen, they might have brazenly attributed their selection to their own eminent worth, not to God's grace. Moreover, if those fishermen had not come first, who would have "caught" us? Nowadays a person is considered a great preacher, if he can give a good explanation of what was written by a fisherman.

Sermon 250, 1

After the second appearance of Christ in the upper room, some of the Apostles made their way back to the Sea of Galilee at Tiberias. They believed in a living Christ but they still had to make a living. Sadly, their first efforts to renew their career ended in failure. They fished for most of the night but caught nothing. They were disappointed but I doubt that they were despairing, something unbecoming of fishermen. As Augustine suggests above, such humble acceptance of failure was perhaps one of the reasons why Jesus chose fishermen as his first disciples. Christ's selection of these humble working men was a sign that his grace is given equally to the noble and ignoble—those who have nothing and are worth nothing in the eyes of the world. As Augustine puts it, Christ called "fishers of fish to be fishers of men" (*Sermon 252A, 2*).

April 13

A Heavenly Picnic

The life we are going to have in heaven will be one of perpetual quiet, everlasting happiness, unfailing bliss, without disturbance, sadness, or death. Only those who experience it can know what such a life will be like and only those who believe it now will be able to experience it.

Sermon 259, 1

There are events in this life, infrequent though they may be, when we enjoy a hint of heaven. One such event, described in the Gospel of John (21:1-14), occurred on the shore of the Sea of Galilee at Tiberias. It was a few days after the resurrection of Jesus and the apostles just had an unproductive night of fishing. Jesus appeared to them on the shore and encouraged them to try again. They did, and filled their nets with a huge catch of large fish. Augustine believed that this catch of good fish (none were thrown away) symbolized how, at the end of time, the saints will be brought to the heavenly shore (*Sermon 251, 3–4*). Saint Jerome interpreted the large catch as an indication that Jesus intended to "catch" every human being, no matter their age, sex, or race. When the apostles finally arrived on shore they saw some fish already cooking over a fire, and so they joined Jesus in breakfast. From then on they imagined heaven as a picnic with Jesus and some friends on the quiet shores of a dawn-dappled lake.

April 14

"Peter, Do You Love Me?"

After his resurrection Jesus asked Peter, "Do you love me more than the rest?" and Peter answered, "You know Lord that I love you!" Jesus then charged him, "Feed my lambs, feed my sheep" (John 21:15; 17). The Lord questioned Peter three times in the same way so that his threefold confession might cancel the threefold denial he had made on the evening of Holy Thursday. He was questioned about his love first and only then were Christ's sheep (his church and all its members) entrusted to him.

Sermon 229P, 1–4

On the shores of the Sea of Galilee, Jesus confirmed what he had said to Peter earlier: "You are Peter and upon this rock I will build my Church" (Matthew 16:15-19). It was a good thing that he did not depend on the advice of a management consultant. After all, Peter was the one who tried to walk on water, who cut off the servant's ear in the garden of Gethsemani, who denied three times that he knew Christ, and who saw the empty tomb but still doubted the resurrection. In light of this, John would seem to have been a better choice as pope. He was more of a mystic and, among all the apostles, he alone stood by the cross of the dying Christ. With all his failings and weaknesses, why was Peter chosen? The answer is that Jesus wanted a great lover to take his place, one who could understand the weakness and failures of his flock.

April 15

"But When You Are Old . . ."

Jesus said to blessed Peter: "When you are old, another will gird you and take you where you do not wish" (John 21:18). And so it is when you get old.

Sermon 335B, 3

Though some of us may die young, it is in our nature to grow old (*A Literal Commentary on Genesis*, 6.16.27). Before he left them, I can imagine Jesus saying to his apostles, "If you reach old age, you will then preach my love by your patience and humility—humility in allowing yourself to be cared for by others, patience when their care is not as good as you would like. Believing in me will not protect you from the somberness of old age, but believing in me will help you know that even in your darkest nights you will not be alone for I will be there. In your youth you may be surrounded by others, but when your day in the sun begins to fade, then there will be just you and me alone in the twilight of your life. If you believe that I am with you, that will be enough."

April 16

The Promise of Christ's Ascension

What Jesus did when he ascended into heaven is his promise to you. Just now we can only hope that we are going to rise again, that we will ascend into heaven and there will be with God forever. Jesus-God, who promises us this, says "In order for you to believe that you will ascend to me, I first descended to you; in order for you to believe that you will live with me, I first died for you."

Sermon 265C, 2

We all would like to live forever but everyday experience testifies to our fragility, that slowly but surely we are fading away. The Christian faith assures us that eventually there will be a resurrection when our spirit is united with a new, more perfect body; but it would be nice to have some assurance that, at the end of time, our resurrected body will be raised up to heaven. The experience of the ascension, when the disciples saw Jesus Christ—soul and body—taken up to heaven, gave them such assurance as well as a glimpse into their own destiny. They now knew that they were not meant to be buried in or on this earth forever. They now understood the meaning of the promise Jesus had made sometime earlier: "Where I am you someday shall be."

April 17

We Are the Church!

We are celebrating the day on which the Lord Jesus Christ, glorified after the resurrection by his ascension, sent the Holy Spirit to the first Christians. You my friends are members of the body of Christ. Among you is being fulfilled what was prefigured on that day when the Holy Spirit first came. Just as on that first Pentecost whoever received the Holy Spirit started speaking all languages, so now the unity among you is itself speaking all languages throughout the world. It is because of this unity that you know you have the Holy Spirit.

Sermon 271

The feast of Pentecost is the birthday of the Church. It commemorates the day when the Holy Spirit came into the lives of the first Christians and bound them together in the unity of love. It was the birth of the Mystical Body of Christ, all those who in Christ's Church are united in faith and love with their head, Jesus (*Commentary on Gospel of John,* 32.8). The message of the story of Pentecost is simply this: if you want to see the Church, you need not look for clerics and religious; look at the loving person next to you. Indeed, if you want to see the Church, you need only look inside yourself because, if you have faith and love, you too are a member of that Body of Christ vivified by the Holy Spirit so long ago on the streets of Jerusalem.

April 18

We Are Christ's Body

When Christ begins to dwell in our inmost being through faith, when we have confessed and invoked him and he has begun to take possession of us, then is formed the whole Christ, head and body, in which the many become one. Christ tells the good news of himself now through his members. Through them he can attract others who will be joined to those who have spread his Gospel. From this, one body is formed under one head, living one life in one Spirit.

Commentary on Psalm 74, 4

The Holy Spirit, who came into the lives of Christ's followers, made it possible for us to be Christ for the world. As Augustine told the faithful of the fifth century, "In Christ we all form one human person whose head is in heaven and whose limbs are toiling on earth" (*Commentary on Psalm 60,* 1). We, Christ's "limbs" that toil on earth, are alive spiritually because of the life-force given us by Jesus and the Holy Spirit. In other words, Christ becomes real to others only through the lives we live. Thus, Nietzsche's challenge still rings true to Christians to this day: "I will become Christian when Christians act more Christian."

April 19

God as Trinity

I now begin to speak of a mystery which is altogether above the power of any human being (including myself) to express in words. Indeed, when I begin to reflect on the triune God, I am conscious of the distance between my mind and the God of whom it is thinking. Therefore I call upon the Lord our God for help to understand and explain my subject and I beg His pardon wherever I go astray.

The Trinity, 5.1.1

The mystery of the Trinity is a mystery that we will never comprehend but it does reveal one fact that we can understand: the depth of God's love for every human being. God is like a parent who so desired to have more to love, that in the person of the Father he created sons and daughters to share his joyful life. Trinity teaches us that God, in the person of the Son, became human in order to restore our friendship with him. Trinity teaches us that God, recognizing that we are still "cracked pots," comes to us in the person of the Holy Spirit to give us the grace and strength needed to get to heaven. The mystery of the Trinity is at the center of our faith and hope because it tells us how much we are loved by the infinite God, a God who will never leave us alone until we reach our final home with him in heaven.

April 20

Love and Friendship

What is it that moves any of us if not some kind of love? Consider even the most shameful deeds (adulteries, villainy, murders, all kinds of lust). Are they not all the work of some sort of love? Should we then be told, "Don't love anything?" Of course not. If you did not love anything, you would be lifeless, dead, detestable, miserable. Go ahead and love but be careful what you love.

Commentary on Psalm 31/2, 5

The difference between love and friendship is that we may love another person deeply but they do not become our friends until they return our love. Love means to desire something or someone; friendship means to have that desire fulfilled and returned in such a way that it creates a "union of hearts." The perfection of love is to desire something because it is good in itself, not because it is "good for us" (*83 Diverse Questions*, 35.1). The perfection of friendship is to have a pure love for another, and to have it returned with the same purity. However, there are no guarantees that another will return our love. The best we can do is create the necessary condition for friendship, which is to make sure that our loves are not out of order. If we love ourselves, our possessions, or others in a perverse way, we are rendered incapable of friendship. How to correct this is obvious: to become capable of friendship, we must first purify our love.

April 21

God Gives the Power to Love Well

What does the Holy Spirit bestow on us? Listen to the apostle: "The love of God has been poured out in our hearts." He continues, "We have this treasure in earthen vessels." Why in earthen vessels? "That the dominant power of loving may be seen as God's" (2 Corinthians 4:7). Thus, in order for you to love God, let God dwell in you; let him prompt you to love him, kindle you, enlighten you, rouse you.

Sermon 128, 4

By creating us social animals, God has given us the power to love, to desire those things we need to live and be happy. However, to control our love for things, to restrain our love for self, to love other humans as ourselves, and to love God above all, we need help. This help was given us by the Holy Spirit at Pentecost. The gift of tongues, though an important gift, was not as important as the gift of loving well. This most important gift, we must admit, has been diminished in practice. That we have not always loved well is because this gift was poured into "cracked pots," earthen vessels that sometimes leak. Many of us love poorly, but some have perfected this love. I am not necessarily talking here about great saints. The power to love well is shown every day by ordinary people; their example gives the rest of us hope.

April 22

God Lives in Those Who Love

The Apostle John writes "If we love one another God dwells in us and his love is brought to perfection in us" (1 John 4:12). Begin to love; you will be perfected. Have you begun to love? God has begun to dwell in you. As John continues "In this we know that we abide in him and he in us, because he has given us his Spirit" (1 John 4:13). How do we know that "he has given us of his Spirit"? Ask your heart; if it is filled with love, you have received the Spirit of God.

Commentary on the Epistle of John, 8.12

A sign that God lives in us is found in our ability to love another perfectly—loving them for the good we see in them, and not for the good we hope to get from them. This is so because the reason we imperfect humans are able to rise above our natural selfishness is because the Spirit of God works within us. Even though we do not now see God, by loving other human beings we make ourselves worthy of seeing him (*Commentary on the Epistle of John,* 17.8). In a way we are like the disciples at Emmaus, welcoming Christ in the guise of a stranger. As Augustine comments, "They received him with gracious courtesy and hospitality restored what unbelief had taken away" (*Sermon 235,* 3).

April 23

The Need for a Friend

> Some of the goods of this world are dispensable, others are necessary. Necessities amount to these two things: to have health and to have a friend. These are the things that we should value highly and not despise. Health and friendship are goods of nature. God gave us existence and life. That's what I mean by "health." God also gave us a need for friends so that we would not be alone.
>
> *Sermon 299D,* 1

We humans are not meant to be like turtles, solitary wanderers meeting only briefly with others of our kind to continue the species. Nor are we meant to be like animals rushing through life anonymously in herds. We are meant to be united to some other human being in oneness of heart. As Augustine remarked, "When a person has no friend, nothing in the world seems friendly" (*Letter 130,* 2.4). However, nature gives us only the need to make friends, not the ability to make friends. Friendship may rest on love but it is more complex. It entails more conditions, the least of which is that we are loved in return. God has told us through Jesus that he wants to be a friend to every human being. This is consoling, but for many of us it would be nice to have a human friend too!

April 24

A Letter to an Absent Friend

My dear friend, you are the kind of person whose absence is too unbearable to be borne bravely. I am depressed at not being able to see you but the sadness gives its own peculiar satisfaction. If I cannot help rejoicing when you are near, how can I avoid being sad when you are far away? It would be dreadful if I could do that. My only joy in your absence is that I am unable to avoid feeling lonely. My consolation now is in embracing my sadness.

Letter 27, 1

Augustine's letter to a distant friend may seem a bit "over the top" but it does express both the ecstasy and sometime distress that goes with being one in heart with another human being. It also hints at the ecstasy we shall feel when we are one in heart with our divine friend in heaven, surrounded by all those whom we have called friends in this life. We can understand the sadness Augustine expresses above if we have ever been in love with another. When they are present to us, it seems that our life expands—we are "blown up" with the joy of simply being with them. When they leave us, it is as though the wind is taken out of our sails. Sadly, we must be prepared for such separations in this life for, though truly united in heart with our friend, we remain different persons with different destinies.

April 25

Friendship Begins at Home

Friendship begins in the home with the married couple and their children and from there moves on to strangers.

But since we all have one father and mother (Adam and Eve) who can be a stranger? Every human being is neighbor to every other human being. Even those you do not know share your humanity. Is this person known as a friend? Let them stay as a friend. Is this person your enemy? Let them become a friend.

Sermon 299D, 1

Augustine believed that the best chance for true friendship was in a home where the spouses loved each other and their children. Perhaps reflecting on his own experience of having an unplanned son, he thought that even an unwanted child cannot help but be loved once it is born (*Confessions,* 4.2.2) and that every baby leaps from the womb prepared to be friends with anyone who cares about it. Augustine was too much of a realist to say that every family was a union of friends. However he did argue that if friendship does not exist in the home, it will be difficult to create it elsewhere. Once soured by an unhappy home, it is hard to establish friendships with the rest of the world. It can happen, of course, but it takes great trust to give your heart to strangers when it has been already crushed by those who knew you best.

April 26

The Pain of Unrequited Love

If we will not believe anything we cannot see, how can we come to believe that we are loved by a friend? We cannot see love. Friendship must then perish since it exists only when love is mutual and how can we accept that we are loved by a friend when we demand that their love itself (and not simply its effects) be seen to be believed?

On Faith in Things Unseen, 2.4

One of the problems in establishing a friendship, is that it depends on mutual love. If love is not returned, then friendship cannot exist. In my youth I was not above sending unsigned love notes to various fair maidens and, though I mooned over their indifference for a while, I could hardly have expected anything different. They did not know I even existed. Unrequited love is much more painful when friendships end because one party ceases to love the other (*The Trinity*, 9.4.6). Such breakdowns are most wrenching when they occur within the family, when spouses suddenly "fall out of love," when children suddenly begin to hate their parents. Unfortunately, we cannot make another love us, no matter how hard we try. The consolation of our faith is that, with respect to God, we do not need to try. God will love us no matter what we do. If there is unrequited love in our relationship with God, it comes from our end of the relationship.

April 27

Friendship: A Leap into Darkness

Where on this earth can one find someone whose character gives us an absolutely certain sense of security? No one is known to another as he is to himself but we do not know even ourselves well enough to predict how we shall be tomorrow. There is so much about the human heart that is unknown and unknowable that the Apostle warns us not to judge anyone before the time when the Lord comes bringing light to the hidden things of darkness and revealing the true feelings in each of our hearts (1 Corinthians 4.5).

Letter 130, 2.4

Friendship must be based on truth; it cannot rest on a fiction. But how can we know the truth about another? How, indeed, can we know the truth about ourselves? As Augustine says, "We are all enclosed in flesh so that our hearts cannot be seen. Each heart is closed to everyone else" (*Commentary on Psalm 55*, 9). We may be tempted to claim to make an exception for friends—that we may have some notion of their motives (*83 Diverse Questions*, 71.5); yet, on the other hand, we find we are unsure if we know them well enough to consider them a friend. Believing that someone is a friend requires faith. We can never know exactly what is going on in the heart of another, even a friend. To gain a friend we must leap into the darkness and hope for the best.

April 28

Heavenly Openness

In heaven everyone will see the thoughts which now only God sees. There no one will wish to conceal what they think because no one will think evil. Just now our thoughts are only known by ourselves; they are hidden in darkness from our neighbor. In heaven your neighbor will know what you are thinking. Why be afraid? Now you fear to reveal your thoughts because sometimes your thoughts are wicked. In heaven you will have only good thoughts. Just as now you are willing to let others see your face, in heaven you will be willing to let them see your conscience.

Sermon 243, 5

Augustine once remarked that one of the great benefits of having a true friend is that we are not afraid to pour out our true feelings to them (*83 Different Questions*, 71.6). We are able to reveal not only our joys but also our anxieties, not only our virtuous feelings but even the feelings we are ashamed to admit even to ourselves. Such openness is a refreshing ideal, but the reality is that charity sometimes requires a limit on our openness. It can be cruel to impose on a friend a truth about ourselves they cannot handle, a truth that will not help them but destroy them. In such cases the prudence suggests that we let "sleeping dogs lie." In heaven all will be revealed, but there is no use in creating a hell for a friend now by revealing a truth they cannot bear.

April 29

Friendship for One in Need

> If poverty pinches, if grief saddens, if pain overcomes us, if exile darkens our life, if any other misfortune fills us with foreboding, let there be good friends at hand who know how to "weep with them that weep" as well as "rejoice with them that rejoice." With such good friends such bitter trials are lessened, the heavy burdens are lightened, the obstacles are met and overcome.
>
> *Letter 130,* 2.4

Augustine's letter to a dear friend who had recently lost her husband expressed sentiments that he learned from experience when he too lost a friend to death. Remembering the loss some years later, he confessed that "The consolation of friends did the most to repair the damage and give me strength after my friend's death" (*Confessions,* 4.8.13). He experienced the truth that friendship adds to our joy in good times but it is proven in bad times (*On Faith in Things Unseen,* 1.1.3). We know our friends by how willing they are to come to our support in times of need. "Fair weather friends" are hardly friends at all. In contrast, friendship to friends in need proves the sincerity of our love. It is nice to be loved for ourselves but sometimes the beginning of such love is in being needed.

April 30

Bearing a Friend's Burden

Let us bear each other's burdens in this life so that we can
achieve that life that has no burdens. Take the example of
deer. When deer swim across a channel to an island in
search of pasture they line themselves up in such a way
that the weight of their antlers is borne by another. The
one behind, by extending its neck places its head on the
one in front. Since the one at the head of the line has no
one to support its head, when it tires it gives up its place
to the one behind and retreats to the last place in line.
Through this method of bearing one another's burden
they are able to cross the channel to the island. It is an
example of the truth that bearing a friend's burden is the
best proof of friendship.

83 Various Questions, 71.1

Augustine's message is that if we are ever to get to heaven,
we need a little help from our friends. Of course our primary
helper is God himself, but God can work through others, such
as counselors—who remind us of where we are going and how
to get there—or friends, who support us when we are too weak
to go on. We need friends whose goodness and happiness give
us the hope that says the world is not as bad as it seems. We
need good friends who can give us the hope that says we are
not as bad as we sometimes feel. With a little help from our
friends we can make it through to the land where God lives.

May 1

Letting Others Bear Our Burdens

I confess that I readily throw myself upon the love of my friends when I am wearied with the scandals of the world. Indeed I feel that God is there in my friends and I cast myself upon Him and rest in Him without care. In that carefree state I no longer fear the "tomorrows" made uncertain by human fragility.

Letter 73, 10

Sometimes it is harder to accept help from others than to give help to them. To admit that we need help demands humility and sometimes it is hard to develop that virtue after having enjoyed health and success. It is embarrassing for one who has been self-possessed to suddenly find that they are dependent on others to carry, clean, put them to bed, and get them up in the morning. St. Augustine's thoughts on this show great humility. He was one of the most powerful figures in the African Church and yet he readily admitted his occasional helplessness. His message to us goes something like this: "If you are willing to accept the strength of God to help you help others in your days of strength, you must be ready to accept the support of God coming through others on your days of weakness."

May 2

Love Makes Old Things Seem New

Is it not a common experience that when we show certain lovely vistas to a dear friend for the first time, our own delight is renewed by their delight at the novelty of the scene. Our reawakened joy is heightened by the passion

of our friendship. It seems that the more we love them,
the more do old things become new for us.

On Catechizing the Uninstructed, 12.17

One of the side-effects of falling in love is that suddenly the
world seems brighter, the sky bluer, and the air fresher. Regarding this a stretch of highway 1A in New Hampshire, comes
to mind. It twists and winds following the contours of the rocky
shore, in one place rising high above the sea. At the very top
there is a wayside rest from which all you can see is the blue
sky and the emerald sea crashing against the rocks below. I
imagine that someone who must travel that road every day
eventually becomes indifferent to the beauty of the scene.
Experiencing the view for the first time with a loved-one, however, might renew one's appreciation. I suspect that the same
thing happens in heaven. For the first time we will see the
world, ourselves, and our loved ones through the eyes of God.
In so doing, as Augustine says above, "In the passion of our
love, old things will become suddenly new."

May 3

Fear of Losing the One We Love

If a woman says to the man who loves her "Don't wear
that sort of cloak," he will stop wearing it. If she tells him
in the midst of winter "I like you best in your short tunic,"
he would rather shiver than offend her. He is not afraid
that she will send him to prison or bring in torturers if he
does not obey. The one and only thing he's afraid of is
that she will say to him, "You will never see me again.
You will never again see my face."

Sermon 161, 10

Augustine understood our fear of losing someone we love deeply. When he lost a friend in death he said it was like losing half his soul (*Confessions*, 4.6.11). Fear of losing a loved one is part of the price of love. Sometimes we will take extreme measures to avoid losing a loved one, sacrificing everything to keep them. There is nothing wrong with this as long as the things we sacrifice do not stand in the way of our coming to God. Love is no excuse for sin; love is no excuse for hurting the innocent. Love is a wonderful thing, but it becomes destructive if it makes us act against the will of God. Augustine thought it a shame that many are not afraid of hearing from God what we fear hearing from our human loves: "Do what I want or you will never again see my face."

May 4

Friendship: Agreement on Things Human and Divine

Cicero (*De Amicitia* 6.20) defined friendship as "The agreement on things human and divine, accompanied by kindness and love." Indeed, there can be no full and true agreement about things human among friends who disagree about things divine because it necessarily follows that he who *despises* things divine esteems things human otherwise than he should, and that whoever does not love Him who made man has not learned to love man aright.

Letter 258, 1–2

Compatibility is necessary for deep friendship, and friendship is the foundation for marriage. Friends need not agree on everything, but they must agree on the important things in life. A marriage cannot survive if there is a disagreement on such fundamental things as fidelity or children. A believer cannot be friends with someone who attacks or ridicules their faith.

Augustine preached to his congregation that true friendship occurs between two joined in their love of God, or because one hopes that, someday, the other will come to love God (*Sermon 336*, 2). God is present in every human who loves because it is his Holy Spirit that gives us the ability to love each other properly. God is the glue that binds lovers together through time and eternity (*Confessions*, 4.4.7), whether they believe in him or not.

May 5

Universal Friendship

Friendship should not be limited; it should embrace all those to whom love is due. Friendship is easier with some than others but it should reach out even to enemies through our prayers for them. There is no one in the human race to whom love is not due, either as a response to their love for us or because they share a common nature with us.

Letter 130, 13

It is important to be clear on what Augustine says here lest we dismiss his thought as unrealistic. First, he is saying that we must love every human being by wishing them only good things. Second, we should be prepared to accept as friends those who have the qualities that make friendship possible. As he says, "One must not reject the friendship of anyone who offers himself as a friend. It may not be possible to receive him immediately but he should be desired as one worthy of being received and he should be treated in such a way that someday he can be received" (*83 Diverse Questions*, 71.6). Among those incapable of friendship might be an infant or someone who hates you. All one can do is wait to accept their friendship when circumstances change. Love of neighbor is commanded by Christ, and so too is friendship, when possible.

May 6

False Friends

In heaven all the "thoughts of our hearts" will be out in the open, but now they are hidden. Someone is considered to be an enemy but perhaps he is a friend. Someone else looks like a friend but is possibly a hidden enemy. What darkness we live in! This one roars at us and he loves; this other one whispers "sweet nothings" in our ear and he hates. Judging by their words, I should flee from a friend and cling to an enemy.

Sermon 49, 4

Augustine's caution about friendship rests on the fact that we cannot know what goes on in the minds of others. You might object, suggesting that a friend is someone who shows us mercy. Augustine responds, "Not everyone who spares is a friend, nor is everyone who strikes an enemy. Love mingled with severity is better than deceit with indulgence" (*Letter 93, 4*). Parental discipline is for the proper growth of a child. The affections of a stranger may be for wicked reasons. To give our heart to a friend demands an act of faith that they truly care for us. It is a leap of faith that must be taken if we are going to live in this cracked world. What Augustine says of international relations equally applies to personal relations: "If we never depend on the peace promised by the oaths of barbarians, where on earth can we find peace? The peace that we enjoy will always depend on the sworn oaths of barbarians" (*Letter 47, 2*).

May 7

The Thirst for Peace

The delight of peace is such that even on the level of
earthly and temporal values, nothing that we can talk
about, long for, or finally get, is so desirable, so welcome,
so good as peace. Peace is so universally loved that its
very name falls sweetly on the ear.

City of God, 19.11

We all hunger for peace and this is the reason why it is hard
to achieve. Perfect peace means "never being hungry" (*Commentary on Psalm 33/2,* 19), having all of our human hungers—
for life, meaning, love, and freedom—completely satisfied. In
this life such satisfaction is impossible. Augustine does not
deny that we can satisfy some of these hungers at least some of
the time, but our satisfaction is always limited by the place
where we live, this inn for travelers. As he says "It is true that
here on earth you can sometimes find bread to ease your hunger but once the bread is gone the feeling of warfare raging in
your empty stomach returns" (*Commentary on Psalm 33/2,* 19).
Perfect peace is impossible in this life because this life is impermanent. Thus, it is worth noting the psalmist: "O Lord, make
me realize the shortness of my life so that I may begin to
achieve wisdom of heart" (Psalm 90:12).

May 8

The Nature of Peace

Peace is the tranquility that results from like and unlike
things being ordered in their proper places. The peace of
the body comes when all its parts work together in an

orderly balance. Peace in our appetites comes from their controlled satisfaction. Peace in our soul comes when action follows conviction. Peace between body and soul is when the soul respectfully rules the body. Peace between a human and the Creator comes from an ordered obedience based on faith. Peace between individuals comes from ordered friendship. Peace in the home comes from the ordered harmony of authority and obedience among its members. The peace in the political community is an ordered harmony of authority and obedience among citizens. The peace of heaven lies in a perfectly ordered and harmonious relationship between those who find their joy in God and each other in God.

City of God, 19.13

We might simplify Augustine's long list above by simply saying that perfect peace in this life depends on everything and everyone conforming to the proper order of things. We can expect such peace in heaven but experience tells us that it will not be realized in this world; in the meantime, we must try to bring order and peace at least to our little part of the world.

May 9

Internal Peace

Our bedroom is our heart. It is there that we toss and turn if we have a bad conscience; it is there that we find rest if our conscience is clear. In public places people have a lot to put up with from disputes and controversies and troubles at work. When they get weary of the turmoil, they hurry home to rest. But if they cannot find rest either abroad or at home, what are they to do? They should retire to the bedroom of their heart and not allow the stench of a bad conscience to drive them out.

Commentary on Psalm 35, 5

Peace in this world must begin deep inside each individual, but achieving such peace within is not easy. Each day we face the inner conflict of a body slowly falling apart and a soul dreaming of being more than it can be. Disorder in life starts deep inside each one of us. We are often at odds with ourselves (*Commentary on Psalm 33/2*, 19). Sometimes we are torn apart by guilt, conflicting urges, passions, addictions, and anxiety about an idealized future. Such inner strife can spill out and poison our friendships, family, and society at large. When we are at peace with ourselves we can bring peace to our family, community, and the world at large (*City of God*, 19.13).

May 10

Fear of Examining Our Conscience

It is truly difficult for people to go home when they have a disordered house. They rush downtown with enthusiasm but when the time comes for them to return to their own home, they get terribly depressed. Going home means facing aggravation, recriminations, fighting, and turmoil. When there is no peace at home, there is a natural desire to run away. Well, if people are miserable going home to a dirty house, how much more miserable are those who are reluctant to face their own conscience, afraid of being overwhelmed by the wickedness they find there.

Commentary on Psalm 33/2, 8

Having been told that peace begins within, there may arise the fear that if we examine our conscience too closely, we will be shocked and depressed. Certainly none of us has a completely clear conscience. All of us will find there some guilt for past evils freely chosen. Some of us will likely find secret desires. Many of us will find a multitude of emotions: pride, hurt, envy, anger, and the desire for revenge. Of course we will find some good things too, but the bad things are more noticeable. Perhaps it is because when you slog through a swamp it is difficult to appreciate the clear blue sky above. To find peace we need to enter our conscience and bravely begin to clean up our somewhat soiled "house."

May 11

The Strife Within

Peace is a condition where there is no strife, no adversity. Are we in that state yet? Is there anyone who is not plagued with temptation? But suppose there is. They still have to fight daily against hunger and thirst. In this life hunger and thirst fight against us, bodily weariness fights against us, the lure of sleep fights against us, the burden of the body fights against us. We want to remain standing but are tired out and have to sit down. If we go on sitting for a long time, that too causes fatigue. What kind of internal peace can there be when we continue to face such resistance from vexations, craving, wants and weariness? This is not a condition of perfect peace.

Commentary on Psalm 84, 10

Creating internal peace will always be difficult because we live in a disintegrating body; we must cope with our unruly flesh and weakened spirit. Only a person who is free of hunger, thirst, illness, and fatigue can find complete peace within oneself. Even for the most virtuous, peace will be a daily battle, full of obstacles to overcome (*Commentary on Psalm 84*, 10). Moreover, we are plagued by guilt, temptation, and anxiety about the future. The best peace we can achieve in this life is by enduring gracefully the trials of living in a body that is not always friendly or well-behaved.

Conflict with Others

Let us try to be of one heart here in this life. Let us try to love our brothers and sisters as we love ourselves and be at peace with them. This does not mean that disputes will never arise. Quarrels have broken out between intimate friends, even between saints. Even Barnabas and Paul sometimes disagreed (Acts 15:9). But such disagreements were not so violent that they destroyed unity of hearts. They were not so vicious that they destroyed love.

Commentary on Psalm 33/2, 19

Perfect peace requires the permanent absence of strife and dissension. But where in the world can you find such harmony? In the really existing world of multiplicity the best you can expect is a tranquil order between like and unlike things satisfied with their place in the universe (*City of God,* 19.13.1). Unfortunately, in this world there will always be disorder and struggle. There will be disputes and quarrels even between the most fervent lovers, between husband and wife, between parent and child. Of course, we could resolve to avoid such conflict altogether; this side of death, however, this amounts to wishful thinking. We are too different from each other and too much a mystery to each other for this to happen. Peace depends as much on the grace of God as on human good intentions (*City of God,* 15.4).

May 13

The Sad Fact of War

The human race is unified in that there is a common
human nature shared by all. However, every individual is
driven by their craving to achieve their private ambitions.
Unfortunately the things they seek are such that no one
can get enough of what they want. As a result the world
in which we humans live is in a constant state of war
between those who fail to gain what they want and those
who succeed.

City of God, 18.2

The sad paradox of this life is that we live in a beautiful world
that is plagued by war. It seems that at every period of human
history there have been wars going on throughout the world—
tribe against tribe, nation against nation, indeed religion against
religion. The cause of this is that we humans are "cracked" and
we sometimes resort to violence to get our way. As a result God
had to impose on us such rules as "do unto others . . ." and
"do no harm." If we lived in a perfect world, the only moral
rule would be to love others. The fact that we have principles
telling us to limit the harm we do to each other is a sign that we
live in a world where love and peace will not always be realized, and where we may be called upon to stop others from
harming the innocent.

May 14

The Roots of War

The City of Man (this world) is, for the most part, a
quarrelsome city with opinions divided by foreign wars
and domestic squabbles which seek a victory that either

ends in death or a momentary break from further conflict. The reason is that often when a nation raises the standard of war, it dreams of being lord of the world even as it is consumed by its own wickedness.

City of God, 15.4

Hobbes' sober observation that "Man is a wolf to man!" on some days seems all too true. If there is any injustice in the statement, it is against the wolves, who kill only for survival. Humans sometimes kill just for the fun of it. Surveying his own violent society led Augustine to say, "Neither lions nor dragons have ever waged such wars with their own kind as human beings have fought with each other" (*City of God,* 12.23). Why is this so, if everyone wants the happiness of peace? The reason is that each one wants *their* peace, which comes into conflict with the peace of others. Not everyone enjoys the means to live well, be respected, and be free. Such wants are the seeds of conflict. The challenge is to recognize that simply managing conflict is sometimes the best we can do.

May 15

Just Wars

Wars are always unfortunate but it would be more unfortunate for the unjust to triumph over the just. The necessity of going to war to prevent this certainly may be regarded by good people as being a blessed course of action.

City of God, 4.14

Living in a violent world, the challenge for peace-loving people is how to deal with conflict. Augustine had no reservations about using violence to come to the defense of others. Indeed, he believed it was the responsibility of a just authority to protect the innocent, especially those under our care. War is always regrettable, but it would be more regrettable to allow evil nations to dominate innocent ones (*City of God*, 4.14). Such wars against unjust aggressors Augustine called "righteous wars" (*Against Faustus the Manichean*, 22.75). Great leaders, Augustine believed, were those who, after trying to bring order with a "word" rather than a "sword," are not above using the sword "to conquer a seemingly invincible foe and thereby bring peace and order to the community" (*Letter 229*, 1). As citizens we have the responsibility to choose leaders who will work for peace and who will wage wars as a last resort and only for the right reasons.

May 16

Unjust Wars

The real evils in war are the love of violence, the cruel passion for revenge, the blind hatred of the enemy, the sometimes insane resistance to an overpowering attack, the hunger for power, and other things of this sort.

Against Faustus the Manichean, 22.74

Augustine believed that it was just to wage war against an unjust aggressor (*City of God*, 22.6) or to regain rights unjustly denied (*Questions on the Heptateuch*, 6.10), but he also believed that few have been waged for right reasons. Many were waged to dominate the weak (*City of God*, 4.6), were driven by extreme nationalism, were aimed at distracting the nation from evils at home, or were begun simply because the ruler wanted to make a name for himself. Even when wars were begun with the best of reasons, they became unjust when carried out in an unjust way. As individuals we must take steps to avoid the little wars that we sometimes wage against each other for wrong reasons.

The seeds of violence have been sewn in each of us. Such seeds must be managed otherwise they might grow to destroy all around us.

May 17

Christus and War

We should not return evil for evil but sometimes we must act with a kind severity when we are trying to make the disorderly change their ways. Thus, an earthly state following the teachings of Christ will wage its wars with kindness and base the peace that follows on godliness and justice, being sensitive to the needs of the conquered.

Letter 138, 2.14

Some object that all wars were forbidden by Christ when he commanded to "turn the other cheek." Augustine responds, "Christ's command not to resist evil was intended to forestall our taking the kind of delight in revenge which feeds on another's misfortune. It was not meant to encourage us to neglect the correction of others" (*Letter 47*, 5). Of course it is best if war can be avoided; but, when war is necessary, charity requires that it be carried on in a kindly spirit. To say that war must never be waged, even in self defense, is to suggest that there is no such thing as justice, that therefore there are no wrongs to be righted. Augustine believed he was being true to Christ when he maintained that war is sometimes a sad necessity in this cracked world; the best that can be hoped for is that it will be waged in a spirit of charity, aiming not at vengeance upon an enemy, but at bringing about a just peace.

May 18

The Wonder of Married Love

Let peace be a sweetheart and friend like a beloved with whom we share our heart in an inviolate nuptial bed, a beloved in whose company we find trust and rest. May peace be like a beloved whose embrace comforts us and with whom we live in a friendship that cannot be dissolved.

Sermon 357, 1

Augustine is almost poetic when he talks about the love that exists in a good marriage. In such a marriage "we are joined to another side by side, walking together and looking towards the goal of our earthly journey" (*On the Good of Marriage,* 1.1).

The greatest peace available in this world, he thought, is like the love between husband and wife, a love created by God himself in Eden. Man and woman were given to each other so as to find the deepest form of friendship. This friendship would then partner with God in bringing reflections of God into this world. What makes for a good marriage is trust (*On Faith in Things Not Seen,* 1.2.4). It is a union of friends who pledge a lifelong love, but their love can only be believed, not seen. On some days it may be hard to believe it is there. Indeed, the depth of their love is most perfectly manifested in their trust that it will be there in troublesome times to come.

May 19

The Three Goods of Marriage

The good that is present in marriage is threefold: fidelity (*fides*), offspring (*proles*), and sacrament (*sacramentum*).

Fidelity means that there must be no relations with any other person outside the marriage bond. Offspring means that children are to be lovingly received, be brought up with tender care, and given a religious education. Sacrament means that the marriage bond is not to be broken.

A Literal Commentary on Genesis, 9.7.12

Fidelity is a consequence of the special nature of the friendship that is the foundation of marriage. In it, the two become "one flesh" (1 Corinthians 6:15-16), joined together in the intimate union of soul and body. A person can have many friends, but there is a special faithfulness and tenderness that can only be shared with one's spouse. Marriage provided the first natural bond between humans (*The Good of Marriage,* 1.1), so marriage continues to be the bedrock of any society. The affection between husband and wife is reflected in God's great song of love for the human race: "Arise, my beloved, my beautiful one, and come! See, the winter is past, the rains are over and gone. Flowers appear on the earth, the dove is heard in the land. Arise, my beloved, my beautiful one, and come!" (*Song of Songs,* 2:10-13).

May 20

The Miracle of Birth

God willed that the miracle of giving birth would remain a human power even after the fall from grace in paradise. No individual is obliged to exercise this power and (sadly enough) it is not given to some. Still, God continues to give to most humans the same sacred power of procreation that he first gave to Adam and Eve.

City of God, 22.24.1–2

Augustine believed that one sign that God did not give up on the human race after their fall from grace in Eden was that he allowed them to continue to conceive and give birth to children. Marriage provides the stable environment in which children are conceived, cared for, and prepared for the life ahead. Augustine hears Christ saying: "I entrust the care of the little ones to the grown-ups. Speak for those who can't pray, pray for those who can only cry. Look after the welfare of those who cannot yet take care of themselves" (*Sermon 115,* 4). Perhaps thinking of the unexpected birth of his own son, he observed, "If children come, we cannot help but love them" (*Confessions,* 4.2.2). It is the challenge of parents to make sure that this is true for their own children.

May 21

Holy Matrimony

> The bond of fellowship between married couples is so strong that, although it is important for nurturing children, it cannot be undone even if there are no children. I do not think that this union would be so unalterable if it were not the symbol of something greater than any human institution. As it is, if there is a civil divorce, husband and wife are still wedded to each other even though now separated.
>
> *On the Good of Marriage,* 7.7

The third special good of the bond of marriage is that it is holy. As Augustine writes, "Once marriage is entered into in 'the Church' it creates a sacred bond that can be dissolved only by the death of one of the parties" (*On the Good of Marriage,* 15.17). The stability of a loving union between husband and wife provides the best environment for raising children. As Augustine observes, "We go from infancy to wisdom through intermediate stages of foolishness" (*Against Julian,* 5.4.18). The guidance of a stable family is to protect us from our "stages of foolishness." However the sacredness and indissolubility of the marriage bond cannot rest just on the human need for security. Augustine says marriage must be a sacred symbol of something greater. The vowed union of husband and wife becomes a symbol of Christ and his church, a union which lasts not simply until death, but even into eternity.

May 22

The Trials of Married Life

When in life is there ever no fear, no grief. Are you to marry a wife? If she is a bad one, she will cause you pain; if she is a good one, you worry "Oh dear, suppose she were to die!" Children not born because of miscarriage make you despondent. Children born torment you with all sorts of anxiety. What joy a newborn child brings to people, and immediately they are all fearful they may soon be mourning it as they carry it out for burial.

Sermon 346C, 2

The sad thing about this life is that some seem to resist falling in love, marriage, and children because they fear that things will not work out and that they will be unable to bear the pain. It is indeed true that family life is not without its trials; after all it is a community of "cracked" people. Husbands and wives sometimes do not get along; children can be difficult. There are worries about present finances and future disasters. Even if one's spouse remains the "love of your life" and your children seem to be growing in wisdom and strength, there is the persistent doubt that this will not last forever. In Augustine's own life, a son of great promise died young, which is why we must relish the joys of family life while they last, as well as prepare ourselves for the disappointments.

May 23

A Death in the Family

We ask "Why does God allow infants to live when he knows they are going to die soon?" With good reason we can leave all that to his guidance. If a man who is skilled in composing a song knows what lengths to assign to what tones, so too does God know how to arrange our births and deaths so that we can make our contribution to the wonderful song of passing time.

Letter 166, 5.13

When our spouse dies before us, when our children die young, when the old live on when they pray to die, we ask how God allows such things to happen (*Sermon 296, 8*). The answer is that there is no good time to die; there is only our time, a time determined by God as the best time to go back to him. When I was little I loved the merry-go-round and wanted it to go on forever. I was not afraid because I could see my father there on the boardwalk, waiting to take me home when my ride was over. For each of us the ride ended and we went home with those who loved us. That is the way our death will be. Those we leave behind may be sad for a while but eventually they should be glad when they realize that we have gone home with the Father of us all.

Wandering on the Circumference

Do not marvel that the soul experiences more and more
emptiness as it continues to reach out to so many things
in this world. Consider the circle. Whatever its size there
is one middle point to which all parts of the circumference converge. If you wander off from the center to any
other part, you lose sight of the whole. So too when the
soul wanders out from itself, it is confused by the enor-
mity of things it finds there. Its nature forces it to look
everywhere for that which is one, but the very multitude
of things it finds outside itself stands in the way of it ever
finding the oneness that it seeks.

On Order, 1.2.3

One of the reasons why we have so much trouble in finding
peace in our families, in our nation, in our world at large, is
because none of us are "well tied together." We would dearly
love to find the answers to life, the secret of love, that center
where finally we could find rest. The trouble is that it is hard to
believe that this center lies within us. We spend our days running around the circumference of life experimenting with possessions, lifestyles, ideologies, careers, and people. We seek
unity but find only complexity. Perhaps it is only when we
finally get old and tired that we wearily return to the center
and find there the one God we have been looking for all the
time.

May 25

Wildly Loving

Inappropriate loving is a heavy weight holding down the spirit that is longing to fly. Just as a right and holy love whirls us up to the heights, so a wild and wicked love plunges us down to the depths. Do you want to be where Christ is? Love Christ and be whirled away to the place of Christ. The trouble is that we are surrounded by many goods that call us to love them above all. The world is a beautiful place and it tempts us with the infinite variety of its beauty. It is impossible to count the things that are suggested every day to be loved in an inappropriate way.

Sermon 65A, 1–2

For many of us it could be said, "He loved often but not well." As we leave our centers and whirl about the circumference of our lives—with its variety of people, places, and things—we begin to love this and that, flitting from one passing good to another. Unfortunately, some of these goods are on the same level as ourselves and some are below us. As a result when we attach ourselves to one or the other we cannot fly to the heights where God dwells. There are many good things in this world that are worthy of being loved, but there is only one good that is above all and that is God himself. Only by loving him above all will we be drawn to the heights where we are meant to live forever.

May 26

Give Me Someone Who Loves

The Lord says "No one comes to me except those whom the Father draws." You are not drawn unwillingly if you are drawn by love. Give me someone who loves. They will understand what I am saying. Give me someone who desires, someone who hungers, someone who travels through this desert thirsting and sighing for the fountain of an eternal homeland, give me such a one and they will know what I am saying. But if I speak to someone coldly unresponsive, they will not understand me at all.

Commentary on the Gospel of John, 26.4

Loving in all the wrong places is not as bad as not loving at all. Love is the only power able to draw us out of ourselves. Without it we are no better than a rock, indifferent to the currents sweeping it downstream. To know the loveableness of God, Augustine suggests, requires that we have experiences of loving things in this world for themselves, and not for the good they bring us. If we have come to love a person, family, spouse, child, or even a pet, more than ourselves, we have opened the door to the possibility of loving God above all. In such modest experiences of love we can begin to imagine the ecstasy of being in love with God.

May 27

Sing Your Love by Your Lives

You who have been born again in Christ, listen to God speaking through me: "Sing to the Lord a new song" (Psalm 149:1). You say, "Well, I am singing!" Yes, you are singing but don't let your life contradict your words. Sing with your voices, sing also with your hearts; sing with your mouths, sing also with your behavior. Do you want to sing God his praises? Be yourselves what you sing. You are his praise if you lead good lives.

Sermon 34, 6

In Augustine's day worship and song was strongly valued by Christians. Augustine says that, in addition to this, a good life can be a hymn of praise. As Christians we can praise God by living in accord with Christ's teachings—loving God above all and our neighbor as ourselves. Even with our human loves, we best show our love for them by what we do to and for them. Some may get upset if their husband or wife, their parent or their child, do not constantly repeat every day, "I love you!" There is nothing wrong with that, but it is a useless exercise if our supposed lover makes our life a "hell on earth" by the way they treat us. It is much better to have a love who is mute and kind than one who sings beautiful love songs but is cruel.

May 28

Love of Others Begins with Love of Self

St. Paul writes "You shall love your neighbor as yourself" (Galatians 5:14). Only if you know how to love yourself, will I entrust your neighbor to you to be loved. If you don't yet know how to love yourself, I'm afraid you are only too likely to cheat your neighbor of love as you are cheating yourself. If you love living an immoral life, you do not love yourself. If you hate your soul by loving only your flesh, both will rise together at the end of time but only to be tormented.

Sermon 128, 5

To love ourselves we must live a life in which we are more interested in truth and justice than in uncontrolled satisfaction of our impulses. Our body and our spirit are both good but it is only through our spirit that we can reach out to others through unsullied love for them. It is only through our spirit that we can understand that no matter how inconsequential we seem to others, we are important to God. Convinced of our own dignity and in control of our passions, we are now able to reach out to others in true love, loving them for their goodness, and not because they serve our interests.

May 29

The Joy of Being Old

It remains true that, as Job said, "The life of a man upon earth is a trial" (Job 7:1). Take the case of a child who must be driven by painful penalties to learn their letters or their trade. Their lack of understanding and skill is itself a burden. Who is there who does not shudder at the thought of returning to infancy? Indeed, if the choice were given of either starting over or dying, who would not choose to die?

City of God, 21.14

One can sympathize with Augustine's reluctance to go back and start over. Like most of us, his life had its share of upheavals, foolishness, and sorrows. Despite these, there is a certain peace that comes with old age. New ventures are precluded by lack of time and energy. No one expects us to run a marathon, start a new career, or have a new family. Our children are now on their own. In these last days the time for delusions of grandeur are over. If people are to love us now, they must love us for what we *are* rather than for what we can *do* for them. In our old age we no longer complain and sit quietly in the lap of God and hear his whispered words, "Can a woman forget her infant? Even should she forget, I will never forget you. See, I have written your name on the palm of my hand" (Isaiah 49:15-16).

May 30

<hr />

You Can't Be Old and Beautiful

Let us see what God has promised us. Certainly not earthly riches and honors. He has not promised that we would be healthy nor that we would reach that sometimes decrepit old age which all desire before it comes but complain about when it does come. He did not promise us beauty of body which (even when we have it) can be destroyed by disease and old age. We wish to be beautiful and we wish to be old but we can't have both. When old age comes beauty deserts us. The vigor of beauty and the moaning of old age are incompatible. So what has God promised us? Only this: an untroubled eternal life where we will fear nothing.

Commentary on the Gospel of John, 32.9.2–3

Augustine probably experienced the truth of the passage above. He lived to be seventy-six years of age, and there is no evidence that he did much preening in his last years. His point is that we should not have unrealistic expectations about the glories of any of our ages. All of them have their own set of problems. God has promised us only two things: first, if we do our best to be decent in this life, we will achieve a life after death that is beyond our wildest expectations; second, in the midst of the turmoil and disappointments of this life he will be with us and indeed in us, giving us the strength to get through.

May 31

<hr />

Everyone Can Be Beautiful Inside

God sees you within. He loves you within and you must love him within for he fashions your inner beauty. Consider the words of the psalm: "All the glory of the king's daughter is within." What is the inner face of beauty? Nothing else than the beauty of conscience. There Christ looks at us; there Christ loves us; there Christ punishes us; there Christ bestows on us the crown of glory.

Commentary on Psalm 44, 29

The consolation of those of us who are beyond the days when make-up or plastic surgery can remedy the "ravages of time" is that the real beauty of a human being is within. All of the primping and preening cannot hide the inner ugliness of the cruel, selfish, and self-absorbed. No matter how pretty they may be on the outside, we are repelled by their inner ugliness. But we have also known average-looking persons who radiate an inner beauty to all those who know them. The good news is that God is concerned only about our inner beauty, and this is something over which we have some control. Through our love of God and neighbor, we are transformed into human beings through whom God's beauty shines.

June 1

In Praise of God's Creation

Thanks be to You, O Lord! We see heaven and earth and the light and darkness which adorns them. We see the heavens through which the birds of the air take their wandering flight. We see the beauty of the waters in the expanse of the sea. We see the dry land that is the mother of plants and trees. We see the great lights shining above, the sun illuminating the day, the moon and stars comforting the night. We see the water spread all about us swarming with fish. We see the earth populated by various land-animals. Finally, we see human beings made in your image and likeness and charged with protecting the rest of creation by their wisdom. We see all these things and each is good and the whole of them taken together is very good.

Confessions, 13.32.47

Augustine believed that all things that exist or will exist were created by a single act of God, an act in which all things in nature germinated from the seeds God planted. As he describes the process, "From the beginning God created in the roots of time all those created things that would later exist" (*A Literal Commentary on Genesis,* 5.4.11). We, like the rest of creation, existed from the beginning but not in the "roots of time." Our roots are in the eternal knowledge that God had of us and the eternity of his decision to "make" time for us, and to make us a part of time, so that we might choose to spend the rest of our eternal life with him.

June 2

"It's a Beautiful World!"

Just think of the world in which we live! Think of the thousands of beautiful things for seeing and the thousands of materials just right for making things. There is an infinitely changing beauty in the sky and the land and the sea. What varieties of color do we see in the changing moon and sun and stars! There are the soft shadows of noon forests, the shades and smells of spring flowers, the different songs and exotic dresses of the birds. How amazing are the animals who surround us, the smallest ant even more amazing than the huge bulk of the whale! Think of the grand spectacle of the sea as it clothes itself in different colors, sometimes green, sometimes purple, sometimes the bluest of blue. And how grand it is when there is a storm (especially grand when you are not sailing on the heaving surface of the sea but are caressed by its soft mist as you stand safe and warm on the shore).

City of God, 22.24

What is less than beautiful in nature has been done by human beings, often for profit or pleasure. God has given us the right to use nature to preserve and enhance our lives but this must be done with respect because nature, like ourselves, is a place where God dwells.

June 3

Loving this World too Much

If a husband gave a ring to his wife and she began to love the ring more than the husband who gave it to her, would she not be a kind of adulteress in her heart? Certainly she should love what her husband gave her, but if she should say, "The ring is enough for me; I no longer wish to see his face," what sort of wife would she be? The husband gave the ring so that he might be loved the more. So too with God. He has given you all these beautiful created things so that through them you might love him. If you love the created things and neglect the Creator who made them, would not your love be considered adulterous too?

Commentary on the Epistle of John, 2.11

The trouble with living in this world is that most of the time "It is a smiling place with many things of beauty, power, and variety" (*Sermon 158*, 7). Our love of this world makes us like kids at a rock concert, unwilling to leave, crying out, "Encore! Encore!" Such enthusiasm can be good, but some love this world so much that they forget about the God who made it. We are not meant to stay here forever. Too much love for the world leaves us nostalgic in our old age, rather than hopeful for the God who created it.

June 4

Not Seeing Creation's Goodness

The reason why creation is good is because it was created by the good God. Still, some are unconvinced. They argue that parts of creation are unsuitable and even harmful to our poor weak human bodies. They mention things like fire, cold, and wild-beasts. They do not consider how wonderful such things are in themselves and how marvelously they make their unique contributions to the beauty of the whole universe. They do not consider how valuable such "dangerous things" are if used wisely. For example, poison is death-dealing when improperly used but when used properly it can be a health-giving medicine. On the contrary, some of the things we like (food, drink, sunlight) when used intemperately become harmful. Wisdom dictates that we should not foolishly find fault with things before we try to find out their true usefulness.

City of God, 11.22

Augustine says that we tend to assume that the universe is meant to be our servant, and when it does not serve us well we call it evil. The fact of the matter is that the universe treats us badly only when we treat it foolishly, when we build homes in flood-plains, when we set fires in forests, when we "bait bears" and then complain that they attack us. We are only part of creation and we must respect the rest for the goodness and beauty that only they can contribute to the whole.

Nature Proclaims the Beauty of God

Question the beauty of the earth, question the beauty of the sea, question the beauty of the air, question the beauty of the sky, question the far-flung ranks of the stars, question the sun making the day splendid with its radiant beams, question the moon soothing the darkness of the night with its gentle rays, question the animals that move in the waters, that stroll about on dry land, that fly in the air . . . question all these things and they will answer: "Look, we are beautiful!" But who could have made these beautiful passing things if not the God who is beautiful and unchangeable?

Sermon 241, 2

Augustine says to us: "Let your mind roam through the whole creation; everywhere the created world will cry out to you: 'God made me!'" (*Commentary on Psalm 26/2*, 12). Augustine believed that natural and human beauty are reflections of the divine. Indeed, the God of beauty is with and in us. He works in the universe maintaining and governing all that he has made (*A Literal Commentary on Genesis*, 4.12.22). Indeed, God tells us, "I am with you in this beautiful world and someday I will take you to the infinitely more beautiful world that lies just beyond the doors of this life."

The World: A Turbulent Sea

In the turbulent sea that is this world the perverse and depraved lusts of human beings make them like fishes devouring each other. They desire other people's death so that they can inherit their property. They make money at the expense of others. They seek high rank and in the process ruin others. They encourage others to sell their hard-earned possessions so that they can buy them. How cruel are we humans to each other! How eager are the powerful to swallow others! No sooner has a big fish devoured a smaller one than it itself is devoured by one even bigger. Such ugly things happen every day before our eyes.

Commentary on Psalm 64, 9

A sign that Augustine was no "Pollyanna," an unmitigated optimist, is that after speaking of the world's beauty, he speaks of its flawed nature, a nature diminished by human action. By *world*, Augustine means people who love this life too much, those who act primarily to satisfy their desire for pleasure, wealth, and power—indeed, for anything that promises to serve their self-interest (*Sermon 170, 4*). They are unable to love God and neighbor because they have never gotten beyond loving themselves. As realists we must recognize the sometimes ugliness of the world; as Christians we must avoid contributing to it.

June 7

Living in a Wrinkled Bed

Weakened by our various ailments, we all look for something to rest on. Good people find rest in their home, in their spouse, in their children, in the modest pleasures of their life, in their little piece of property, in the plants they have set in the ground with their own hands, in the buildings they have constructed. But because God wants us to be in love only with eternal life, he mingles bitter elements with these innocent pleasures so that even in the midst of our joys we are not totally comfortable. God allows "the sheets on our bed to be wrinkled" so that we will not fall in love with this earthy barn instead of longing for the true home that awaits us in heaven.

Commentary on Psalm 40, 5

There is no question that in many ways this life is like lying on an uncomfortable bed. If we were guilty of some great crime, we could understand our discomfort, but most of us have avoided a life of villainy. Why then do we suffer so much? Augustine's explanation is that God allows the world to trouble us so that we keep some level of discomfort and yearn for a better life to come. Despite the sometimes bitterness of this life, we still love it and need to be weaned from it as a child is sometimes weaned by putting something bitter on its mother's breast (*Sermon 311,* 14). The greatest cruelty would be to allow this life to become so sweet that we would never want to move on.

June 8

The Best Possible World?

O God, I finally came to understand that even rotting things are good. After all they could not decay if there were not something good there to decay. I realized then that you made everything that exists and that everything you made was good. When I finally was able to see the whole picture, I no longer wished for a better world.

Confessions, 7.12–13

It is more important to focus on the eternal life of ecstasy than to find fault and disparage this life. There is much in this world that is beyond our control, but our life after death is within our control. Through God's grace it is possible to overcome our immaturity and impulses in this life, and become "glued to God" in the next. The beauty of this future possibility caused Augustine to declare, "O God, those who find fault with any part of your creation are just crazy!" (*Confessions*, 7.14.20)

June 9

Loving Good Things Immoderately

There is truly a fascination caused by beautiful bodies like gold and silver and other such things. Earthly honor also has its own special value as does the power to rule. This life itself possesses its own appeal. Friendship among human beings brings a sweetness through the loving bond that unites hearts. Sin comes about only when, because of an immoderate desire for such lower things, the higher good is deserted. True, these earthly things have their delights, but they cannot be compared to the God who made them all.

Confessions, 2.5.10

Our problem with this world is not that it is bad, but that sometimes it overpowers us with its appeal. We begin to love it too much so that it becomes the primary object of our love; when this happens we become trapped here by the delightful things that surround us. At the same time, Augustine says, "When we are commanded 'Do not love these things' this does not mean that we should no longer eat or drink or beget children. It only means that we should limit our desire so that these things do not shackle us by our love for them" (*Commentary on the Epistle of John*, 2.12). All things in this world are good because all reflect the goodness of God. But it would be a shame if we became so enthralled by God's reflection that we no longer yearn to see him face to face.

June 10

Every Age Has Its Temptations

No period of life can be free from trials and temptations. The moment babies are born they seem to prophesy a life full of misery with their tearful cries. They are already affected by temptation, not personally of course, but in temptations suffered by their parents. Perhaps old age is an exception. On the contrary, many bad old people, in whom we find a maelstrom of greed and the insatiable craving of the belly, end up drowning themselves in drink. What are we to say about the young? Youth is over-confident about its strength, boastful about its handsome appearance, and aims at making a show with the glitter and gloss of temporal possessions. Indeed, being young is a dangerous time, a time of being inflamed with lust, swollen with hope for temporal things, and bursting with pleasure.

Sermon 391, 1–3

Augustine warns us that we must be constantly vigilant against sliding from virtue into vice because the struggle between good and evil is constant and within ourselves. Yet in fighting bravely against the temptations we face every day, we are preparing ourselves for the day when we shall stand face to face with our God and be able to say to him, "Well, Lord, I fought as best I could!"

June 11

"Give Me Chastity But Not Yet"

Many years (perhaps as many as twelve) had flown by since that nineteenth year when my reading of Cicero's

Hortensius had aroused a zeal for wisdom. Yet I still delayed devoting myself to that search even though I was convinced that just searching for wisdom was preferable to the bodily pleasures available to me. From my very early years I had sought chastity from you but had prayed, "Give me chastity and continence, but not yet!" I feared that you would hear me quickly, and that I would be cured of the lust I wanted satisfied rather than extinguished.

Confessions, 8.7.17

Augustine's words describe his situation when he was in his early thirties. He had a developing career in the imperial court of Rome. Despite growth in wisdom, he still could not control his sexual desire. It took him two more years to manage his sexual desires enough so that he could be baptized. His experience illustrated the power of the sexual drive given to us by God so that children could be conceived and friendship between spouses established. He still felt the power of sexual temptation as an old man committed to celibacy (*Sermon 128*, 11) and he repeated a cautionary tale of an eighty-five year old man who suddenly ran away with a lyre player (*Against Julian* 3.11.22). In this present cracked condition, Augustine believed, it is possible at any age to misuse the sacred power of sexuality that God had implanted in humans in paradise.

June 12

Reaching Out to the God Above

I sought my God in creatures but did not find him. I sought him in myself and I did not find him there either. Now I realize that God is above my soul. For my soul to reach God it must pour itself out above itself. Let the onlookers who deride me go on saying, "Where is your God?" I will answer that there above my soul is the home of my God; there he dwells; from there he looks down upon me; from there he created me, governs me and takes thought for me, arouses me, calls me, guides me and leads me on. From there he will lead me to my journey's end.

Commentary on Psalm 41, 8

Nothing can be given to those who demand proof of God. The best we can do is show them that our belief in God is reflected in the lives we lead. Certainly this is unsatisfying, even to ourselves. Our desire is to see and be united with God. But since he is "above," in order to have an experience of him we must get out of our skins, our souls must be poured out. To do this we must free ourselves from anything that can hold us down to this world. After that we can reach out to the God who dwells above by our desire and prayer.

June 13

"Unfinding" God

The soul must be careful not to form any idea of God that its imagination may suggest. It must first learn to "unfind" the one it wishes to find. What is this I've just said: "It must first learn to *unfind* God"? What I mean is that when we search for God and the beauty of the earth impresses us, we must go beyond it and continue the search. The same thing must happen when we are struck by the loveliness of the sea or the tranquility of the air we breathe. The soul must say to itself, "This is not my *God*; it is the *work* of my God." Even when we are seduced by the heavenly light of the sun, don't think God is anything like that. God is much more than any of these.

Sermon 360B, 7-8

The trouble with this world is that the many signs of God are so splendid that we easily mistake them for God. Falling in love is an example of this, in which we say, "This is enough for me. My love is truly divine and I need look no further!" While acknowledging the beauty and wonder of such things, Augustine reminds us that we must go beyond them to the one who made them wonderful. The good things in life are not meant to be our goal; they are rather arrows encouraging us to go further in our search for God.

June 14

Ask What You Will

When God says to you, "Ask what you will," what request will you make? Think hard! Expand your greed as far as you can! Ask for the whole earth and all its people as slaves. Then ask for the sea, even though you can't live in it. Ask for the air as well, even though you cannot fly. Lift your longing even to the sky and say that you want the sun and the moon and the stars. All these things are precious in their own way but nothing is more precious than the God who made them. What he wants to give you is himself. If you have discovered anything better than that, go ahead and ask for it.

Commentary on Psalm 34/1, 12

God has promised that he will give us whatever we want. Unfortunately many of us do not know what our true wants are. Sometimes we learn about our true wants only after we have exhausted the list of things that we think will satisfy and bring us peace. We soon find out that wealth, power, or love do not satisfy us. They may be precious in their own way, but their satisfactions are temporary. They end when we die. That is why when God says to us: "Ask what you want and I will give it to you," we should respond: "If possible, Lord, give me some of the good things of this life but above all give me yourself."

June 15

The Good Things of Life

The earth with its lofty mountains and gentle hills and plains and pleasant fertile fields is good. A well-built house which is well-proportioned and spacious and bright is also good. All living things are certainly good and good too is air that is temperate and salubrious and food that is hearty and wholesome. Certainly health without pains and weariness is good, and good too is a handsome man and lovely woman when they are well-proportioned and cheerful and have a pleasing complexion. Especially good is the spirit of a friend when united to us in the sweetness of agreement and the security of love. A just human being is very good. Even riches are good because of the good things they can do. The sky is good with its sun and moon and stars and good are the angels in their happy obedience to God. Good is talk that teaches pleasantly and counsels wisely and good too is poetry that is harmonious in its rhymes and rhythms and weighty in its content. But why add any more? Take away the "this good" and the "that good," and think of good itself. This is the God who is to be loved, not as this or that good, but as good itself.

The Trinity, 8.3.4

The passage above should prove to the doubter that Augustine did *not* believe that there was nothing good in this world. But he would add that all of these true goods are nothing compared to the good God. All things are good except for reflections that drag on too long. And so I end mine here.

June 16

We Are All Aliens

The true Christians are those who understand that on
earth they will always be aliens. Our native land is above
in God's heaven where there are no strangers. If we are all
moving on, we should now perform good works which
cannot be lost so that we can find in heaven our good
works waiting for us. For example, in this life we should
recognize our duty of hospitality, a work that will bring
us to God. In this life we should receive strangers kindly
because we are aliens just like them. Why are you afraid
of losing what you invest here by generosity? Christ the
Lord is the keeper of such good works.

Sermon 111, 4

Recognizing our alien status helps us to understand why we
sometimes are so uncomfortable. Even the best motel cannot
match the comforts of home. We are surrounded by strangers,
those who do not know us for the wonderful persons we really
are. Some of them strike us as truly strange because they do
not look, talk, or act like us. We may develop xenophobia—the
fear of foreigners—and long to return to our own kind. The
paradox in such thinking, as Augustine reminds us, is that we
are all aliens in this life, destined soon to move on to our heavenly home. Knowing that, we should indeed be hospitable to
those around us because we, like them, will soon be moving on.

June 17

Longing Stretches Our Capacity

If you wish to fill a pocket and you know how big the
object is that you will put into it, you stretch the pocket.

By stretching it you make it more roomy. So God, by post-poning the joys of heaven, increases our longing and thereby stretches our soul and makes it more spacious. But our longing will train us for receiving heaven only to the extent that we have pruned our longings away from love of this world. We must empty out the space that is to be filled with God. You are to be filled with the good; pour out the evil.

Commentary on the Epistle of John, 4.6.2

When I was a little kid I remember sitting in the back seat of our old car on the way to the seashore badgering my father with the cry, "Are we there yet?" The longer we rode, the more I yearned to arrive. And so it is with this life. We want peace and happiness, and we have been promised we will have them when we finally arrive at the "shores" of heaven. The longer the journey takes the more our capacity for these good things increases, especially as we experience the continuing wars and loneliness and sicknesses of this life. Our longing grows. We are stretched thin, and we cry out to our God, "Lord, are we there yet?"

June 18

Licking the Dust of the Earth

As long as you go on licking the dust of the earth by lov-ing it you cut yourself off from the God above. What is it that makes a person happy? You seek gold because you think gold will make you happy but gold will not make you happy. You imagine you will be happy with honor from men and worldly triumphs but worldly triumphs won't make you happy. Whatever else you seek by lick-ing the dust of the earth, you do it in order to be happy but nothing of earth can make you perfectly happy. It is because you want to be happy that you reach out for earthly things but such things bring their own sort of misery.

Sermon 231, 4

Augustine's words do not mean that it is wrong to seek some sort of happiness in the things and people of this life. He simply means that they will not bring us perfect happiness. However, in reaching out for love, security, or respect in this life we reach out for goods that we will possess perfectly in heaven. When we experience love, appreciation, and the "good life" here, we are encouraged to seek the infinite love, respect, and life from God that we will experience in our heavenly home. We will always be "licking the dust" in our earthly life, but this does not mean that we must end our search for happiness here.

June 19

Christ Shows the Way to Happiness

What are you seeking? A happy life. Well, it is not to be found here. Christ came down and experienced all those unpleasant things that are part of our lives and said to us: "I did not turn up my nose at the nasty things of your life; believe that I am inviting you to my life. I am inviting you to the company of the angels, to the friendship of the Father and the Holy Spirit. I am inviting you to be my brothers and sisters. I am inviting you to my life. Are you reluctant to believe that I will give you my life? Remember that I died for you." So now, while we are living in this perishable flesh let us die with Christ. By our love of being just let us live with Christ.

Sermon 231, 5

If humans were meant to have a perfectly happy life here, Jesus would certainly have had such a life when he became human. Instead, he experienced the depth and breadth of humanity and, by so doing, taught us how to endure life's challenges. By his death he freed us from the suffering of the next life that humans brought upon ourselves; by his resurrection he gave an example of the glorious life that is possible for every human at the end of time. Moreover, he promised that our faithfulness in this world would be rewarded with glory in the next.

June 20

Heaven: Seeing God

St. John writes: "Most beloved, we are now children of God but what we shall be is not all that clear. We do know that on some future day we shall become like God. We shall see the Lord as he truly is" (1 John 3:2). Thus, there is being prepared for us a surprise that is simply beyond imagining. At present we may get some vague hint but like seeing an enigma's reflection in a darkened mirror. No one could ever describe in word the sweetness and the beauty of the gift that our Lord is preparing for those who care about him and hope in him. What in the world can this gift be? Nothing else than to be like the angels and truly see! For the first time we shall see the Lord Our God!

Commentary on Psalm 36/2, 8

The essential happiness of heaven is that we shall finally see God clearly and be embraced by his love completely. Though there is no clear analogy for this experience, the closest would be the reunion with a loved one from whom we have been long separated. The ecstasy of such a reunion is beyond description.

It follows that our reunion with God will be all the more beyond description. God is the infinite goodness that we have been seeking throughout our lives. This is the union for which our nature calls out. Finally we will be satisfied and, best of all, our ecstasy will never end.

June 21

Heaven: Being Drunk on God

What shall we be like when we come to see God face to face? All the psalmist can say is "They will be inebriated by the rich abundance of your house." When he saw people taking too much wine and losing their senses, then he knew how to express the experience of God. When we experience the joy of being with God, the human mind will almost vanish. It will become drunk with the rich abundance of God. God's mercy will flow with mighty force to submerge and inebriate those who now hope in him. It is like a torrent that inebriates the thirsty. Thus, let those who are thirsty now continue to hope. The day will come when they will be intoxicated by the reality. Until then, let them continue to thirstily hope.

Commentary on Psalm 35, 14

In trying to express the feelings of those in heaven, Augustine uses the analogy of drinking. In such a state people are overcome with a euphoria that robs them of inhibitions. Sometimes the experience so overcomes the mind that it cannot be remembered the next day. Being "drunk on God" means something like that. We are "taken out of ourselves" by the joy of being with God. Best of all there is no hangover. And we need not remember what we did the day before because there is no "day before," only *this* eternal day on which we continue to be intoxicated by the presence of God.

June 22

Heaven: Resurrection Stories

The time of our trials and affliction is signified by the
forty days of Lent before Easter. The time of happiness
which is coming later—the time of rest, of good fortune,
of eternal life, of the kingdom without end—is signified
by the fifty days after Christ's resurrection. Two times are
indicated by the Church calendar: one before the Lord's
resurrection, and one after. Our present time of trial is
symbolically represented by the days of Lent. The time of
happiness and quiet in God's kingdom after resurrection
is symbolically represented now by our song, "Alleluia!
Praise the Lord!"

Sermon 254, 5

In trying to imagine what heaven is like, Augustine suggests
that we reflect on the days between Easter and the Ascension
when the disciples walked and talked to the risen Jesus. Scripture gives us many images of heaven. They include a room of
friends into which Christ enters (John 20:19-23), a garden in
which we find Jesus (John 20:11-18), a walk, talk, and dinner
with Jesus (Luke 24:13-35), fishing on a quiet lake while Jesus
watches us from the shore (John 21:4), a picnic on the beach for
which Jesus supplies the fish (John 21:9). Heaven is like all
these glorious scenes, and much more.

June 23

What Will We Do in Heaven?

What will we do in heaven? I answer that our whole
activity will consist in singing "amen" and "alleluia."

Refuse to be saddened by the thought that if you remained standing and saying every day "amen" and "alleluia" you would collapse with weariness. In heaven you will cry out "amen" and "alleluia" not simply with sounds from your throat but with the devotion of the heart. What then does *amen* mean? What does *alleluia* mean? *Amen* means "it is true!" *Alleluia* means "praise God!" Those things that Paul said we now see "through a mirror as in a riddle" (1 Corinthians 13:12) we shall then see with an inexpressibly different feeling of love. We then will shout "Why, it's true!" And, because we shall see the truth with perpetual delight, we will be moved to praise God by shouting "alleluia!"

Sermon 362, 1

Augustine's church congregation was disappointed when he told them that for all eternity they would be shouting "amen!" and "alleluia!" Suddenly heaven did not seem all that exciting. He eased their fears by telling them that "amen" is equivalent to crying out, "It is true! I now know all the things I always wanted to know!" In heaven we will finally see all the mysteries of life revealed in God. Overcome with the infinite beauty of God we will cry out in joy, "Alleluia!", "Praise God!" In our excitement we will then know that our eternity will be spent in a continuing revelation of the wonders of God and the wonders of his beautiful and complex creation.

June 24

Will We Get Bored in Heaven?

What are we going to do in heaven? We must not be afraid of getting bored. Do you find it boring now to be well? If you don't get tired of good health, will you get tired of being healthy forever? Again, does your heart ever get tired? As long as you live your heart goes on beating. You do some work and you get tired. You rest and then go back to work. Through all of this your heart never tires. Just as your heart never grows tired in your condition of good health, so your tongue and heart will never grow tired when you are enjoying your condition of immortality. Your relaxing activity in heaven will be to praise the Lord and you will never get bored doing this.

Sermon 211A

Boredom seems part of the human condition. Even the most pleasurable activity will over time become boring. Even death seems preferable to a life "but dimly lived." Considering the occasional boredom of this life, it is not surprising that we get frightened at the prospect of living forever. We say to ourselves, "How in the world can I find something interesting to do on a day that never ends!" Augustine's analogies about health and a beating heart are his way of saying that heaven is about vitality without distress. It is hard to get bored when one is "feeling good" forever.

June 25

Waiting in Heaven for Our Bodies

That life which the souls of the blessed martyrs enjoy before resurrection is only a small part of the bliss that has been promised. Complete happiness comes only after the body is reunited to the soul and the whole person finally receives the reward for a good life. Think of the difference between the joys (or woes) of those dreaming and those who are awake. There is a similar difference between the joys (or woes) of a soul after death and those of the whole person after resurrection. The rest enjoyed by souls without any bodies is one thing; the glory and happiness of being like the angels with heavenly bodies is quite another.

Sermon 280, 5

The passage above shows that Augustine was not a Platonist. The body for him was not just an unfortunate appendage to our glorious spirits; the body is an integral part of being human. Indeed, without my body I would not be me. There is no doubt that the souls of the just will be in a heavenly state after the necessary "cleansing" in purgatory has been achieved, but their joy cannot be "complete" because they themselves are not yet "complete." Their joy will be tinged with expectation until their happy spirits are joined once again with their now burnished and perfected bodies. They will be in heaven but their state will be something like the way we feel when we arrive at a party before our loved one. We are indeed in a place of happiness but our joy will not be complete until the one we love joins us.

June 26

My Heavenly Friend, My Body

What are you afraid of? Why are you anxious about your body? Jesus promised "Not a hair of your head shall perish" (Luke 21:18). It is true that Adam by his sin condemned your bodies to death but Jesus "will bring to life your mortal bodies" (Romans 8:11). Remember that Paul wrote "You will be delivered from the body of this death" (Romans 7:24). This will happen not by doing away with your body but by receiving another one that cannot die. If Paul had not added "of this death" and had just said "you will be delivered from this body," you might erroneously come to think, "You see, God does not want us to be with the body." But Paul said "From the body of this death."

Take away death and the body is good. Let death, the last enemy, be removed and my body will be forever my friend!

As I sit here squinting at the text through watery eyes, trying to find a comfortable place on the chair for my arthritic hip, it is consoling to hear that in heaven for all eternity I will not need to worry about such things. My body will be my friend. Augustine describes this friendly state by saying, "Whatever the spirit commands, immediately the body will do. And the spirit will never choose anything improper either for itself or for its body" (*City of God*, 22). The reason is simple: friends do not hurt friends.

June 27

The Mystery of Our Resurrection

In heaven (after the dregs of sin have been wiped away) we will no longer get tired. Hunger will not interrupt our singing because the only body that gets hungry is one that is dying and "weighing down the soul" (Wisdom 9:15). No longer will we get thirsty or get sick or grow old or drop off to sleep. We will not feel any kind of weariness or fatigue. Our bodies will have the vitality of the angels. We should not be surprised that our present body will be the source of our heavenly bodies on the day of resurrection. Remember that at conception God fashioned and shaped us who previously were nothing! What's so hard about God making an angel out of a human being, seeing that he made the first human beings out of mud?

Sermon 159B, 15

For most of us, by the time our resurrection occurs our old bodies will be dust. How then can it come back, especially in a new and pristine condition? We are told that it will be truly our body, recognizable to all who knew us. Augustine tells us not to worry about how this could happen. The God who brought it about that our bodies were first formed out of unlikely materials supplied by our mother and father will have no difficulty "reforming" us on the day of resurrection. In any case, resurrection is God's problem, not ours. All we have to do is enjoy it.

June 28

The Beauty of Our Heavenly Body

Every fiber and organ of our imperishable body will play its part in praising God. On earth these varied organs have their own special function, but in heaven function will be swallowed up in rapture. The muffled notes of our bodily organs will swell into a great hymn of praise to the supreme Artist who has fashioned us. The movement of our bodies will be of such unimaginable beauty that I dare not say more than this: our bodies will have the poise, grace, and beauty that is appropriate to a heavenly place where nothing unbecoming can be found.

City of God, 22.30

We know that in heaven our body will be perfect! What follows from that is speculation and Augustine was not above such speculation. He believed that even the old body we have now is a miracle of order and some parts, such as the beard of a man, seem to be there only to enhance beauty. Augustine believed that all our body parts will be present in our heavenly body, not because they are needed, but because they contribute to the beauty of the whole. We will come back in the body that we had, or would have had, in the "prime of our earthly life" with the stature we had on earth. All defects and blemishes will be eliminated. We will shine like the sun (*City of God,* 22.20). We will finally be the truly "beautiful people" we now sometimes pretend to be. God's reflection in us will for the first time come through brightly and clearly.

June 29

In Heaven with My Friends

In heaven, no longer upset by our sins and vices, we will love God perfectly because we will see him face to face (1 Corinthians 13:12). We will also love our friends perfectly because we will have nothing to hide. All the thoughts in our hearts will be open to each other. Never again will we be upset by the fear that others are thinking evil of us.

Against Two Letters of the Pelagians, 4.10.28

In his *City of God* (19.13) Augustine speaks of heaven as the everlasting glory and honor of enjoying God and loving our human loves in God. It is a comforting thought. In this life we are commanded to love God and neighbor in order to be complete as human beings, which is why it stands to reason that love of neighbor continues in heaven. Of course our essential joy will be in seeing and being embraced by God, but added to that will be the joy of seeing and being embraced by our human loves. Best of all, we will be able to be completely honest. No longer will we need to hide our thoughts for fear that they will hurt our loved ones. We will see the clear reflection of God in each other, and in God we will love each other even more.

June 30

Heaven: Summing Up

In heaven your peace will come from possessing God. Here what is wine cannot be bread and what is light cannot be drink. But in heaven God shall be all of these things for you. You shall eat of him so that you will never again be hungry. You will drink of him so that you will never again be thirsty. He will illumine you so that you will never again be in the dark. You will be supported by him so that you will never again fail. All of him will possess all of you but you will not be cramped for space. You will possess all of him and he will possess all of you. You and God will be one.

Commentary on Psalm 36/1, 12

There are few things we can say with certainty about heaven with the exception of this: in heaven all our desires will be fulfilled and we will have perfect peace. Though our capacities for receiving God may differ, all of us will be full. Whether we die young or old, we will receive the same *denarius,* the reward of being eternally at peace with God (*Sermon 87,* 5–6). Every once in a while we may get a hint of that peace when we hold in our arms someone we love, but even that is far less than the peace of heaven. Indeed, rather than going on trying to imagine what heaven is like, it is more profitable to concentrate on doing the things we need to do to get there. Then and only then will we know what heaven is like.

July 1

Rules for Living: Restraint and Endurance

There are two things commanded in this life by the Lord: restraint and endurance. We are told to restrain ourselves during the good times of life and to endure the bad times. We need restraint in order to curb our untoward desires and control our attachment to life's pleasures. Just as it is the task of restraint not to be attached to the good times of life, so the task of endurance is to survive bravely the bad times. Whether at present we "never had it so good" or "never had it so bad" we must continue to look forward to the coming of the Lord who will give us what is truly good and pleasant and protect us from what is truly evil.

Sermon 38, 1

Augustine observed that despair and love of life are two obstacles to completing our journey to heaven. Life's challenges can lead to despair, which in turn tempts us to seek salvation elsewhere. The second obstacle is finding things of this world so enjoyable that we "sit down on the road," we stop our spiritual journey altogether. To reach heaven we must keep on the road, we must move through the good and bad times that are sure to come along.

July 2

Life: A Mixture of Good and Bad

The good and bad things which are mixed together in the potpourri of this life do not affect only the good or only the bad. What you describe as "good things" are had by the good and bad alike. Both good and bad enjoy bodily health. Both good and bad have riches. Children are a gift common to the good and bad alike. Both good and bad live long lives. On the other hand both good and bad suffer hunger, disease, sorrows, losses, oppression, bereavements. So it is easy to see that both the joys of the world are enjoyed by good and bad people alike and that the sorrows of the world are also borne by both the good and the bad.

Sermon 38, 2

Augustine's point here can be disturbing for those who struggle to live good lives and who suffer in poverty, illness, and loneliness while wicked people appear to prosper. We may be tempted to blame God for such injustice, but before we do we should remember two things. First, this is not the world that God wanted. It was created by the misuse of human freedom. Second, reward for the good and punishment for the bad is promised in the next, eternal life, not this passing one.

July 3

Life as Rising Smoke

Now is the time to grow tired of your captivity in these "Babylonian" days. Here comes that heavenly mother, Jerusalem, to meet you on the way with a cheerful invitation to "choose life and love to see the good days" (Psalm 34:12), days which you will never have in this world. Here, after all, your days "are fading away like smoke" (Psalm 102:3). For them, extension has meant becoming less. As they grow in length they have become fewer. They rise up and then vanish away.

Sermon 216, 4

This image of our life as rising smoke, beginning thick and dense and gradually dissipating, seems quite accurate when you come to think about it. When we begin our existence we are thick with unused possibilities. Our life is dense and thick because the fire that feeds it is at its peak. At the prime of our physical lives, and with intellects unhampered by disappointment and bad habits, we feel we can become and achieve anything. But as life goes on our fire tends to smolder, our smoke thins out. This is not bad so long as we do not cling to what once was. Rather we should allow our spirit to rise to the heavens too, joyfully responding to the heavenly invitation, "Come here and live forever!"

July 4

The Gift of Freedom

When God made human beings, although he made them very good, he obviously did not make them equal to himself. However, since a person is better who is good freely and willingly than a person who is forced to be good, it was fitting that God would give free will as an appropriate gift to human beings.

83 Diverse Questions, 2

Most of what we do on a daily basis is freely chosen. Of course we are influenced in our choices. The things we choose must "delight" us in some way so that we are drawn to them, for example because they give us pleasure or fulfill our needs. We are sometimes drawn to choose out of necessity, but we are not forced to choose. This is especially true when it comes to choosing to be good people. As Augustine says, "God has so excellently fashioned the human being that should they will to retain this excellence no one could forcefully hinder him" (*83 Diverse Questions,* #4). We may not be totally responsible for who we are, due to external factors, but we will be responsible for what we become in the life to come if we reject the grace that draws us to heaven. In the words of Augustine, "God who made us without ourselves will not save us without ourselves" (*Sermon 169*, 13).

July 5

The Good Things in Life

God's gifts are in part earthly and in part heavenly. In this life God causes his sun to rise over the good and the bad, and pours his rain on the just and unjust alike. The mercy of God brings us into existence, distinguishing us from the beast by making us rational animals capable of knowing God. Then it gives us the ability to enjoy the light, the air, the rain, the crops, the changing seasons, earthly comforts, bodily health, the affection of friends and the safety of our own homes.

Commentary on Psalm 35, 7

There is no sin in seeking and enjoying the good things of this life. But there is a danger involved. This world is often so good that we are tempted to desire nothing more. At the same time, we think our comfort is God's reward for our virtue. We are mistaken in this, however, because we will not enjoy our current comforts forever, and they are enjoyed by many who are not as virtuous as ourselves. Our good life is not God's reward for our goodness. We need to remind ourselves that whatever good things we have in this life are but a prelude to the life we will have forever on the other side of death. It is there that our virtue will be rewarded (if we humbly admit that our virtue is by the grace of God).

July 6

Life: More Fragile than Glass

What could be more fragile than a glass lamp? And yet it can be preserved and last for centuries. Though it is liable to accidents, glass does not have to fear getting sick or growing old. We are even more fragile and weak than glass because we are threatened not only by accidents but also by illness and the ravages of time. You may spend your life avoiding fatal blows but can you avoid your inevitable final exit? You may escape accidents happening to you from outside, but can you avoid attacks from within? Now any kind of disease may suddenly infect you and even if you avoid these, eventually old age will come and there is no way to escape its disabilities.

Sermon 109, 1

It does not take long to realize how fragile we are. As a song from the musical *Porgy and Bess* reminds us, "We ain't necessarily so." If God should lose sight of us, cease to pay attention to us, we would instantly go out of existence (*A Literal Commentary on Genesis*, 4.12.22). We are like luminescent air, fighting to retain the light that makes us sparkle. We cannot shine on our own. We escape the darkness of non-existence only so long as divine light stays with us and in us. However, Augustine's words are not meant to be depressing. Rather they should prompt us to break out in a song of praise for the God who continues to burn brightly in us despite our fragile nature. Like fragile glass lamps, we can carry the light of God to the world.

July 7

Pouring Out Life to Save It

Do you love your soul? Lose it! But you will say to me,
"How can I deliberately lose what I love?" Well, you do it
all the time in your daily life. For example, a farmer loves
corn and yet he eventually scatters the corn which he had
stored with such care in his granary. He worked hard to
harvest it but when the time comes for sowing, he will
bring it out and scatter it. Because he loved corn so much,
he poured it out on the ground. You too, if you love life,
must pour out your life. If you love your soul, lose it! The
reason for this is that when you lose it for God's sake in
this life, you will find it in the life to come. If you love
your life, you must pour it out to save it.

Sermon 313D, 2

Augustine's words are an invitation to imitate the Creator.
God at the beginning of time loved life so intensely that he
wanted to share it with others and so he scattered life throughout creation. Though all from seeds, each of us is a unique
reflection of God's goodness, each of us has gifts that are different from those of every other human being. We have a capacity
to love that is special to us; over a lifetime we have gathered
knowledge and experience that no other human being has. We
must pour our gifts, love, and self out onto the world around
us. Unless we "scatter" ourselves now, we will not be able to
enjoy the heavenly harvest.

July 8

Life Is a Pain

Few are those who suffer no pains in this life. Only a few
reach old age without losing their peace of mind or their

health. Most of us can agree with Job's sober observation that "The life of man upon earth is a pain" (Job 7:1). Children begin life knowing nothing and unable to do anything and must be forced to learn their letters or a trade. We begin life by crying, not laughing, and that is a prophecy of how the rest of life shall be. How true it is that "A heavy yoke is upon the children of Adam from the day of their coming out of their mother's womb until the day of their burial in the earth" (Sirach 40:1).

City of God, 21.14

Augustine's words above should not be interpreted to mean that he had an unhappy childhood. Indeed, from what he writes it appears Augustine had a happy childhood. In time, however, he came to experience sexual passion, poor health, grief, loss, and old age. All of these painful times strengthened his conviction that anyone who pursues this-worldly desires will be disappointed. Christ's promise, that someday we will be perfectly and eternally happy, will only be fulfilled in heaven. There is nothing wrong in enjoying the good times of this life as long as we continue to desire and work for the better times that are to come in heaven with God.

July 9

Pain Now, Joy Hereafter

Let us begin by reminding ourselves of our love of this present life. After all, this life is still loved whatever it is like. Even those who live wretched, miserable lives are frightened that it will come to an end. Think of the things we must go through in this life. Every day we struggle and run around and bustle about and gasp for breath. You can scarcely count the things that have to be done to live every day: sowing, plowing, planting, sailing, grinding, cooking, and weaving. And after all these things are done, your life comes to an end anyway. So learn, brothers and sisters, to seek eternal life. There you will not have to endure these things but will reign with God forever.

Sermon 84, 1

We are attached to this life just now because it is the only one we know. We struggle each day to make a living and to make our life livable while fearing the time when we can no longer maintain our livelihood. Augustine observes that some, in their old age, prefer to die but will accept eagerly even the most bizarre suggestions from their doctor as to how to live a few days more (*Sermon 84, 1*). But this desire to live, Augustine says, is a good thing because it can lead us to the promises of Christ—that we will live forever a life without tribulation, a life surrounded by love. Only then will our passion for life seem not unreasonable because it will be fulfilled.

July 10

This Life Is Like an Oil Press

The world now is like an oil press and we all feel its pressure. If you are dregs, you run off down the drain; if you are the good oil, you remain in the vat. Pressure is applied by famine, war, poverty, need, epidemics, robbery, greed, and unrest in the cities. Some people grumble, "Look what great evils there are in these Christian times!" That's the dregs collapsing under the pressure of the times. But now hear the voice of those who like good oil have been purified and strengthened by the pressure. They cry out, "O God, blessed be your name. You foretold that these bad times would come and you promise that good times are to come. Train us well through the pressure of these bad times so that we may receive the heavenly inheritance you have promised."

Sermon 113A, 11

Augustine was also an optimist in that he believed that diffi-cult times could strengthen us as we wait for the bliss of heaven. But his experience of war, terrorism, and revolution made him a realist. His faith gave him his optimism, which allowed him to view the pressure of chaotic times as a catalyst for spiritual per-fection. The disruption of his daily life made him look forward even more strongly to the peace promised to those who do not give up on God in the midst of the pressure of their times.

July 11

Life: A Boxing Match

Here we have a fight on our hands and God is watching from the stands. Our fight is with all our vices and Satan, the prince of vices. He challenges our soul to a single combat. Whatever evil or unlawful thing may be sug-gested to your thoughts, whatever dark, unwholesome desire wells up from your flesh against your mind, these are the weapons of the enemy who is challenging you to combat. Your foe and your protector are both invisible. You cannot see the Satan with whom you are locked in combat but you can know through faith the God who protects you.

Sermon 335K, 3

We have many battles in life with outside forces, but our most dangerous battles are those that are waged inside our souls. These are the most dangerous, not just because they can tear us apart in this life, but because they can threaten our peace in the next. Augustine's image of life as a boxing match reminds us that, to find evil, we need look no further than inside ourselves. Even the best of us must sometimes battle lustful thoughts, anger, hatred, greed, and inordinate selfish-ness. For each of us our salvation depends on how many of these battles we win. God may have a ringside seat, but does not intervene, does not stop the fight from happening. But, by his grace, he supports our fight against the evil temptations within.

July 12

Winning the Fight

None of us should engage in combat with the temptations that vex us and presumptuously rely on ourselves. Don't be careless and slack about fighting but also don't proudly rely only on yourselves. Whatever it is that troubles you, battle it bravely and don't give in. But then call upon the God who watches from the sidelines. God uses you as his instrument in the battle. It is he who insures the victory. By fighting bravely and acknowledging God's help, we can compete without anxiety and, when the contest is over, we can rest in the holy quiet of heaven. The God who permits the battle to continue, watches you in your fight, helps you when the going gets tough and will crown you with the victor's laurels when you win.

Sermon 335K, 6

In order to win the fight against our weakness, we must "fight like the devil" and ask God for the grace to succeed. Fighting like the devil means to do our part in stifling the evil desires by cutting off their nourishment. As pornography nourishes lust, so certain people and situations nourish our anger. Both must be avoided. But after doing this we need to pray to God for the grace to win the battle. God is not a spectator; he is the captain of the team and the one who will ultimately be responsible for our victory.

July 13

Life on the Road

Paul teaches that this life of ours is like traveling abroad
from our home country. He says "As long as we are in the
body, we are traveling abroad from the Lord" (2 Corinthians 5:6). Since we are still traveling in a foreign land,
we ought to keep in mind what our home country is—
that country to which we must hasten by turning our
backs on the attractions and delights of this life. This
homeland towards which we travel is the only place where
we can find true rest because God does not wish us to find
rest anywhere else but there. The reason is simple: if God
gave us perfect rest while we were still abroad, we would
find no pleasure in returning home.

Sermon 346B, 1

Augustine's image of this life as being "on the road" explains why we sometimes get tired, dissatisfied, and confused.
With travel there are always multiple things that can go wrong.
This was surely the case for Augustine. He traveled abroad
only once and was never tempted to make that trip again.
However, he believed that the anxiety caused by being far from
home had its purpose: if we got too much satisfaction in this
place, we might never want to move on. We were not created
to be at home in this life; it is only the way to get home.

July 14

A Warning to Those on the Road

When we become believers in Christ, we are still not home
safe but have only begun to walk along the road towards

161

it. We still may be held back by the delights of the road itself and not drawn forward by love for our home country. We move forward by love of God and neighbor. If we don't love at all, we become stuck on the road; if we still long for this world, we are looking back. Our face is no longer turned towards our heavenly home. What is the use of being on the road if we are going backwards and not forward? What's the use of being a Christian on the right path if by loving the world we are looking back and returning to the place from which we started?

Sermon 346B, 2

The main road to heaven is through belief in Jesus Christ and following his command to love God above all and other human beings as ourselves. Such love fixes our eyes firmly on our heavenly destination. But being on the right road is not a guarantee that we will finally get to our destination. Through laziness we may sit down, or we may return to the pleasures of this world. The message is clear: being baptized a Christian is no guarantee that we will get to heaven. To get there we must act like a Christian, trying every day to live as Christ wants us to live.

July 15

Road Work

How are you supposed to act here on the road to heaven? What should be your occupation? Surely it is to praise the God you love and to bring others to love him together with you. If you were passionate about a charioteer, would you not pester other people to become your fellow-fans? A charioteer's fan talks about his hero wherever he goes, trying to persuade others to share his passion. With the same passion you should not begrudge God to anyone.

Grab someone else, as many people as you can, everyone you can get hold of. There is room for all of them in God and all of you will together possess him whole and entire . . . From the stench in the building I realize that I have talked too long but I can never keep up with your eager demands. I only wish you were just as demanding in seizing the kingdom of heaven.

Commentary on Psalm 72, 34

Augustine's words at the end of the sermon indicate that he was sometimes long-winded, but he was so because his people demanded it of him. His congregation was especially excited with the topic "heaven and how to get there." In this passage he tells us that, if we are truly excited about the message of Christ, we will want others to join us in following him down the road to heaven. We do this, not by preaching the Word, but by living it.

July 16

Carrying Christ on the Road

Don't be ashamed of being the Lord's donkey. If you are carrying Christ, you won't go astray walking along the road to heaven. Do you remember that young donkey that was brought to the Lord on Palm Sunday? That's what you are. But don't feel ashamed. Let the Lord sit upon you and take you wherever he wants. We are his beast of burden as we make our way to the heavenly Jerusalem. With him seated on us we aren't weighed down; we are lifted up. With him guiding us we cannot go wrong. We are going to him and we are going through him. How can we lose the way?

Sermon 189, 4

The paradox of being a Christian is that we are on the way to join Christ in heaven while carrying Christ on the road. Christ has told us that he is with us, keeping us on the road. If we allow him to be a vibrant presence within us, there is no danger that we will lose the way, even though sometimes we do not know exactly where we are going. On Palm Sunday the donkey that carried Christ had no idea about the way to Jerusalem. But, under the gentle guidance of Jesus, he made the journey successfully. And, as he made his way down the road, the crowds could see that he was carrying Christ and cried, "Hosanna!" perhaps because they saw for the first time that God was living with them on the road.

July 17

The Desire to Get Away

The psalmist cries out, "Who will give me wings? Then I will fly away and find rest." He was either hoping for death or longing for solitude. This does happen, my friends. A desire for solitude does often arise in the mind of a servant of God from no other cause than a host of troubles and difficulties. You may be trying to correct a misguided person for whom you are responsible and find that all human effort and vigilance seems wasted. If you cannot correct them, all you can do is to try to endure them. If such a burdensome person is one of your own, where will you go to get away?

Commentary on Psalm 54, 8

There are times in our life when the needs of others demand much of us. We may be tempted to escape, but their needs do not allow for it. In such situations all we can do is try to endure the burden as long as we can. But we must be realistic too. There is a limit to what we can endure alone and there is no shame in asking for help. We should pray to God for the grace to endure the burdens of our life, and to know when we can bear them no longer. Even Augustine had to take a six month sabbatical from his busy life so as to preserve his mental well-being.

July 18

Action Versus Contemplation

There are three types of life: the contemplative, the active, and the contemplative-active. People can live the life of faith in any of these but everyone must make time both to seek the truth through contemplation and perform the actions that charity demands. No one should be so committed to contemplation as to give no thought to the needs of their neighbors. On the other hand, no one should be so absorbed in action as to give up contemplating God. The desire for contemplation should not end up as empty-headed leisure but be dedicated to the discovery of truth both for one's own sake and in order to share it with others. Those dedicated to action should seek earthly power and position in order to contribute to the eternal salvation of those committed to their care. Even though they may be dedicated to truly good works, they should not give up their delight in contemplation. If they do, they may lose their taste for it and be overwhelmed by the burden of their active life.

City of God, 19.19

Virtuous contemplation for Augustine was reflecting on the mystery of God; virtuous action was that done out of love for neighbor. Both are necessary for salvation. The contemplative sitting in his cell must not ignore the needs of the world; the person involved in charitable action must spend some time in contemplation. A balance of the two allows us to avoid burnout, on the one hand, and self-indulgence on the other.

165

July 19

In Praise of Martha

Martha and Mary were sisters related by blood and equal in holiness (Luke 10:38-42). Both were dedicated to the Lord. Martha welcomed him as travelers are welcomed. She was the maidservant receiving her Master, the invalid receiving her healer. You are indeed blessed, Martha, because of your service, by your seeking peace through good works. But when you come to the heavenly homeland you will find no traveler to welcome, no one hungry to feed, no thirst to relieve, no sick to visit, no quarrelers to reconcile, no dead to bury. There will be none of these tasks there. What Mary chose in this life will be realized there in all its fullness. "The Lord will make his servants sit down and he will wait on them."

Sermon 103, 2 & 6

By attending to Jesus, rather than helping Martha with the meal, "Mary has chosen the better part." But why was it better? Because it represented the type of life all of us will enjoy in heaven sitting at the table of the Lord and being served by him. On the other hand, Martha's direct service to the Lord is commendable for when we care for the poor and needy in our own day we are taking care of him (Matthew 25:40).

July 20

The Need for Reflection

Let us leave a little room for reflection, room too for silence. Enter into yourself and leave behind all noise and confusion. Look within yourself. See whether you can find some delightful hidden place in your consciousness, a place free of noise and argument where you need not be carrying on your disputes and planning to have your own stubborn way. Hear the word of God in stillness. Perhaps then you will understand it.

Sermon 52, 22

If our passion for good works gives no time for reflection, then our action becomes thoughtless (*83 Diverse Questions,* 58.2). Augustine learned this lesson from experience. In the midst of his own active life he wrote to his friend Nebridius: "I find it impossible without the aid of some relief from care and toil to taste and relish what is really good. Believe me, there is need for much withdrawal of oneself from the turmoil of things which are passing away, in order to someday fear nothing" (*Letter 10,* 2). For Augustine, frantic activity can only make us tired; reflecting on God deep inside ourselves may bring us peace.

July 21

Advice to Contemplatives

Do not prefer your peaceful retirement to the needs of the Church. Just as a man has to pick his way between fire and water so as to be neither burned nor drowned so we should steer our way between immoderate pride in our works and sloth masked under the title "contemplation." You must so love your quiet contemplative peace that you continue to withdraw yourselves from all worldly distractions. Likewise when you are doing good work through prayers or fasting or (above all) by putting up with each other in charity, do all of these things for the glory of God. Such a life will not be dried out by activity nor cooled by sloth. And (as Paul wrote): "If you do these things, the God of peace will be with you" (Philippians 4:9).

Letter 48, 1–4

The above advice that Augustine sent to a group of monks applies to all who are drawn to a life of contemplation and quiet research. It is a good life if done for the glory of God, but at the same time those engaged in it must be open to action, if called upon. Certainly a researcher who jealously guards his knowledge rather than sharing it with others is not worthy of great praise. One may be inclined toward one rather than the other, but circumstances may demand that we go beyond our comforts so that we might serve the wider church.

July 22

A Warning to Lazy Christians

Christianity does not forbid doing a little work. Prayer is certainly an absolute necessity for all of us but this does not mean that we are justified in giving up all work for the sake of it. What hinders a person from meditating on God and singing his praises while performing a bit of manual labor? Don't say that you need your leisure for holy reading! Remember that the one who reads good books only advances in virtue to the extent that the good reading is put into practice.

On the Work of Monks, 17

Augustine wrote the words above to a group of monks who believed that, rather than trying to earn their living, others should provide for them while they devoted themselves to prayer and contemplation. Augustine had little sympathy for such indolence. Although he would have dearly loved a quiet life of reflection, he felt compelled by God to continue his daily tasks of preaching and teaching and listening to the troubles of others (*Sermon 125,* 8). This was demanding and thankless work, but in the end, God wants great hearts—those willing to labor and pray on God's behalf.

The Rest of the Innocent

Every one of us looks for something to rest on in this life because it is too great an effort to be constantly reaching out for heaven. Thus, a good man finds rest in his own home, in his household, his wife and his children, in his modest way of life, in his small property, in the young plants he has set with his own hands, in a building that has been put up through his initiative. Innocent people find their relaxation in this life in things like these. But because God wants us to continue longing for heaven he mingles bitter elements even with these innocent pleasures so that even in them we experience distress.

Commentary on Psalm 40, 5

Fortunately, there are sources of enjoyment in this world that do not require of us sin or disreputable acts to generate them. Such innocent joys include receiving the gaze of our beloved, watching our children grow, and enjoying the fruits of our labor. Such good days cannot last forever, but perhaps that is good too because it makes us look forward to the eternal good times promised by the Lord. In the meantime God gives us the gift of memory so that we can remember without regret such wonderful days.

July 24

The Joy of Heavenly Birth

Your birth into heaven will not be like your birth on earth which led to such woe, weeping, and death. Rather it will be an easy birth characterized by happiness, by joy, by eternal life. There your infancy will have the quality of innocence, your childhood reverence, your adolescence patience, your youth virtue, your middle age merit, your old age nothing less than the white hairs of wisdom and understanding. You will have all these six ages of life at the same time and in them you will be permanently renewed. They will carry you through to the seventh age of perennial quiet and peace. There your immortality will be serene; there your serenity will be forever.

Sermon 216, 8

By the time Augustine wrote this sermon he had gone through the insecurity of the child, the confusion of the adolescent, the passions of the young adult, the fatigue of middle age, and the disability of the aged. He believed that in heaven we shall be in our prime, but all of the good parts of each age will be piled upon each other, with none of the bad. It is no wonder that, given the choice between dying and returning to youth, Augustine would choose death. There were too many good things awaiting him to wish to stay longer than necessary here on earth.

July 25

Living in a Violent World

When some difficulty arises in accomplishing what we desire, we become angry. Not only do we get angry with other people, we also sometimes get so angry with a faulty pen that we break it. Dice-players will do the same with "unlucky" dice, painters with their tattered brushes, and in general anyone who suffers any frustration with the tool he is trying to use. After a while our anger makes us bilious and the rising bile causes us to get angry over and over even without an apparent cause.

Letter 9, 4

Like us, Augustine lived in violent times, times when children killed their mothers, husbands abused their wives, thieves plundered shipwrecks, mobs roamed the streets (cf. *Sermon 259, 3; Letter 34, 3; Confessions, 9.9; Sermon 302*). Augustine wrote that violence is the result of our not getting what we desire: "Every person on earth is driven by his passion to pursue his self-interest. Unfortunately, there are not enough existing goods to satisfy everyone completely (and) as a result this world suffers a chronic condition of war in which those who win oppress those who lose" (*City of God, 18.2*).

July 26

The Good and Bad of Anger

Great thinkers of the past recognized that passions such as anger and sexual desire must be bridled and checked and redirected towards reasonable goals: anger towards prevention of public disorder, sexual desire towards fulfillment of parental duty. In Paradise before sin occurred these passions were never so roused against the commands of the rational will that reason was forced to put them in harness. It is different now. Even the most moral people need to control these passions. The present condition is not that of healthy human nature; it is a sickness induced by sin. However, even now in most cases when a man is angry he will not become violent in word or action unless he chooses to do so.

City of God, 14.19

Augustine describes anger as the passionate urge to overcome obstacles which hinder our freedom of action (*Letter 9, 4*). This means that anger can be good, such as our angry response to the news of the murder of innocent children. But how are we to deal with the anger that causes evil in the world? To be sure, we must control our own anger so that we not contribute to the violence of our times. But we must also redirect our passion towards battling the evils that prompt violent anger: the unjust conditions that frustrate the disadvantaged.

July 27

The Dangers of Anger

We must take care that our anger is not so vehement as to turn into hatred. Anger is not hatred. You may be angry with your son but you do not hate him. We do not yet hate those with whom we are angry but if the anger remains and is not quickly uprooted, it grows into hatred. John says "Whoever hates his brother is still in darkness" (1 John 2:11). Our eye is confused by anger and it may develop into hatred and blind us. The psalmist says "My eye is confused by anger, my soul too, and my belly" which means "Everything inside me is in turmoil." It is sometimes legitimate to be angry with wicked and perverse people but we must not lose our temper with them even though the tension from "holding ourselves in" may upset our insides.

Commentary on Psalm 30/3, 4

There are three dangers in getting angry. First, anger over time can become hatred (*Sermon 114A,* 6). Second, anger can result in losing our temper and violent acts. And third, our anger may make us sick: "As vinegar corrodes a vessel if it is left in it too long, so anger corrodes the heart if it goes over to the next day" (*Letter 210,* 2). In our cracked condition we cannot avoid getting angry sometimes (*Sermon 211,* 1) but in most cases we can manage it (*Sermon 315,* 10). We must make every effort to do this so that we not contribute to the hatred and violence in the world today.

July 28

Hatred Kills the Soul

If love is life, hatred is death. When a person begins to
fear that he may hate the one he used to love, he is afraid
of death and the death he fears is one more dreadful
because it is a death that slays not the body but the soul.
What harm can an angry person do to you in view of the
security the Lord gave you when he said "Do not be
afraid of those who kill the body" (Matthew 10:28). In his
rage the enemy may kill the body, but by hating him you
have killed the soul. He killed the body of another; you
have killed your own soul.

Commentary on Psalm 54, 7

When we hate we become prisoners of that hate, unable to
reach out in love to other humans or to God. We imprison our
self in a hate-filled cell of our own making. Augustine put it
this way, "He who hates his brother walks about and comes
and goes as he pleases. He is bound by no chains. He is not
physically confined to a prison cell. And yet he is bound by his
guilty state. His prison is his heart" (*Sermon 211, 2*). It is not
easy to avoid such imprisonment, given the many opportuni-
ties to hate. All we can do is to remember that God lives in
those who tempt us to hate, and will someday pass judgment
on them. By "leaving them to Heaven" we make it more likely
that we will get there ourselves.

July 29

The Evil of Revenge

Why vent your rage on those who have harmed you? You
answer: "Because they are evil!" If you vent your rage on

them you are adding yourself to their number. You are objecting to their evil and you are adding your evil to theirs. Do you want to overcome evil with evil? Then there would be two evils needing to be overcome. Suppose you vent your rage on a person by killing them. After death none of your punishment touches them. All that exists then is your malice in killing him. That's mindless madness, not avenging justice.

Sermon 302, 10

Augustine's words above were addressed to members of his congregation who had joined a mob who took revenge on a criminal by lynching him. He told them, "There are the authorities to deal with him. What business is it of yours to vent your rage like that? What authority have you received? This is not a case of public punishment but of private revenge" (*Sermon 302,* 13). Revenge is not punishment. It serves no purpose, other than to bring satisfaction to the one who seeks revenge. We may never forget, but we should try our best to forgive. At the very least we must not take the law into our own hands.

July 30

Winning the War Within

God's promise that he will "banish war even to the ends of the earth" seems not fully realized. Wars still go on. They are fought between nations, between sects, between Jews, pagans, Christians and heretics. His promise must therefore refer more to the wars waged against evil within ourselves. When we come to see that we cannot look to ourselves for any help at all, then the wars that rage within us are quelled. We must stay unarmed without any aid from ourselves and then God will take up our cause. He will equip us with weapons such as truth, self-control, salvation, hope, faith and charity. God has made you weak in order to make you strong with his strength.

Commentary on Psalm 45, 13

In these days of war and violence there is only one war that is within our control: the internal war between what we *want* to do and what we *should* do. Augustine's words remind us that, by God's grace, we can do battle against hatred, lust, greed, ambition, and despair. With God's help we can win that eternal life that he wants for us. We may never conquer earth; we can conquer heaven.

July 31

Passing Time

In this life not a single day will stand still for us. Each of them flies quickly away. Each seems to be gone before it even comes. Take this day on which I speak to you; much of it has already disappeared. We can't even hold onto this moment where we are now. It flies away and another one comes only to fly away in turn. What is it you love so much in this life? You embrace it and hold onto it and try to keep it. But it does not stand still and it does not let you stand still. All those things you considered precious fly away. Do you want to find a stable place to stand? Stand with the Lord Jesus who remains forever and listen to him. With him you can stand secure forever.

Sermon 65A, 13

A most unhappy reality is this: we can stem neither the flow of time, nor the drifting away of those we have loved. True, those we love and have loved are separated from us for a while as the currents move us in different directions; but the happy fact is that we will all meet at the same destination. There the

river of our times empties into that eternal sea where God
waits to embrace us.

August 1

Jesus Frees Us from Time

When the fullness of time arrived, Jesus came to free us
from time. Freed from time, we will come to eternity
where time does not exist. There "today" is everlasting
and is not preceded by a yesterday nor closed out by a
tomorrow. In this age the days move. Some pass away
and some come. Even the moments in which we are
speaking drive one another away. One syllable passes on
so that the second syllable may sound. Nothing stands
still in time. This is the reason why we ought to love Jesus
who created time so that we may be finally freed from
time and made secure by him in eternity.

Commentary on the Gospel of John, 31.5.3

Whatever the present moment is like, we tend to be anxious
about the future. Our anxiety stems from the fact that we
cannot predict whether the future will bring pleasure or pain.
A characteristic of eternity, an eternity made possible for us by
the sacrifice of Jesus Christ, is that it is without anxiety because
there is no "next"; with eternity there is only the "now," a now
filled with joy.

August 2

The Wisdom of the Ant

It is when times are tranquil that people should harvest
the word of God for themselves and store it in the depths

of their hearts. They should imitate the ants who store the riches of their summer's labor deep inside their nest. There is time and energy to do this in the serenity of our summer months. Winter with its troubles will inevitably come and if we cannot find provisions within ourselves we will starve to death.

Commentary on Psalm 36/2, 11

Augustine says we should develop our spiritual lives when things are going well. There are times when God appears hidden, times of loss or suffering, when the world is gray with the winter's dark. We need to fill up with God's Word, to strengthen our faith, during our fruitful summer days so that we have the spiritual reserves from which to draw for the winter days. Also, the ant is a social creature which lives and flourishes in colonies. So too are we. It follows that in the good times of our summer days we should deepen the love we have for our friends. Strong friendships fashioned in the joy of summer can support us when the dark and lonely doldrums of winter set in.

August 3

Looking Ahead

Let's not allow past things to hold us back from hearing about what lies ahead; let's not allow our involvement in present events to prevent us from thinking about the future. Let us look forward to the things that are to come and forget about the past. All those great good things that we work for now we shall enjoy fully at the resurrection of the just. So don't let the sweetness of the past hide the word of God from you. Don't let the pressures of present things so tie you down and impede you that you end up saying "I don't have time to read; I don't have time to listen." To say this is to bury your head in the sand. Don't let your past or present prevent you from looking to the future.

Commentary on Psalm 66, 10

The difficulty in looking to eternity is that the past and the present seem more real. When we are young, we neither think much of the past, nor worry about the future; we are focused on the here and now. The older we get, the more time we spend reminiscing about a past that is increasing, while our future is decreasing. But the more the past consumes our attention, the less we look forward to the eternal future promised us by Jesus.

August 4

Singing My Life-Song

When I am about to sing a song, it exists only in anticipation. As I begin to sing, the notes are plucked off and committed to the past. In my present moment, my attention is concentrated on the process of singing notes still anticipated and sending them into the past where they live in memory. The longer the song continues the more the notes in memory increase and anticipated notes decrease until finally the realm of expectation is used up. The song is now finished and no longer sounds. It is only remembered. The same process happens in the song we sing with our lives where the various notes are the things we do through our times.

Confessions, 11.28.38

My whole life is like a song I sing to the universe and to God. In the beginning it is all expectation. I have not yet sounded the notes that I am to sing. As I live longer more notes sound and then join the melody, which exists only in memory. As more and more notes are added, there are fewer to come. The days of my life shorten and I prepare myself for the final sounds of the song of my life. Whether the song will be a hymn of triumph or a cacophonous failure remains to be seen, but what it will be is within my control. My time is passing but my song continues to sound.

August 5

Sing Me a Happy Song

If we really and honestly love the martyrs and follow in their footsteps, with the help of God's grace should we not also become God's friends? Our happiness has the effect of praising God because it is he that turns us from being miserable into being happy. You see, we can make ourselves miserable all by ourselves but we don't have the ability to make ourselves happy.

Sermon 335H, 2

To the reflection above, I would add: "Though we can make ourselves miserable all by ourselves, we are often helped by other people." Some people singing the "song of their life" seem only capable of singing dirges. Moreover, many of these sad songs are of their own making. The paradox is that, often, those who have suffered the death of a loved one, a disabling illness, or the loss of a good job, are usually not the ones who spread their misery to others. They suffer in silence out of love for those around them. Out of love for our neighbor we should all pray, "Lord when I get depressed stop me from singing a sad song to those I meet. Give me the grace to keep my mouth shut when I am upset by the burnt toast at breakfast."

August 6

Things Are Passing Away

You never stop hoping for temporal things and yet are
frequently disappointed in your hopes. You are excited by
them before they come, corrupted by them when they do
come, tormented by them when they inevitably leave. Are
not all temporal things the sort that glow brightly when
coveted, grow dull when acquired, and fade away when
lost? It is better by far to use the good things of this earth
as we need them on our pilgrimage but avoid making
them the center of our heart's joy so that we not be buried
in their ruins when they collapse. It is better by far to
make use of this world as though we were not using it in
order to reach the God who made it and remain in him for
all eternity.

Sermon 157, 5

It is sad that in this life we should cling so tightly to money,
honors, property, and power. At the same time it is under-
standable because these are the only things we know. It is sad
that we become so acquisitive because all temporal things are
destined to fade away. Such things make our earthly pilgrimage bearable, but they do not last. Better to embrace that which
is eternal: the eternal love of friends and family, and the love of
God who waits to embrace us in the next life.

August 7

Greed: The Root of Evil

It has been said that "Greed is the root of all evil" (1 Timothy 6:10) and also that "The beginning of all sin is pride"

(Sirach 10:13). How can these two statements be harmonized? Surely we find greed in pride because through pride a person has "exceeded the limit of his nature." And what is it to be greedy? Is it not "to seek more than what is needed"? Scripture tells us that Adam fell through pride but is this also not greed? What is more greedy than a person for whom God does not suffice?

Commentary on the Epistle of John, 8.6

For most of us, greed is expressed in our desire for such temporal things as money, power, and status. Adam's temptation was to be "more than God," to be obedient to no higher power. As Augustine observed, "Having God did not suffice for him." Though we sometimes pretend to be God, it is not a temptation that dominates our daily lives. We would be quite satisfied with wealth and possessions. But in time, such possessions easily become like "birdlime on our spirit" preventing us from flying to the heaven where God awaits (*Sermon 112*, 6).

August 8

The Lust for Money

Look at what people are ready to suffer for the sake of money! They sail the seas despite the storms. They seem ready to die rather than be poor. And yet when the storms come they throw all their goods overboard so that they might live. For a moment they prefer life to money but then, when they are saved, they reproach God saying "Why didn't you drown me in the sea with my goods?" Look at the things the lovers of money endure for their beloved. Some wear themselves out with toil and break down under their labors; others are butchered by bandits; others drowned in the waves; others die a thousand deaths from worry.

Sermon 299F, 5

Augustine believed that greed was one of the persistent temptations of human beings. Speaking of old age, he observed, "From personal experience I have noticed that with the decline of sexual desire, avarice increases" (*The Good of Widowhood*, 20.26). He also noted that being poor was no protection because, "Avarice means wanting to be rich, not being rich" (*Sermon 85*, 6). Avarice causes us to do anything to anybody in order to get a bit more money. It is sad when our happiness comes to depend on such a paltry thing. Final happiness comes only in heaven and it cannot be bought by any amount of money.

August 9

How Much Land Does a Man Need?

You know how a greedy person acts when they get a coin. They say "It rolls away; it is able to be destroyed. I must keep my hold on it by buying something permanent." And so he buys a farm but does he truly *have* it? The time will come when he will die. Who will then own what he once bought? Then he will have no farm nor will the farm experience his presence except perhaps the presence of his body in the grave. That will be truly strange; his farm will possess *him*, but he will not possess it.

Sermon 335C, 8

Augustine's words remind me of a story from Russian literature that tells the tale of a man who could have as much land as he could circle in twelve hours. The catch was that he would lose everything if he did not return to the starting point. He ran a great distance, anxious to get as much land as possible, only to realize that he had to run faster to get back to the starting point. Exhausted, he fell across the finish line where he died and was buried. This raises the question as to how much land a man needs. Answer: about six feet! The lesson for us is that we must not get attached to the things we use in this life because when we die we will leave them all behind.

August 10

The Worries of the Wealthy

Who is happy? You say "The man who has everything in abundance and seeks nothing more." But is he not afraid of losing what he has? How then can you say that he wants for nothing? He may not lack possessions but he does lack security in them. And who in this world can give him the assurance that what he has will not be destroyed? Many a man has gone to sleep rich and awakened a pauper. No one can give him such security. A sensible person knows this and is therefore afraid.

Sermon 359A, 6

It seems that the more things we have, the more we have to worry about. Of course, it is reasonable to worry about our possessions, say, in the face of a hurricane. With the potential for global destruction, it is not unreasonable to worry about what is precious to us. But possessions will never bring perfect happiness. When we don't have them we are anxious to get them; when we have them we fear losing them. The conclusion must be that we will never be perfectly happy in this life. But Christ's encouraging promise is that we can have perfect happiness in the life to come.

August 11

The Anxiety of the Avaricious

Avarice requires of us exhausting efforts, dangerous adventures, bothersome trials, tribulations, which we endure. To accomplish what? That you may have the gold to fill your bank account, lose your freedom, and gain anxiety. You were probably more free when you were a "have-not" than when you became one of the "haves." You have filled your house with your wealth and now robbers are feared. You have acquired gold; you have lost sleep. Avarice commands us to "do this!" and we do it. God's only command is that we love him. "You seek gold but perhaps you will never find it. If you seek me, I will come to you. Who has ever really loved me and has not gained me?"

Commentary on the Epistle of John, 10.4.1

Augustine compares what the avaricious must do to possess what they seek to what the virtuous must do to possess God. Avarice commands us to suffer all sorts of tribulations to get gold, honor, and love. Once obtained, such possessions bring a whole new series of anxieties. On the other hand, the only thing we need do to possess God is to love him.

August 12

Avarice: The Dropsy of the Heart

The avaricious person has a raging thirst. He is like a person suffering from dropsy: the more he drinks, the thirstier he gets. If you are avaricious, you have dropsy of the heart: the more you have, the more you need. When you had less, you wanted less, you could enjoy yourself with fewer things. But because you have now been filled, you have also been stretched. You have become grossly opulent. But you go on drinking; you go on being thirsty. You say "If I can get this, I'll be able to do that." In fact, when you get this, all you have more of is "wishing" for more.

Sermon 177, 6

When I think about the sickness of avarice, I think of the miser living in a run-down house while having millions of dollars stuffed in his mattress. In its worst form, it is the impulse to possess rather than use. Augustine speaks of a man who began by desiring a farm and ended up desiring all the land and the islands of the sea. But this was not enough for him. "Having made the earth his own, he would happily have gone on to seize heaven if he could" (*Commentary on Psalm 39, 7*). To possess all that is good, we need only to love God and neighbor.

August 13

Extravagance: The Opposite of Avarice

There are two opposing vices that may take hold of us: avarice and extravagance. Avarice tells us to save, while extravagance tells us to spend. Avarice says, "Save up for yourself, save up for your children. If ever you are in need, no one is going to give you anything." Extravagance takes the opposite line, saying "Live while you are alive; treat yourself well. You are going to die and you don't know when. Nor do you know whether the one you plan to leave your estate to is going to get it or will pray for you once you are dead. So treat yourself well now while you can." My friends, the Lord calls you to freedom; don't be enslaved by vices such as these.

Sermon 86, 6–7

There is nothing evil in owning, using, and enjoying possessions. But it is wrong to use them in a way that blinds us from our true destiny in heaven. Thus, we need to avoid both avarice and extravagance in our use of this world's goods. The miser accumulates possessions to create security. For the spendthrift, there is no security in this life so we might as well enjoy ourselves now. In the end, however, we will all be judged by how wisely we used the goods of this world.

August 14

Getting "Stuck"

John says "Do not love the world nor the things that are in the world" (1 John 2:15). He did not say, "Don't have the things of this world." You have possessed them. You have loved them and now you are stuck. Love of earthly things is the birdlime that entraps spiritual wings. How can you fly to the true rest of heaven when you have gotten so stuck? You have unwisely wanted to rest here and now have gotten badly stuck. To avoid this you must follow God's command "Do not love the world!"

Sermon 112, 6

No doubt, there are those of us who get stuck in situations with little hope of escape through no fault of our own. At the same time, there are those of us who create our own situations. Either we have loved the wrong things, in the wrong way, or loved them too much, believing that they will give us the peace and happiness we seek. They are good in themselves, but they do not direct us to the God who allows us the perfect "rest" in heaven.

August 15

Almsgiving: A Wise Investment

To those who are rich, I say make amends for your sins
with almsgiving. Don't sit on your gold like a hen on its
eggs. If you are going to be put in your grave naked, for
whom are you amassing all these things? Why not be
generous with your wealth? For a morsel of bread, for a
coin, for an old coat, you will receive eternal life, the kingdom of heaven, endless bliss. Give such earthly things to
the poor and you will get back the God who made heaven
and earth. Without him the rich man is just a beggar and
with him the poor man is rich beyond imagination.

Sermon 350B, 1

Of course there is much that can be done politically and
socially to alleviate poverty. On a personal level, we are called
to give. As Augustine suggests in the passage above, giving is
a wise investment. Almsgiving is the only way we can take our
wealth with us when we die. It helps the poor in this life and
will be credited to us in the next. It is a safe investment because
it is guaranteed by the words of God himself who said that
whatever we do for the least of our brothers, we do for him.

August 16

The Right Order of Love

You value gold; God created it. You value beautiful
bodies; God is their creator. You value pleasant vistas;
God created them. If you are neglecting God on account
of what God has created, grant some worth to God himself. He has created everything that you value and love;

how worthy he must be to be valued and loved. Go ahead and love the good things and people of this life, but love him more. I am not telling you not to love earthly things. I am saying "order your love." Put heavenly things before earthly ones, immortal things before mortal, eternal things before temporal, and put loving the Lord before everything else.

Sermon 335C, 13

Why is it such a challenge to order our loves, to love the eternal more than the temporal? I suspect that it is because eternal life seems distant in contrast to this life, which is right in front of us. And there are times when God seems distant. When Augustine's friend died, others told him to pray, but he could not because God seemed too vague compared to the pain of his loss. That is why we must pray when God feels near. In doing this, we create memories of God's closeness, memories from which we may later need to draw.

August 17

The Lust for Power

Christ was born into this world as we were born but he was different from us sinners because the allurements of this world did not hold him prisoner. He did not want an earthly kingdom and the pride that goes with it. Such pride is rightly understood as the "seat of pestilence" because a pestilence is an epidemic which has spread widely and overwhelms nearly all people. The lust for power is like such a pestilence because there is hardly anyone who does not love wielding power or who does not long for human glory.

Commentary on Psalm 1, 1

This desire for power seems to have been present even before sin. The innocent Adam disobeyed because he wanted to be in charge of the garden. In our own age of lost innocence it seems the desire for power has become even more intense. It is good for us to remember this when we are put in some position of authority in life—as a parent, teacher, boss, president, or bishop. We must humbly admit our weakness and pray for the grace to use wisely the authority that has been given to us.

August 18

A Boss Is Just a Human Being

Considering how short life is, does it really matter what government you must obey as long as you are not compelled to act against God or your conscience? As far as I can see, it makes no difference at all to political security or public order to maintain the purely human distinction between conquerors and the conquered. It adds nothing to a nation but empty pomp, an appropriate reward for those who wage fierce battles out of lust for human glory. When all the boasting is over, what is any man but just another man? Even when honor in this life is merited, it has no lasting value. It is smoke that weighs nothing.

City of God, 5.17

The context of the reflection above was the fall of Rome to the barbarian tribes from the north. Augustine's words were directed to those who made much of the glory and superiority of Rome. However, his words can be applied just as well to anyone who thinks themselves glorious because of their dominance. It is as human beings that we will be judged by God, not by our worldly achievements. His one question will be, "Did you show love for me and for your neighbor in the use of your position?"

August 19

Two Qualities of a Good Leader

Nothing could be better for the world than that those who are in power join a good life to the art of political government. Such humble leaders attribute all their virtues, however many they may have on earth, to the grace of God who bestows them on those who pray for them. Such leaders understand how imperfect they are. They realize that they are not angels.

City of God, 5.19

Augustine gives practical advice when he says that those who want to lead should be virtuous and also be masters of the "art of leadership." These two qualities are often hard to find in the same person. History has shown us many cruel, but effective, leaders on the one hand, and good, but ineffective, leaders on the other. In Augustine we find both these qualities, which was not the case for some of his episcopal confreres. All of us have the ability to be virtuous people but not all of us are natural leaders. It is important that we examine our abilities and humbly accept the position in life that is fitted to us. We can achieve salvation without being a president, pope, parent, or boss; but we cannot achieve it if we are not good.

August 20

The Duty to Serve

Every earthly state makes use of some of the citizens of the "City of God" to administer its affairs. How many of the faithful are there among its loyal subjects and its magistrates, its judges, generals, governors and even among those who have been kings? All these are good people, keeping deep in their hearts the longing for the glorious things of heaven. In a way they are like foreigners in a society that will pass away, but in the meantime (under the command of God) they serve their earthly masters conscientiously.

Commentary on Psalm 61, 8

Augustine believed that there was nothing wrong in God-fearing people serving as leaders in earthly societies. Indeed, he maintained that those who had the talent had an obligation to bear the burden and hardships of public service (*Against Faustus the Manichean* 22, 58). Such good and faithful people were especially useful in the administration of public business (*Letter 151*, 14). The rationale for public service is that the church benefits from the peace secured by the earthly society. Thus citizens of the City of God are obligated to assist the state in its role. Indeed, all of us work out our salvation through our service to each other.

August 21

Advice to the Young: I

Young people devoted to the law of God ought to live in such a way that they avoid all promiscuity, gluttony, and obsessive care and primping of the body. They should avoid lazy sleep and wasting time playing silly games. They should refrain from jealousy, detraction, and envy. They should control their ambition for honor, power, and praise. They should recognize the desire for wealth as a danger to their hopes for wisdom. They should neither be halfhearted nor rash in what they do. When others fail them, they should not get angry or at least so restrain their anger that it is not apparent. Above all, let them hate no one.

On Order, 2.8.25

The reflections of the next three days are from a conversation Augustine had with some young students who wanted wisdom to guide their lives. Augustine begins with lessons on how they should prepare themselves if they want to be considered wise in the eyes of God. Such wisdom requires that we develop our talents, not waste time, and treat other human beings with love. The rules may be simple, but their observance can be difficult in this mixed-up world.

August 22

Advice to the Young: II

You should remember that all those over whom you have authority are human beings like you. If you are subject to a superior, you should be so obedient that they are embarrassed to give you orders. If you are a superior, you should rule others so considerately that they are pleased to obey your wishes. As a superior you should not be unwilling to correct vices but you should be careful to avoid vengeance and be ready to forgive. You should punish only those who are proven guilty but not ignore situations that may become worse. You should not badger those who are reluctant to do what you want. With regard to enmities, you should avoid them carefully, bear them patiently, and end them speedily. In every ordinary relationship you have with others you should observe the rule "Treat others as you want to be treated."

On Order, 2.8.25

In this section of his instruction to his young students Augustine considers how we should live in society. His words have application to all of us in our family, in our job, in our various political and religious societies.

August 23

Advice to the Young: III

You should not seek to undertake positions of authority until you have matured and you should not seek such maturity before you become middle-aged. In all circumstances of life, in every place and at all times, you should seek out friends. You should be well disposed towards those who deserve it but be less concerned about those who are proud. You should avoid pride yourself and always live in a fitting and decent manner. Supported by faith, hope, and love, you should have God as the object of your worship, thinking, and striving. For yourself and your colleagues you should desire peace, a good mind, and a quiet life.

On Order, 2.8.25

The last part of Augustine's instructions to his young students is about their future positions of authority in which they must remember several things: that they are bound by the law of God; they should not take their noble position too seriously; that they recognize that it is by the grace of God that they might succeed. Such qualities will help them achieve their salvation and make it easier for those they serve to work towards their own salvation.

August 24

The Mirror of Princes

We call those Christian rulers happy who govern with justice, never forgetting that they are only human. They think of sovereignty as a ministry of God, and they fear and worship God. They are slow to punish and quick to forgive. They temper with mercy and generosity the unavoidable harshness of their commands. They are all the more in control of their sinful desires because they are freer to indulge them. They prefer to rule their own passions more than to rule the peoples of the world. They rule not out of vain glory but out of love for everlasting bliss. They offer to God the humble sacrifice of their repentance and prayer. In this life they are happy in their hope and are destined to be truly happy when the eternal day comes for which we all hope.

City of God, 5.24

In the passage above Augustine speaks of the virtues of the Christian ruler who tries to apply the teachings of Jesus Christ to the nation he serves. It is a good guideline for anyone put in a position of authority over church or state. It is also a guideline for those in a democratic society who have the responsibility of choosing their leaders.

August 25

Do Not Glory over Others

A Christian should not try to glory over others. If you wish to be better than another, you will begin to envy him when you see that he is your equal. You should wish that everyone be your equal. If for the moment you are superior to another in moral wisdom, you should wish that they too should become morally wise. As long as a student knows little, he learns from you; as long as he is untaught, he needs your teaching. For the time being you are superior because you are the teacher and he is still learning. If you do not wish him someday to be equal to you, he will always be a learner. If this is your desire, you will be an envious teacher but how then can you be called a teacher at all?

Commentary on the Epistle of John, 8.8

Love requires that we not possess the object of our love. Parents must allow their children to eventually make their own lives in the world. Teachers must teach so that someday their students think for themselves. A political or religious leader must move their subjects to the point of responsibility and self-governance.

August 26

Swimming in the Rivers of Babylon

The "Rivers of Babylon" are all those ephemeral earthly things that we love. A farmer loves farming and becomes rich. He will learn that what he loves is but a "River of Babylon." Another says "The soldier's life is the thing! People fear soldiers and tremble before them!" Fool! You are throwing yourself into a raging river even more hungry for victims. Another says: "To be a lawyer is a splendid thing! What is mightier than an eloquence that can argue for a person's life or death?" This is but another "River of Babylon." Another proclaims "Going to sea on business is my ambition. I plan to be always on the move and come home rich!" But one shipwreck can destroy your wealth and you will be left to weep away your remaining life on your chosen "River of Babylon."

Commentary on Psalm 136, 2–3

Whether we are king or slave, rich or poor, smart or dumb, all that we have in this life will eventually be swept away in the flowing river of time. All that we will take with us as we plunge over the great falls of death will be the memory God has of our efforts to lead decent lives.

August 27

A Lesson from Babel: I

Scripture tells the story of what happened when the human race spoke the same language. They said: "Let us build ourselves a city with a tower that reaches to the heavens so that we can make a name for ourselves" (Genesis 11:1-9). That city was called Babylon (that is, "Confusion") but it was never completed as planned by the pride-filled people who had conceived it. The tower they tried to build was to reach the very place of God in the heavens. They did not realize that the only way to build a highway to heaven is by humility.

City of God, 16.4

Augustine believed that there were at least two lessons to be learned from the story of the Tower of Babel: the first is that pride can make us think that we can reach God on our own, indeed that we think we can become God by our achievement. Some are tempted to enjoy dominion over their territory—whether that be in the workplace, classroom, church, or marriage. The lesson of Babel is that God will not stand for such pretense.

August 28

A Lesson from Babel: II

Remember the tower that certain proud people built after the flood? What was their intention? They said: "Let us construct a high tower. We don't want to perish in another flood." They tried to build such a high tower but the Lord confused their speech. They no longer could understand each other. Up to that time they all spoke the same language because one language was enough for a humble people who were of one mind. But then that unity degenerated into a prideful conspiracy against God. God then took action, coming down and mixing up their speech so that they could not form further dangerous alliances by understanding each other.

Sermon 54, 11

The second lesson about pride contained in the story of the Tower of Babel is that pride makes communication between humans difficult, if not impossible. Pride prevents us from understanding another's point of view because we cannot transcend our own point of view. It takes great humility to sit silently and listen to another; sometimes it takes even greater humility to ask, "Now what did you mean by that?"

August 29

Pride: The First Sin

Pride turned Lucifer into Satan and banned him eternally from heaven. This vice is thus no slight evil. It makes those infected with it refuse to bow their necks to the yoke of Christ while they harness themselves all the more tightly to the bondage of sin. This vice is the root of all vices because from it all the others grow. It causes the soul to rebel against God and wander off into the darkness. It was because of this vice of pride that the Lord came to us in humility.

Commentary on Psalm 18/2, 15

Scripture tells us that this is not the world that God intended. But he made humans and angels free, a freedom that allowed us to choose against him. Lucifer, the creature closest to God, proud of himself, saw no reason why he should continue to be subject to anyone. He walked away, never to return, not because he did not want to, but out of resentment. It is a sad story. If in the beginning of time creatures had not become proud, they would have easily entered heaven, loving God for all eternity.

August 30

Pride: The Most Dangerous Sin

There is no greater obstacle to perfection than pride. People may boast of their riches or their beauty or their strength but it is absurd to make much of such passing things. Even during their lifetime they often lose them, and will certainly lose them when they die. When a person has begun to be virtuous, if they become proud of their improvement, they thereby lose all the spiritual progress that has been made. When we are doing wrong, we are in danger of falling into all the other vices. When we are becoming good, it is then that we have most to fear from pride.

Commentary on Psalm 58/2, 5

One of the signs of the insidious power of pride is that it is the only vice that we carry with us when we die. On our deathbed we will no longer get drunk, desire sex, or make deals to increase our wealth, but we might still believe that we are the best thing in God's creation. Pride has no regrets. It attacks us even when we are trying to be good as it makes us think we are good, without need for God's forgiveness.

August 31

The Proud: Evanescent Smoke

"As for the Lord's enemies, no sooner do they boast and exalt themselves than they disappear, fading away like smoke." Comparing the proud with smoke is a fitting analogy. Smoke bursts from its fire and drifts upward in a great cloud. The bigger the cloud gets, the more attenuated it becomes. It is insecure and inflated and eventually it is carried away and disappears. Its size is its downfall. The higher it rises and the wider it spreads, the more diaphanous it becomes until finally it vanishes into thin air. So too with the overblown pretense of the proud. They uplift themselves as though they were righteous or important but, as Paul writes, "Like smoke they will not last because their insanity will soon become obvious to everyone" (2 Timothy 3:9).

Commentary on Psalm 36/2, 12

Like smoke, the proud rise, expand, and then disappear. And their passing usually is not accompanied by a dramatic thunder-clap. Rather, frail clouds that they are, the bigger they get the more insignificant they become until eventually they disappear, leaving nothing behind but the laughter of those who witnessed their madness.

September 1

Asleep on Your High Horse

It is no sin to ride a horse but to toss one's head proudly against God and think oneself high and mighty . . . that is sinful. Because you are rich you have mounted your high horse and have fallen asleep. It was this kind of sleep that overcame Pharaoh when he mobilized his horses. His heart was not wide awake because the rebukes he had heard had left it hardened and such hardness is like slumber. Think how sleepy people are now who still refuse to condemn their old life and awaken to the new. For our part, we heard Christ when he invited us "Arise, sleeper, arise from the dead." Those who hear him are those who do not flaunt themselves and ride high on their rank and power.

Commentary on Psalm 75, 10

The proud sit on their high horse looking down on everyone else. Of course they will be brought down in death when differences in wealth, power, and status are erased. But it would be nice if this could happen somewhat earlier, if—by the grace of God—they would voluntarily dismount and recognize our common humanity. Hopefully they would also recognize that, despite their previous pretense of superiority, God still loves them.

September 2

Curing the Madman

People who have lost their minds through fever are dangerously ill. They laugh and sane people cry. If you proposed a choice between these two things—to laugh or cry—is there anybody who would not prefer to laugh? However in this life where saving, repentant sorrow is necessary, the Lord presented tears as a requirement for future laughter. He said "Blessed are those who cry, because they shall later laugh" (Luke 6:21). Crying is a requisite for the reward of laughter. Everyone prefers tears with sanity to laughter with madness. Such is the value of mental health that is it preferred even with lamentation.

Sermon 175, 2

Pride has the effect of preventing us from knowing we are sick, and for that reason it is the most dangerous spiritual sickness. Hangovers may follow a night of drunkenness; an upset stomach may follow an eating binge; a tortured conscience may follow injury to others; but with pride there are no disturbing after-effects. A symptom of insanity is that one does not know they are insane. It takes a divine doctor to cure this illness and, luckily, such a doctor exists in the person of Jesus Christ. We should pray for the proud that their sickness will not be so severe that they refuse to answer the door when Christ comes with his medicine of humility.

September 3

Through Pride We Lose Ourselves

Pride hinders the soul's vision of itself. A rebuke causes what it was trying to avoid seeing to be set before its eyes. What it had preferred to be hidden behind its back is now brought round and it is forced to confront it face to face. It had looked at itself and been very pleased with itself and become a lover of its power. By loving the world the soul forgot what it really was. It had lost the ability to look honestly at its own actions and thus justified all its evil deeds. Through its selfishness and self-indulgence it became insolent, proud in its wealth and positions of rank and power.

Sermon 142, 3

One of the sad things about being proud is that our pride causes us to lose sight of our true self. So enthralled are we with our virtues that we cannot see our vices. As Augustine says, we try to put our defects "behind our back" so that we will not see them, and we become enraged when anyone calls them to our attention. The result is that people stop being honest with us; instead they tell us what we want to hear because we are incapable of hearing the truth. It is truly a shame because without the truth the proud person will never find their true self.

September 4

Swollen Heads

Christ invites us to enter heaven when he says "Enter by the narrow door" (Matthew 7:13). You make an effort to enter but your swollen head prevents you. The door's narrowness irritates your swollen head and the irritation makes it swell all the more. You must get the swelling down if you want to enter. But how are you to do that? You must accept the medicine of humility. Your bulk is swollen, not big. If it is big it is solid; if it is swollen it is just so much empty air. Get the swelling down to be genuinely big. Do this by not taking pride in the pomp and circumstance of things that slip away and crumble into nothing.

Sermon 142, 5

Notice that Augustine does not say that we will not get into heaven if we are too fat, but only if we are too "fat-headed." The obstacle to our salvation is in our head, not our body. It is our head that tells us we are not responsible for our actions, that tells us we can do no wrong because we determine for ourselves what is right or wrong. Over a lifetime we come to believe our own fictions. Only a healthy dose of humility allows us to see who we really are: weak humans dependent on God's grace for the good we do.

September 5

Rules for Rulers

A ruler must understand that he is the servant of those
ruled. You will remember the scene where the disciples
seemed to want superiority over others. Jesus placed a
small child before them and said: "Unless a person becomes like this child, he shall not enter the kingdom of
heaven" (Matthew 18:3). What he was teaching them was
the need for humility. Pride was the original sin, the cause
of all our sins. Pride is what changed an angel into a devil.
Pride was the first great temptation of man. Adam had
been made in the image of God; he wished to *be* a god. He
reached out for what he was not and lost what he was.

Sermon 340A, 1

To be pope, president, or parent means to be a servant of
those over whom one presides. A ruler may be appointed by
humans but the authority to rule has its source in God. God is
the only one who, by nature, has the right to rule anyone. He
supports human authority over others only for the good of
those ruled. Thus a president must seek the common good; a
pope must seek the salvation of the faithful; a parent must seek
the welfare of the children. What Augustine says of Adam is
true for the ruler who tries to act like God: "He reached out for
what he was not and lost what he was."

September 6

The Divine Doctor

If you follow in the way of the humble Jesus, you will be
exalted with him one day. As sick as you are, you will

regain your health if only you don't turn your back on him. Remember that the only reason why Jesus-God humbled himself and descended to you was in order to heal your weakness. You were trapped in your illness. Only the greatest of doctors could get to you and heal you. You were too weak to get to the doctor yourself, and so Jesus-God came to you. He brought you the medicine of humility because he knew that it was primarily pride that kills the human soul.

Sermon 142, 2

This idea of Jesus as a Divine Doctor was especially attractive to Augustine because of the spiritual illnesses that afflicted him during the first thirty years of his life. It was comforting for him to think that Jesus-God came into this world not to pass judgment but to try and cure us of our spiritual ills before our final judgment. However, we must do our part: we must take our medicine. We must not act like we sometimes do with our human doctors—ignore their advice and then complain how bad we feel.

September 7

Do Not Despair!

Do not despair. Remember that you were loved when there was really nothing lovely about you at all. You were loved when you were ugly and deformed. You were loved before you were worthy of being loved. You were first loved and only afterward became lovable, worthy of being loved. Can you imagine what Jesus will do for you when cured, consider that he died for you when you were still sick and ungodly? If you really are greedy and want to possess everything, seek everything through humility. Through humility you will possess the Jesus-God who made all these things and thus in possessing him you will possess them too.

Sermon 142, 5

Two obstacles that prevent us from accepting Jesus, the Divine Doctor, are pride and despair. Pride makes us think we are not sick; despair makes us think we cannot be cured, and so we try to get as much out of this life as we can, thinking there is nothing on the other side of death. Augustine's words above encourage us not to despair because of our spiritual ugliness. Jesus has seen it all before. Indeed, he died because of it. Despite our spiritual hideousness, Jesus wants us to possess him and is even now waiting at the door of our soul, hoping we will let him in with his medicine.

September 8

Sickroom Martyrs

Think of the sick person who is very weak, gasping for breath, hardly able to move his tongue much less his arms and legs. But still he says to himself: "God will take me when he wants to. If he decides I must die, whether I am happy or sad about it, let me submit to God's will. I will die shortly and the only question is how I will deal with it." Many people have been crowned with victory for fighting the wild beasts in the amphitheater. Many also have been crowned with victory on a bed of sickness. They seem hardly able to move and yet in their heart they have great strength as they fight their last battle. The battle is hidden but so too is their victory.

Sermon 4, 36

Although the days of martyrdom in amphitheaters are long past, there are still many modern martyrs. We find them in the seriously ill, who bear their suffering without complaint and look to death without fear, who offer their suffering as a partial repayment for the suffering that Christ took upon himself for their sake. We should pray in the days of our strength for the grace to bear up under the suffering of that final illness which will challenge us to live with hope and love for the Christ who waits with our crown as we struggle to complete our sacrifice.

September 9

Obeying the Doctor

> The soul is well able to get sick by itself but quite unable to cure itself. So too the body. People have the power to get sick but not the power to get better on their own. If they do things that are injurious to health, the day comes when they fall sick. When they have fallen sick, they don't get better automatically. They were able to get sick themselves by over-indulging but in order to get better they need the help of a doctor. They had the power to lose their health but not the power to recover it.

Sermon 278, 2

Augustine's words apply primarily to the spiritual sicknesses that wrack our soul. In paradise the "healthy" Adam had it within his power to stay healthy but he chose to sin and thereby infected himself, and the rest of the human race, with disease, decay, and death. The only deliverance from our condition now is by the healing practice of a physician. To become healthy physically means to know what pill to take in the morning; to be healthy spiritually means to know what grace to pray for as we begin our day.

September 10

Sources of Spiritual Illness

The reason why no one can be without sin is because they do not choose to avoid it. Humans do not choose to do good either because (1) they do not know what the right thing to do is, or (2) because they do not find delight in doing the right thing. We choose good to the degree of our certainty that this is what we should do and to the degree of our delight in doing good once discovered. Ignorance and weakness: these are the sources of our inability to always choose good and avoid evil.

Merits and Remission of Sins and Infant Baptism, 2.17.26

Augustine says in his *Commentary on Psalm 99* (#11), we are all born "cracked" and these cracks show themselves in our ignorance in discovering the good and our weakness in choosing to do it. It was not so in the beginning when Adam had a clear mind and delighted in doing what God wanted. But then he sinned. Thereafter all humans pass on a spiritual gene which prevents us from recognizing and doing the good. Our sight is affected by a cataract of the spirit. We have lost the "taste" for the good, which makes it harder to choose. The pleasures of dissipation, greed, and selfishness often outweigh the delights of abstinence, generosity, and selflessness. We can still do evil without help but it takes grace from God for us to discover the good and delight in doing it.

September 11

The Inn of the Samaritan

The whole human race is like that man who was lying in the road half-dead, left there by bandits (Luke 10:30-37). The man was an Israelite. Bandits had robbed him, seriously wounded him and left him lying on the road. A priest came along, like him an Israelite, but walked past him. Then a Levite (also an Israelite) came along and likewise ignored the wounded man. Finally, a Samaritan passed by, one far removed from the injured man in nationality, and he mercifully helped him. The Samaritan represents Jesus because "Samaritan" means "Guardian" and this is what Jesus has done, coming from afar to save and "guard" us (Philippians 4:5).

Sermon 171, 2

The story of the "Good Samaritan" explains much about our present condition. Wounded on the road, we have been picked up and taken to a place of healing with the promise that our rescuer (Jesus) will come back someday to take us the rest of the way home. Living in this place of healing, it is no wonder that on some days we neither feel nor do well. We have been rescued but we are still not healed. When we are healed, he will then come to take us the rest of the way home to heaven. All we need do now is to let him into our hospital room when he knocks.

September 12

Saved but Not Cured

A drunkard is baptized. He has heard that drunkenness is included on the list of sins barring people from entering heaven (cf. 1 Corinthians 6:9-10). By his baptism all his past sins of drunkenness are forgiven, but the habit remains. The thirst for a drink still tortures him. It tries to penetrate his will and drag him away as its prisoner. If he does not give in to the temptation, it will gradually become less and less because it gets its strength from submission to it.

Sermon 151, 4

Augustine uses the example of a "drunkard" to make the point that being baptized does not mean that we are cured of our bad habits. After baptism, a drunk is still tempted to take a drink, a libertine is still tempted to have an affair; a greedy person is still tempted to cut corners to make a dollar, a selfish person is still tempted to ignore the needs of others. It was only by the grace of God that we have been saved; it is also only by the grace of God that we can fight successfully against the temptations that will still plague us.

September 13

There But for the Grace of God Go I!

This life bears witness to the fact that the race of fallen men is a race that is indeed "cracked." Consider our love for all the vain and poisonous things that cause so many heartaches, troubles and fears, our joy in conflict, strife and war, and so many plots of enemies and sycophants. Consider such things as fraud and theft and robbery; the pride we take in depravity, our envy and ambition, cruelty and murder, lawlessness and lust. Think of all the shameless passions of the impure: fornication and adultery, incest and unnatural sins, rape and countless other filthy acts. Look at the sins committed against religion: sacrilege and heresy, blasphemy and perjury. Consider the evil we do to each other: calumnies and cheating, lies and false witness, violence against persons and property. Indeed, if anyone were left to live as he pleased and to do what he desired, he would go through practically the whole gamut of sinful acts listed above . . . those which I wrote down and others that I forgot to mention.

City of God, 22.22

One might suspect that Augustine had a bad day when he wrote the passage above, but if you read the morning paper you begin to see that he was not far off the mark. Indeed, the miracle of today is that there are so many good people! And it indeed is a miracle because we are only able to overcome our evil tendencies by the grace of God!

September 14

Waiting for the Doctor

It was only to be expected that after paradise human beings would have days that were hard. The human race after Adam was gravely ill and because of this the Divine Doctor had to take over the case of the patient lying ill in the huge bed that is this world. But just as any very skilled doctor first observes the turns the illness takes and in its milder stages works through assistants, so our Divine Doctor first sent his prophets to examine us. They foretold that the illness was getting worse and the patient was more agitated. Clearly now the presence of the Doctor was required and that he come in person.

Sermon 346A, 8

When we are sick, we fail to appreciate the nurses and procedures before we see the physician. We want to see the doctor face to face, to receive the encouragement that we can indeed be cured. We are unconcerned about the pain, because at least he is speaking about a cure, whereas the nurses only spoke about the symptoms. The condition of human beings after losing paradise was one of waiting for the doctor to come, a condition in which we knew we were ill, but did not know what the sickness was. The prophets were able to describe the sickness but the final cure had to wait for the Divine Doctor, Jesus Christ.

September 15

The Doctor Comes

The Divine Doctor came. He came as a human being, sharing our life and death so that we might receive a life without death. As we continue to restlessly twist and turn, panting and covered with sweat, some complain: "Ever since this doctor came, I have been subject to frightful distress. It would have been better if he had not come into my house." That's what those say who are still involved in the vanity of the world. Why does this make them sick? Because they won't accept the doctor's medicine of moderation. Stupid patient! The doctor has not made your illness worse; he comes to bring you relief.

Sermon 346A, 8

It does no good to see the doctor if you do not follow his advice—take the pills that he prescribes, stop smoking and drinking, give up coffee, and get more exercise. The trouble is that, in the short term, the cure is often more painful than the disease. The good news is that the Divine Doctor has come with the medicine that will cure us so that we can enter heaven. The bad news is that the taking of this medicine of moderation is often painful.

September 16

Painful Cures

In this life we are plagued with infirmity and disease. They weigh us down; they crush us. I believe that if God were speaking to us, he would say "Submit to the doctor's knife! Let it penetrate the rotten sore so that the evil contained there can burst out." Just think of the things we suffer from human doctors! They immobilize us in splints, lance our wounds and then purify them with fire. Because the doctor promises possible health we not only endure the painful surgery; we beg for it. This being the case, don't you think that you are being cured of your spiritual illness when you suffer hardship in this life? Don't you believe the words of Scripture: "In fire gold is tested and worthy men in the crucible of humiliation"? (Sirach 2:5). So put up with what the Divine Doctor applies to the patient when he acts like a goldsmith applying fire to the gold being refined.

Sermon 23B, 11

Augustine confesses that his early life was characterized by sexual promiscuity. If such sin is a malady, then the cure was celibacy. This was painful medicine, however, and it took him many years to gain control of his sexual desire. But such distress is a natural side-effect of the painful medicine we must take to develop a healthy spiritual life.

September 17

Scorning the Humble Doctor

You should become humble because the good God humbled himself for you. When we get sick, the best doctors look for the root causes. Unskilled doctors may take care of the symptoms but if the underlying illness remains it soon bursts out carrying additional distress. In the Scripture the diagnosis of the Divine Doctor is clear: "The beginning of every sin is pride" (Sirach 10:13). The doctor himself came to you but you ridiculed him. You murmured "What sort of God is this? One who was born, suffered, smeared with spittle, crowned with thorns and then hung up on a cross?" Despicable soul! You see the humility of your doctor; you don't see the pride-filled wound that he has come to cure. You are displeased with the humble doctor because he is an affront to your pride.

Sermon 360B, 17

Because of our pride, we seek out the hospital and doctor with the best reputations, one with an aura of invincibility. We want our doctors to be god-like and sometimes it is hard to accept a divine doctor who came as a weak human being. We say with the scoffing Nathaniel, "What good can come out of Nazareth?" It is a shame that this is so. We do not realize that our illness was so severe that the doctor had to die in order that we might have a chance to live.

September 18

Killing the Doctor

Patients insane with anger sometime strike their doctors. If they are very strong, they may even kill the one who seeks to cure them. Our Doctor (Jesus) was not afraid of being killed by his insane patients. Indeed, through his death he brought the remedy for their frenzy. Notice how he did not get angry with those who injured him. He felt sorry for them and wanted to heal them as they raged against him. Hanging on the cross, he looked at those who were venting their rage against him and prayed: "Father, forgive them because they do not know what they are doing" (Luke 23:24).

Sermon 360B, 18

In our more sophisticated times, it is unusual for an unhappy patient to kill their doctor. It is more likely that they will sue. We get angry with our doctors if we do not like their remedy. This is what happened to Jesus. His message of detachment from possessions and service to the poor caused those he came to cure to become insane with hatred, and so they beat him and killed him. They killed their divine doctor not realizing that this is what he intended all along. His death was the final medicine by which he would cure the human race of the terrible wounds inherited from Adam, the wounds that prevented them from entering heaven.

September 19

Believing in the Medicine

Imagine a person blind from birth who doesn't know what it is to see light. The doctor tells them "I am going to apply some rather strong ointments which will cure your blindness, but it will be painful." The terrified patient then cries out: "I am not going to put up with such agony unless I first see what you are going to show me." The doctor answers: "How can you see before you can see? Take the medicine and then you will be dazzled by the brilliance of the light you hear others talking about." If the patient agrees, he will be cured. If he does not agree, wishing to see before believing in the cure, he will prove to be both ridiculous and an enemy of his own health.

Sermon 360B, 14

Believing must always come before seeing in the cure of physical or spiritual illness. Yet we insist upon the opposite. We want to see how the medicine will work before it begins working; we want an experience of sobriety before undergoing treatment, or a sense of how health will feel before we become healthy. We want to "see" before we will "believe." Of course this is impossible. To be cured of any physical or spiritual illness we must first trust the doctor and the prescription.

September 20

A Patient's Song

O Wonderful Healer, you care for us all:
Soothing our painful swelling,
Supporting our fading strength,
Cutting away the useless in our lives,
Keeping only the truly necessary,
Saving those given up for lost,
Giving beauty to those warped and bent by life.
Who can despair of life, seeing how the Son of God has
    come down to help us?

The Christian Combat, 11.12

Given Augustine's sinful past, he was uniquely sensitive to our "cracked" condition, and our need for God's grace. At the same time, he argued for human responsibility, that we must cooperate with God's grace. For example, he said we must avail ourselves to healing, always resisting the temptation to pride or despair. This in turn reminds us of the need to persevere in prayer, which keeps us on the narrow path. Of course, we must strive for charity at all times. And we need to be joyful, singing songs such as the one above, the hymn Augustine once sang to the only doctor he trusted completely, Jesus the Lord.

215

September 21

A Fork in the Road

All who come into this life are compelled by the turning wheel of time to pass on. You must keep walking or you will be dragged along. As we travel on our journey we will be met at a fork in the road by Jesus. And he will say to us, "Don't go to the left. It looks like an easy and delightful road to pass along, but at the end of that way lies ruin. But there is another way which involves innumerable labors, and hardship. This is a road difficult to follow but when you reach its end you will experience the very peak of joy."

Sermon 346A, 1

Augustine speaks of the moments in our life when we are confronted with critical choices. He uses the metaphor of the easy road, which gives pleasure, and the hard road, which is a call to duty. To choose the hard road is not to say that life will not be without its pleasant moments; but the road of duty is a directed life, one in which duty to God and to others takes precedence over personal wants and desires. It is a road on which we are challenged to maintain our human dignity as well as to treat others with dignity. Christ stands at the fork giving us direction, but it is up to us to make the choice.

September 22

Cleaning the Eye of the Heart

Our bodily eyes need to be cleansed to make them able to see the light that shines during daylight and shines at night from glowing lamps. If our eyes have misted over or have been hurt by something getting into them, seeing light will be painful. In a similar fashion, to be able to perceive the eternal light (that is God) the eye of the heart needs to be cleansed. Just as our bodily eyes are hindered from seeing by an inflammatory secretion, so too the spirit-eyes of our heart are dulled by past iniquity. Consequently, just as our bodily eyes need to be cleansed to see physical light, so too the inner eyes of our spirit need to be cleansed before we can see that light which reveals the wonders God has prepared for those who love him (1 Corinthians 2:9).

Sermon 360B, 3

To suggest that God is everywhere invites the question as to why so few see him. The reason for this, Augustine says, is because the eyes of our heart and spirit have been clouded over by our involvement in this world, which has caused a mist that covers our eye. It can only be cleared by way of detachment. Then if we earnestly try to focus our attention, we will begin to see the dawning light of God embracing the world.

September 23

The Advantage in Being Mortal

The reason why (after Adam's sin) humans were infected with mortality was to train them in humility. In being mortal they were forced to face the fact that they could not live on earth forever and that at some time or other this life would come to an end. They were thus encouraged to humble themselves before God and strive to lay hold of that unending future life even as this present life was rushing away.

Sermon 360B, 5

Being mortal is like living in a motel. We know we must check out someday and thus should not get too attached to the facilities. Of course the difference is that in life we are never sure when we will check out. We must be prepared to leave at any moment, and this is a good thing. It encourages us to live wisely, practice detachment from possessions, and be truthful with ourselves. We are indeed altogether mortal; we should try now to be as completely moral as we can be.

September 24

Lessons from the Barber's Chair

We cannot hold onto something that is slipping away. Can any of us hold onto our age, so that children won't grow up and young adults won't grow old? Already in this time I have been speaking to you we have all aged a little. Our mind knows about these changes in our condition but minute to minute you cannot see them happening. In the same way you can't see your hair growing but we know it does. This is the reason why we search out barbers every few days. Well, just as our hair is growing but its growth cannot be seen, so too at this very moment we are all getting nearer to old age even though we cannot see it happening.

Sermon 360B, 5

Augustine's comparison of life with hair is interesting. Hair grows unnoticed until finally we realize we must do something about it. Likewise, we wake up one morning and discover that we are old, just as we wake up one morning and discover we need a haircut. Augustine's metaphor invites other connections: baldness and death mean no more growth, only a new form of life; we color our life just as we color our hair; we try to comb the snags out of our lives to be more presentable. However, the main point of Augustine's reflection is that our life is passing and there is little we can do about it other than to accept and make the best of it.

September 25

Hold onto a Life that Endures

We love this life despite the fact that it is vanishing, slipping away with equal speed in our youth and in our declining years. So how much better is it for us to hold onto something secure, the life that we will enjoy when this life is over? After all, what is really long if it comes to an end? Moreover, this life is not only short; it is also uncertain. We can die at any age. Therefore, it is just good sense to kneel humbly before God, to confess our sins and groan over them, to tell our Divine Doctor of our sickness so that we may be cured.

Sermon 360B, 6

The slippage of time suggests that it makes good sense to reach out to the life that is eternal. Just as when we are young we try to do those things that will prepare us to be a success in the future, so too should we work now to insure our success in eternity. Jesus has told us the things we must do: "Love God above all; love our neighbor as ourselves." In trying to do that as best we can now, we will insure that the eternal present, that is our future, will be one filled with joy.

September 26

The Greatness of the Human Soul

The human soul is invisible but it wields great power over the physical world. It cannot be seen but we stand amazed at the visible works it accomplishes. Think about the wonderful things you see every day. Look at the order that the human soul has imposed on the world, at the beauty of cultivated fields, uprooted thickets, fruit tress planted and grafted in the countryside. Look at the organization of society, the grand structure of buildings, the variety of arts and crafts, the number of languages. Consider the depths of our memory and the power of eloquence. All these are works of the soul. How many and how great are these visible wonders even though their source, the soul, remains invisible!

Sermon 360B, 9

Here, Augustine focuses on the visible and material wonders that are the fruits of the human spirit. He does not mention such things as selfless love, sacrifice for others, and the ability to forgive—all things we cannot quantify but are no less real. Taking account of the works of the invisible human soul can lead us to belief in the invisible God whose visible creation is all around us, not the least of which is ourselves. Indeed we humans are capable of so many wonderful things through the imagination and creativity of our human spirit.

September 27

Why Christ Chose Fishermen

Jesus came to save both the poor and the rich, both the peasant and the prince. But when it came to selection of his apostles, he did not choose princes or the wealthy or the learned or those of noble birth. Instead, he chose fishermen, simple people through whom his grace could shine most clearly. If he had first called a king, the king might have thought that it was because of his regal position that he had been chosen. If he had first called a scholar, he might have thought that it was because of his brains that he had been chosen. To call the world to humility, the message had to be carried by humble people. And so it was that Christ did not convert fishermen through an emperor but emperors through a fisherman.

Sermon 360B, 24

There have been saints who were kings, philosophers, and great preachers, but not because of their intellects or eloquence. What made them saints was God's work through them. God chose them for the same reason God chose the humble fishermen as the first apostles, men who knew that it was not by their achievement that they were chosen as apostles, but by the grace of God. Likewise, the good that we do is not of our making, but because of God's grace working through us.

September 28

Loving Neighbor; Loving God

If anyone says "I love God" and still hates his brother, he is a liar. Listen to the Gospel: "He who does not love his brother whom he sees, how can he love God whom he does not see?" Does he who loves his brother then also love God? Well, we are told that God is love. If God is love, whoever loves love must love God. Therefore, love your brother and be free of anxiety because you cannot say, "I love my brother" and not love God. If you have love, then your eye will be cleansed more and more by that love so that eventually you can see that God in whose presence you will always rejoice forever.

Commentary on the Epistle of John, 9.10

The sentiments expressed above were reflected in the last years of the life of Saint Thérèse of Lisieux, the "The Little Flower." After years of ecstasy, feeling the presence of God close by, she suddenly entered her own "Dark Night of the Soul" in which God seemed absent. Rather than give into despair, she decided that she would devote the last years of her life to loving those around her and, in so doing, love God. As with the Little Flower, such love draws us out of ourselves, opens up our heart, allowing an opening for God's grace to enter.

September 29

Benevolent Love

All pure love wills only good for the person loved. We ought not to love our beloved in the way a hungry man says, "I love thrushes." He says that he loves them but his goal is to destroy them. Whatever we love to eat, we love in order to consume it and be refreshed by it. Would it be right to love humans in this way? Far from it. We should have a friendly benevolence towards them, doing good for them when we can. And even when we can't give them anything, if we want good to come to them, this is enough to have pure love for them.

Commentary on the Epistle of John, 8.5.1

Pure love reaches out to a loved one because of the good we see in them. It is a love that wants, but does not demand. It is a love that seeks union with the beloved, but does not consume them, nor does it diminish their identity. The temptation in love is to possess our beloved so that their energies are fixed exclusively on us. As Augustine points out, this is false love. It is not the love that God has for us. God's love for us is one that expands our lives far beyond our wildest dreams.

September 30

Love Is Not Always Easy

Do not suppose that it is easy to preserve love, that you need not do anything to keep it, that you can always afford to be gentle with the beloved, a gentleness that sometimes masks a "not caring" what the loved one does. That is not how you preserve love. Do you love your children when you won't discipline them? Do you love your neighbor when you never correct them? This is not love but apathy. Love must sometimes arouse you to correct the loved one. When you find that they are good, rejoice with them; when you find that they are going in a wrong direction, admonish them.

Commentary on the Epistle of John, 7.11.1

Loving all others as ourselves is not easy. First of all there are some who are far from "lovable." Rather than wishing them good, we are tempted to wish they would go away and stop bothering us. On the other hand, there are those we love so much that we are afraid to confront them with the truth of their destructive behaviors for fear of losing their affection. In such cases true love demands that we try to do something that allows them to confront their mixed-up lives. In this we imitate Jesus who loved human beings but admonished them, even when he knew it disrupted their comfortable lives.

October 1

The Glory of Love

If only we could truly love, we would not be anxious
about anything. If we truly loved, how could we do evil
to anyone? How can anyone bring evil to someone they
love? If we truly loved, it would not be possible to do
anything but good. Indeed, my friends, we can never be
filled enough with the power, beauty, and nourishment of
love. Indeed, if it so delights us here in the midst of our
pilgrimage, imagine how it will cause us to rejoice once
we reach our homeland!

Commentary on the Epistle of John, 10.7.1-3

Augustine's words here apply to both love of God and love
of neighbor. If we truly loved God, we would never do anything against his will. We would do only that which is good.
Moreover, awareness of God's love for us gives us cause for
rejoicing on our pilgrim way to heaven. His words also have
some application to our love for each other here on earth. In
the joys of earthly love, we easily forget what is truly good for
our beloved. We can lead them astray or follow them as they
go astray. Still, it is true that the love we have for our loves, and
the experience of their love for us, can be a source of great joy
as we continue our pilgrimage through life.

October 2

Loving Enemies

We should love all humans, even our enemies, not because they are friends but in order that they may be like
friends. We should burn with love for all who are already

our friends and pray for those who are still enemies that they might become friends. When we love someone in the right way we make them a friend, one who is joined in some way to us in unity. If we lived the way we should, we would love our enemies in order that they might become our friends.

Commentary on the Epistle of John, 10.7.3

Love means to see the good and wish the good of another. It means that we are prepared to see good even in the most disreputable person, a good made possible by the recognition that there is in them a special reflection of God. Such a love makes it more possible to love our enemies. The model for such love is Christ on the cross, praying, "Father forgive them because they do not know what they do!" There is no doubt that, if pressed, he would have gone even further, praying, "Father forgive even those who know exactly what they are doing!"

October 3

The Need for Tolerance

What can be more disturbing than to find that those for whom you had high hopes are leading bad lives? You say: "What a fine fellow that person was! How is it that he has fallen so low? Perhaps everyone is cracked like him." It is only because you are self-righteous that you suspect everyone is unrighteous. You ask our conscience, "Am I as cracked as the rest of humanity?" and your clouded conscience replies, "Oh no, not you." Well the truth is that if you are not cracked, you are the only one who isn't. When you think yourself without fault, your pride is worse than the wrong-doing you despise in others. There is really only one sensible way to act. Don't think badly of your neighbor. Strive humbly to be what you would like them to be and then perhaps you will stop imagining that they are all that different from what you pretend to be.

Commentary on Psalm 30/3, 7

We easily overlook how unlovable we are to those with whom we live. We all have rough edges that are rubbed against by those around us. We disapprove of the ways others act and whose beliefs are different from ours. What are we to do about it? Augustine's advice is clear. Put up with them! If they are going astray, we should urge them to correct their lives. But even if they won't, we must continue to love them even though we may find it impossible to accept them as they are.

October 4

Putting up with Others

The apostle urges us, "Bear with each other in love, careful to maintain the unity forged by the Spirit in the bond of peace" (Ephesians 4:2-3). "Bear with each other" he says. Is there nothing in you that anyone else has to put up with? If there really is nothing, I am amazed. But if there is nothing, that means you must have all the more strength to put up with other people, if there is nothing in you that others have to endure. If you are no bother to others, you must be well able to bear with all the rest. "But I can't," you answer. But such an answer shows that there is at least one thing about you which troubles other people.

Commentary on Psalm 99, 9

The apostle Paul seems unnecessarily sarcastic when he says that he would be simply amazed if there were nothing in us that others had to put up with. He obviously does not know what fine, generous, kind, understanding, selfless, and just beautiful people we are! Such regard for ourselves suggests that there is much in us that others have to bear. The most difficult people are often those who think of themselves as saints, who see themselves as morally and spiritually superior to those around them. We should remember that Jesus died for us despite our pretense of being better than we are.

October 5

The Temptation to Become a Hermit

Is there any place to which we can withdraw, to get away from the distress caused by others? Where can we hide? Should we seek a solitary place where we have no one to "put up with"? Such intolerance proves that we have made no progress at all towards sanctity. Paul tells us that we must "bear with one another in love" (Ephesians 4:2). If we turn our back on other humans and hide ourselves away where no one can see us, how can we help others? Could we have reached the stage of perfection we claim if no one ever had helped us? Are we going to blow up the bridge to sanctity, just because we think we have crossed it? Remember what the Lord said through Paul: "We must bear with one another in love!"

Commentary on Psalm 99, 9

After fifty years of living in community there are days when being a hermit seems quite attractive. I suspect that this happens among members of any association of human beings. There is always the temptation to fly away, leaving the disagreements, conflict, and scandals behind. Of course this is impossible and, even if it were not, it would not be advisable. We cannot love God and turn our back on our neighbor, no matter how difficult they may be. Even Saint Simon Stylites, living on his fifty-foot pillar, would not have been a saint if he had ignored all those who came for help. Like it or not, we will get to heaven as a disagreeable group or not at all.

October 6

Searching for a Safe Harbor

Someone says: "I will go into seclusion with a few good people. Then I will not be bothered by the annoying rabble of this world." To join with a few good people in a safe harbor far from the world is indeed an attractive dream. But would you find there the peace you desire? Remember you are still subject to temptation and even a safe harbor must have an entrance somewhere. This means that it is open to the wind and this can cause the ships to crash against each other and be wrecked. To survive, the ships must truly love each other and carefully adapt themselves to one another to avoid collisions. People in that harbor must live a life of fairness and charity.

Commentary on Psalm 99, 10

The dream of escaping the turmoil of human society is indeed attractive. The young Augustine once had the dream of going away to a quiet place with like-minded friends to discuss philosophy. Unfortunately, their wives would not let them go. Later on, after having established his religious community, he realized that the dream of a "safe harbor" was just that—a dream. Even if we could find such a harbor we would bring our baggage with us. Whether we are trying to form a family, create a business or church, we will always be affected by the raging sea around and inside us. There is no safe harbor in this life, only groups of good human beings trying their best to get along.

October 7

Trying to Form a Perfect Society

In trying to form a perfect society, you may say: "I will be careful not to admit any bad person. I can recognize them when they apply." But how can you know them when they do not know themselves? Many promise that they will be good but, when thrust into the kiln of life's fire, they crack. Can you shut out evil thoughts even from your own heart? We all do battle against temptations such as avarice or lust or gluttony. Such temptations assail us all. We try to conquer them but are very lucky if at least one does not break through our defenses. How then can we find absolute security in this life? The answer is only in the hope given by God's promises.

Commentary on Psalm 99, 11

Augustine's words were aimed at anyone who dreamed of creating a perfect religious community, but they equally apply to those looking for a "perfect" spouse or employee. It is an impossible task for two reasons: first, we have limited knowledge of ourselves, let alone others; second, all of us have hidden cracks that will show up only later. Getting married or joining a religious community is always a leap of faith for all parties involved. It is good to remember this so that we will not be terribly surprised when things do not work out as we planned. Any human society in this life is a miracle of accommodation. Only in heaven will we be able to get along perfectly because only there is God the one who reviews our application.

October 8

The Danger of Unrealistic Expectations

When considering a particular way of life, people sometimes have unrealistic expectations. This happens because people praise it by omitting all the negative factors included in it. When any profession is praised without reservation, it may attract idealistic people but when they enter and find there people not living up to the ideals, they are so shocked that they reject the good along with the bad. Thus when someone exuberantly praises the Catholic Church by saying, "They all love each other and try their best to help others," the listeners may not realize that those who are less than perfect have been passed over. Shocked by the bad Christians they find there they ignore even those who are doing their best to live up to the Christian ideal.

Commentary on Psalm 99, 12

Augustine's words of warning to anyone entering a community with unrealistic expectations applies in many areas. Some are shocked entering marriage when they find out that it is not as perfect as romantic novels depict it. Some leave the religious life or the church itself when they find that all there are not saints. But those not living up to the ideal are found in every human association, institution, or profession. We are social animals and we must join with others in society even though some of our compatriots do not live up to the ideals demanded.

October 9

The Church: "A Lily among Thorns"

Some condemn Christians saying: "Christians are misers, usurers, drunkards, gluttons, envious and spiteful to each other." Indeed there are some like this but the description does not fit all Christians. If you want to describe the present-day Church, do it as Scripture does: "As a lily among thorns, so is my beloved among women" (Song of Songs 2:2). Someone hears about the Church and weighs the matter. The lily is attractive, so they enter. They stay close to the lily and tolerate the thorns. Some enter believing that all members are good, especially those with religious or clerical vocations. Others revile these supposedly "holy souls" for being far from perfect. Both those who only praise and those who only criticize are wrong. Those who praise must admit that there are some bad people among church members; those who criticize must not ignore the many who are good.

Commentary on Psalm 99, 12

The church will always be a "Lily among thorns," beautiful in its ideals but somewhat messy in its members. We are naturally distressed when those around us do not live up to their noble ideals, but we should remember that our faith-commitment is not to them but to Jesus Christ. It is through him that we will work out salvation. The occasional "scratching" of the thorns surrounding us cannot be permitted to stand in the way of our dedication to Jesus.

October 10

Putting up with Bad Leaders

Think how fiercely God tests us in this life. As the psalmist says, "You have tested us, O God! You put a heavy burden on our backs. You let men ride over our heads and we went through fire and water" (Psalm 66:10-12). Sometimes leaders are placed over us who are hard to stomach. It is good for us to recognize that in this world created by

Adam's sin we must sometimes tolerate superiors who seem to enjoy "riding over our heads."

Commentary on Psalm 65, 16

It is bound to happen in a society of "cracked people" that sometimes our leaders will be less than perfect. Even when we choose our leaders, their practice does not always live up to their promise. In societies in which an incompetent, if not evil, ruler is imposed, the ruled can at least say, "It is not my fault." Unfortunately when a leader proves to be a bad leader there is little we can do about it. Most of us do not have the luxury of quitting when we have a difficult boss. Even with respect to religion, when faced with an authority that seems uncaring, the only response we can make is the one Peter made to Christ when asked if he too would walk away: "Lord, where shall I go?"

October 11

The Burden of Being a Leader

In those of us who have been selected as bishops, two things need to be differentiated: the fact that we are Christians and the fact that we have been put in charge of others. We are Christians for our own sake; we are in charge of others for their sake. Many people will be saved without ever being responsible for others and their journey is easier because they carry less of a burden. We bishops as individuals will be judged on our Christianity but, because we have been put in charge of others, we will be judged also on the quality of our stewardship over those we led. People whom God puts in charge of others must not use their authority for their own advantage but for the good of those they rule. A bishop who just enjoys being the boss and seeks his own honor and looks to his own convenience is feeding himself, not the sheep.

Augustine in the passage above is speaking about all those who have leadership positions in the church, but his words apply to anyone burdened with responsibility for others such as parents for their children and teachers for their students. The burden of leadership is a great burden for those who lead because so much rides on the kind of leader they choose to be.

October 12

The Virtue of Patience

Patience is the virtue by which a person endures troubles with a tranquil mind. The impatient do not free themselves from the evil that upsets them. Instead they end up suffering even more evil. Patient persons who prefer to put up with evils rather than add to them lessen what they patiently endure and escape the greater evils which, by reason of their impatience, would have overwhelmed them. By putting up with brief and passing evils they do not lose the great good that is eternal.

On Patience, 2.2

The Garden of Eden was a place in which Adam and Eve had everything they needed and did not want what they did not have. That changed with their desire to be God. With that they were cast into a world of conflict, a place in which even their innocent desires were frustrated. Augustine believed that it was fitting that human beings who had lost paradise because of their desire for pleasant times should regain it through endurance of unpleasant times (*On Patience*, 14.11). We are now in such a world where there is much unpleasantness that we cannot control. All we can do is, by the grace of God, patiently endure without contributing to the world's turmoil.

October 13

Why Patience Is Needed

It may happen that some catastrophe strikes suddenly. Our hearts throb as the earth quakes and thunder rolls round the sky. Or we are frightened by a terrifying attack or the threat of robbers lying in wait. There is terror all around and panic strikes home. Above and beyond these dreadful events, we suffer what is going on inside us and what is done to us by those with whom we live. We suffer our own bad qualities and we are obliged to suffer those of other people. No wonder that the psalmist cries out, "O Lord, cleanse me from my secret sins and spare me from the faults of others" (Psalm 19:12-13).

Commentary on Psalm 37, 15 & 16

Through the course of a lifetime, some of us will be spared suffering caused by natural or man-made tragedies. But none of us can avoid hurt and harm caused by those close to us. When friends hurt us or loved ones leave us, it is all the more painful because they betrayed a basic trust. Such hurt is compounded by our aging bodies, and a soul plagued with continuing temptation. Our one and only consolation is that all such troubles are passing and that God will help us endure them or at least pick us up when our endurance fails.

October 14

Stubbornness Is Not Patience

The virtue of patience endures trouble for good reasons but it becomes a vice when it descends into stubbornness. Stubbornness imitates patience; indeed, it is its close neighbor. Just as a person who cannot be forced to do evil is better than one who weakens under the pressure, so too a person who stubbornly cannot be turned away from evil is worse than one who can. Stubbornness prevents a person from ceasing their evil or foolish course of action even by the threat of the most dire consequences. What shall we say of such a person who refuses to yield to pressure? Rather than describing them as having great patience we should recognize that they are just hard-headed stubborn people.

Sermon 283, 7

Endurance under pressure is not always the virtue of patience; it may be the vice of stubbornness. As Augustine says, they are "next door neighbors" and it is sometimes hard to distinguish which neighbor is visiting. To stubbornly endure the criticism of others without asking ourselves whether their criticism is valid is foolish. The virtue of patience is present but only in those who must put up with such stubbornness. All one can do is to walk away and pray that the person's stubbornness will not cause great harm to themselves and others.

October 15

Bogus Patience

Highway robbers spend sleepless nights lying in wait for travelers. Their endurance is to be marveled at but their apparent "patience" should be condemned. Patience flows from wisdom, not passion. Patience is the product of a good conscience. It does not result in robbing the innocent. Whenever, then, you see someone enduring suffering, do not immediately praise their patience. Patience must come from a good cause. Not all those who suffer have the virtue of patience. Only those who suffer for the right reason are crowned with patience's reward.

On Patience, 5–6

It is not always virtuous to put up with an unpleasant situation or unpleasant person. We must endure for the right reason for it to be patience. To wait all night in the rain outside a neighbor's house so that we may attack them is not patience. As Augustine says, "Without charity there can be no true patience" (*On Patience,* 23.20). We endure the bad times in our lives out of love for the God who awaits us in eternity. We practice patience with the confused and wandering lives of those we love, only when we can't do anything about it. If we can do something, but fail to out of fear of offending them, we are not practicing patience. We are practicing cowardice.

October 16

Patiently Waiting for Heaven

Take care that your habits are not corrupted, your hope undermined, your patience discouraged and you yourselves turned aside into crooked ways. On the contrary, by being meek and mild you keep to the straight ways which the Lord teaches you. The truth is, without patience amid the troubles and trials of this life, hope in the future life cannot be kept alive. You cannot maintain unflagging patience unless you are meek and mild, never resisting God's will. Indeed, by being meek and mild you will not only love his consolations, you will also bear up under his discipline. Continuing to hope for what you cannot yet experience, you will wait for it patiently.

Sermon 157, 2

My father would occasionally drive my siblings and me to the New Jersey "Shore," as we called it, for a day at the beach. Given the distance, our excitement and impatience would take over, only to be corrected by a threat to turn the car around, unless we behaved. I learned then the lesson that being "meek and mild" is a better way to get to the good times promised ahead. This is also true with heaven. We are promised we will get there if only we patiently and bravely endure the temporary heat and unpleasantness of these days. We will get to heaven not by complaining about the way we get there but by meekly trusting the God who is driving the car.

October 17

The Heroic Patience of David

By patience we are supported when, amid the troubles of this world, our happiness is postponed. It was with such patience that King David endured the attacks of his son Absalom. Although he could easily have destroyed Absalom, David forbade those who were grieved and upset by such treason to take vengeance on his wayward son. He accepted the moment as a time for humility and bowed to the will of God and drank the bitter wine of his son's disloyalty with the greatest patience.

On Patience, 9.8

King David's love was his son, Absalom, whom he showered with good things all his life. Perhaps that was the root of the problem. Absalom saw such wealth flowing from the monarchy that he began gathering forces to wrest the kingdom from his father. Rather than order that Absalom be executed, King David patiently endured his son's disloyalty. He is a great example of the patience we are to exercise when our loved ones turn against us. We cannot make them love us; all we can do is pray that in their new life separate from us they will find happiness and be able to work out their salvation.

October 18

The Patience of Job

Job was tempted in many ways but stayed steadfast in his patience. At first, he lost all his possessions. Then he was afflicted by the death of his sons. Next his body was attacked with pain from head to foot. He got little help from those closest to him. His wife spent her time cursing God and encouraging him to do the same, but he would not. The paradox is that Adam in paradise consented to temptation while Job on his dung heap held firm. To add insult to injury, friends came suggesting that his woes were because of some great sin. Job suffered in his flesh, and in his heart he endured the pain of the accusations of his wife and friends. But, he did not give in. He scolded his foolish wife, taught his friends wisdom, and preserved his patience.

On Patience, 11-12

Job's story describes misfortune that is not of our own making. In such circumstances, God himself seems to be the only one we can blame. Of course things are made even worse when we get no sympathy from our family, and others look at us suspiciously, thinking, "What evil must he have done to deserve such bad luck!" Hopefully none of us will have to bear the misfortunes of Job. But if some of them come we should pray that we will respond as he responded, "We accept good things from God; should we not accept evil?" (Job 2:10).

October 19

Perseverance

People change both for better and for worse. We are alternately encouraged and saddened by seeing the changes in people every day. We are cheered by people who live good lives and are saddened when people wander away. That's why the Lord did not promise salvation to those who begin well but rather says "Whoever perseveres to the end is the one who will be saved" (Matthew 10:22).

Sermon 51, 1

Even when he was seventy-four years old, Augustine worried whether or not he would persevere to the end. As he said to his friends, "A perseverance whereby a person perseveres clinging to Christ is a very great gift of God. I say 'to the end' because it is only when life is over that the danger of failure is past" (*On Perseverance,* 1). Augustine prayed for perseverance because he feared a moral and spiritual lapse was always possible. At the same time he looked forward to the end of the struggle. The dying Augustine remembered the words of Paul: "If we hold out to the end we shall reign with the Lord" (2 Timothy 2:12). At the moment of death he was filled with joy because he finally knew that indeed he had persevered.

October 20

Walk On!

What does "walking" mean? It means to "keep on going."
So keep on moving my friends. Examine yourself without
self-deception, without flattery. There is no one inside
you before whom you need to be ashamed, no one that
you need to impress. Of course God is there but he is
pleased with your humility. You must be dissatisfied with
the way you are now if you ever want to get to where you
are not yet. When you are self-satisfied, you get stuck
where you are. If you say to yourself, "That's enough;
I need not go farther," it is then that you die. Keep on
walking, don't stop on the road, don't turn round and go
back. Especially don't wander off the road by turning
away from Christ. A lame man limping along the road
goes farther towards God than a sprinter running off the
road.

Sermon 169, 18

Doctors tell us that the best way to stay mobile is to keep
walking. It is hard to do this sometimes. Our aches and pains
sometimes tempt us to sit down and rest, but of course this will
only further immobilize us. In the spiritual order this is equivalent to the end of prayer and the practice of virtue. Just as our
muscles atrophy, so do our spirits and souls. And God does not
come to us if we stop moving toward him. We must walk on to
reach that finish line where everyone who crosses is a winner.

October 21

Hold Out for the Lord!

Let us listen to the voice of the Lord encouraging us from
on high and comforting us. He has taken notice of our

desire and has willingly accepted our plea that we have
sent through Jesus. While we are still plodding along on
our pilgrimage, he has deferred giving us what he promised. He urges us to "Hold out for the Lord!" You will not
be holding out for one who will be unable to find anything to give you. By holding out for the Lord you will
come to possess him. The one for whom you are holding
out will be yours forever. Long for something else, if you
can find something greater or better or more lovely!

Commentary on Psalm 26/2, 23

There are so many good things in this life that only come
after a time and if we lose patience in "holding out" for them,
we never attain them. But all such things, as good as they may
be, are passing. We may "hold out" for them but we cannot
"hold onto them." There is only one great good that we can
hold onto forever and that is the good Lord himself. We must
"hold out for him" until he comes to take us home. Otherwise
all the good things in this life that we patiently "held out for"
will mean nothing.

October 22

Joy in Creation

We should shout for joy when we look upon the whole of
creation: the earth, the sea, the sky, and all the creatures in
it with their own time for birth, existence, and decline. We
watch the stars revolve from east to west as the time
speeds by in hours and years. We see the hints of an invisible something, a spirit or soul, in living things which en-
ables them to seek pleasure, flee from harm, and avoid
decay. In ourselves we perceive a quality of mind that
seems almost divine, a quality whereby we are not only
able to live and see and hear like other animals, but are

able to think about God and distinguish justice from injustice as the eye can tell white from black.

Commentary on Psalm 99, 5

One danger in thinking too long about the troubles we must endure, is that we may forget all those things which we can innocently enjoy. We complain about rainy days but forget that we live in a world where rain is possible, rain that does not burn but cools, a rain that nourishes rather than destroys. And so it is with so many other parts of this world, which seems to have been made precisely for our enjoyment and wonder. It is a great joy to be part of this world if only we could realize it more.

October 23

The Joy of Being Alive

God, the wise Creator has made us the loveliest of all the lovely things on earth. He has given us good gifts that enhance our life now, gifts like the blessings of health and friendship. He has given us gifts that are perfectly adapted to our physical life: things like daylight, air to breathe, water to drink and everything we need to feed, clothe, cure and beautify ourselves. More than this, he gives us a promise that if we use these goods well, we will receive more abundant and better goods, nothing less than an undying peaceful life and all that goes with it: the glory and honor of enjoying God and enjoying our neighbor in God forever.

City of God, 19.13

It seems many of us are born with a natural love of life. Sadly, this joy of life does not last for everyone. In time some seem crushed by disappointment, pain, and rejection. Still, as

Augustine observes, "Whatever it is like, this life is sweet and nobody wants to end it, wretched though it may be" (*Sermon 335B*, 3). We thirst for life, especially a life that is free of pain and is eternal. At the same time we would much prefer to enter eternal life through some other door than the door of death (*Sermon 344*, 4).

October 24

The Joy of Love

I see that when you praise love you shout out. But just as it pleases you when you praise love may it so please you that you preserve it in your heart. Love is praised by you; it pleases you. Well, have it, possess it! There is no need for you to steal it from anyone. There is no need for you to consider buying it. It stands available at no cost. Take hold of it, embrace it. Nothing is sweeter than love. If it is delicious to talk about, what is it like when it is possessed?

Commentary on the Epistle of John, 7.10.2

Love allows us to go beyond our selves as we reach out to our beloved. The love that is returned gives us strength and courage to endure anything for the sake of our love. It is love the drives a parent into a burning building to rescue its child; it is love that drives the martyrs to sacrifice their lives for the sake of God. As Augustine told his people, "Anyone who does not love is a cold individual, frozen and stiff. So let us love what is lovely but let it be a loveliness worthy of being loved" (*Commentary on Psalm 32/2*, 6).

October 25

Flying on the Wings of Love

Don't be afraid of taking upon yourself the yoke of Christ. Christ's burden is so light that it lightens. You won't be pressed down by it; indeed, without it you cannot rise up. Think of the burden of Christ as being like the burden of wings for birds. As long as a bird is burdened by wings, it can fly. Without wings it is trapped on earth. The wings carrying us to Christ are the commandments to love God above all and our neighbor as ourself. To the extent that you use these two wings, you will lift up your heart.

Sermon 68, 12–13

Augustine uses the example of a hunter to make the point that love is a welcomed burden. Out of love for hunting a hunter will endure the heat of summer, the cold of winter, forest thickets, and steep mountainsides. Love makes all these difficulties actually pleasant. These burdens are so pleasant that if hunting were prohibited, the hunter's spirit would be crushed. The paradox, Augustine concludes, is that while a hunter will endure great trials to get at a boar, some of us refuse to endure anything to get at God (*Sermon 68,* 12).

October 26

Joy in a World of Living Things

Just think of the world in which we live! Think of the thousands of beautiful things for seeing and the thousands of objects just right for making things. There are the soft shadows of forests at noon, the shade and smells of spring flowers, the different songs and exotic dresses of the birds. How amazing the animals who are around us, the smallest (the ant) even more amazing than the huge bulk of the whale! How grateful should we be for the gentle animals and silent plants that give themselves so that we might have wool and cotton for our clothes.

City of God, 22.24

Augustine believed that God cares for all living things and all living things share our salvation in being able to live out their lives in this mostly pleasant world. The animals and fish and plants can share our joy in living a vibrant life and creating new generations. Some creatures even become our last friends when all of our human companions seem otherwise occupied. In the providence of God they, like us, die after a life well-lived but, unlike us, they end their lives without anxiety or regret (*Commentary on the Gospel of John,* 34.1.3–4).

October 27

The Joy of Being Me!

Humans go distances to admire the soaring mountains, the giant raging waves of the sea, the broad expanse of the silently flowing rivers, the seemingly infinite expanse of the ocean. They wonder at the limitless paths of the stars but they ignore themselves. They feel no wonder at themselves. The fact, for example that I could not have spoken of the wonders above, unless I could see them in my memory with all of its endless expanse.

Confessions, 10.8.15

One of the greatest joys in life is the fact that God has determined that we should exist as human beings. We wonder at the universe and the various gifts of nature and forget that our appreciation rests on our ability not only to see such wonders, but to *understand* them and, through understanding, to take steps to preserve them. We wonder at the ability of birds to build the same nest year after year and ignore our power of freedom which allows us to build, or not build, our home. It is true that we, of all the animals, can mess up our lives; however we can choose to live heroic lives of faith, hope, charity, and justice. It is a frightening thing to be a human because we can fail; but also we can succeed in a way far beyond the dreams of any other creature.

October 28

A Bishop's Confession

Lord, why should I bother revealing my scrapes and bruises to others as if they could do anything to heal my past failings? Humans seem compulsively interested in hearing about another's blemished life but they are downright lazy when it comes to paying attention to their own faults. It is strange that so many people seem to be waiting to hear from me how I am while paying no attention at all to me when I try to tell them how they are. They don't even know whether I am telling the truth about myself. If they only would listen to the Lord giving a description of their lives, they would be able to say with confidence: "Well, he at least can't be lying."

Confessions, 10.3.3

Augustine wrote his *Confessions* to praise God for rescuing him from the faults of his early life and preserving him from even greater faults after his conversion. His first thirty years of life contained much to be rescued from. Now, as a forty-year-old bishop, his recounting of past deeds and misdeeds apparently had a growing audience, many of whom were scandalized by his accounts. But, as Augustine says, in concentrating on the sins of their bishop, they were able to ignore their own faults.

October 29

A Prayer When God Seems Absent

How mixed up I get, Jesus! And how sad my poor soul becomes when it is trying to rest in peace and you seem not to be in the room! In its solitary space it turns this way and that on its chosen bed, first on its back, then on its side, then on its stomach, only to find more discomfort. Only you, Lord, bring peace. And I know you are always right here, ready to free me from my stupidity and get me going in the right direction. You build up my courage by whispering to me, "Go ahead and run, skipping into your future, I shall hold you in my arms until you win the prize and then go on holding you forever and ever."

Confessions, 6.16

In the early book of the *Confessions*, Augustine describes how he felt on those bad days when he was in his twenties and had lost hope in ever finding any peace. The last sentences describe how he felt on the good days after his conversion when, by the grace of God, he was able to believe in the God of love even when he seemed to be absent. The passage is encouraging for us when we pass through our own bad days when God seems absent and we feel no hope. The message of faith is that God is present always, supporting us on our bad days and giving us a taste of joy on the days when all seems right with the world.

October 30

Passionate Love of God

O God, what do I love when I love you? It is not bodily beauty nor graceful movements nor brilliant light. Nor is it the sweet melodies of songs. It is not the smell of flowers or ointments or fine spices nor is it the taste of honey on bread. When I love you, I don't love something that can be hugged in fleshly embrace. It is not these things that I love when I love you, my God. Yet when I love you I do love something like a light or a pleasant smell or a warm embrace that penetrates deep inside me. When I love you a light shines in my soul and there is an eternal melody and a fragrance that never dissipates and a taste that never loses its savor. And, in some way I am embraced by a hug that I never tire of. This is what it is like to love you, my God.

Confessions 10.6.8

Few of us are able to experience and write so passionately about our human loves, let alone God! No doubt Augustine did not feel this way about God all the time. He, like us, was so consumed by daily obligations that often he had no time to think about God, much less feel passion. Such a passionate feeling is indeed a gift from God. Augustine gives us a taste of how all of us will feel as we stumble into heaven to meet the true love of our eternal life.

October 31

A Day for Unmasking

The whole message contained in the command to the mind to "know itself" comes down to the following: the mind should not pretend that the self has virtues which in fact are not present and does not ignore those vices which in fact are present.

The Trinity, 10.16

In the Christian calendar All Hallows Day is a feast that celebrates our final unmasking when we shall see our true selves reflected in the eyes of Jesus. I have a recurring dream in relation to this day in which I come to the door of heaven wearing the masks that I hid behind in this life. Jesus removes my masks only to find no face at all! The "me" that God created had been destroyed by my pretending to be things I was not. It was then that I understood the meaning of hell: it was Jesus looking for me and finding nothing. I knew then that in this life I must try my best to be true to myself and to the Lord. If I could do that, then, when the day came for me to face Jesus, he would see in my face his own reflection and I would march into heaven with him singing the hymn of triumph, "I live, no longer I, but Christ lives in me!" (Galatians 2:20).

November 1

Who Are the Saints?

The saints are those who are moved by God's grace to do whatever good they do. Some are married and have intercourse with their spouse sometimes for the sake of having a child and sometimes just for the pleasure of it. They get angry and desire revenge when they are injured, but are ready to forgive when asked. They are very attached to their property but will freely give at least a modest amount to the poor. They will not steal from you but are quick to take you to court if you try to steal from them. They are realistic enough to know that God should get the main credit for the good that they do. They are humble enough to admit that they are the source of their own evil acts. In this life God loves them for their good acts and gives forgiveness for their evil, and in the next life they will join the ranks of those who will reign with Christ forever.

Against Two Letters of the Pelagians, 3.5.14

Many of the saints about whom we read seem far above our ordinary experience. Augustine's description is more to our liking because it describes ordinary saints with some virtues and some faults. Their saving grace is that they are humble, willing to admit mistakes and ask forgiveness. Heaven certainly has some "great" saints but I suspect that it is more crowded with ordinary folk like you and me, "cracked" people who tried their best to do God's will.

November 2

Jesus Conquered Death

Jesus came to save us. He died but at the same time he conquered death. He put an end to what we fear so much. He took it on and conquered it. So be of good heart, my friends. What has already taken place in Jesus will also take place in us. Listen to those who have triumphed and now live where death is no more. Hear Paul saying, "When what is mortal has been clothed with what is immortal and when that which will die has been clothed with what cannot die, then the Scripture will come true: 'Death is destroyed; victory is complete! Where, O Death, is your victory? Where, O Death, is your sting?'"

Sermon 233, 3–4

What do Paul and Augustine mean by saying that "Christ has conquered death"? We will still die and we still fear death's coming. Our victory over death is revealed by our faith which tells us that our present life is like a dot on a line that is eternal. True, we must move from that dot of time into eternity, but through the sacrifice and example of Christ we now know that, like him, we will rise from the grave to an eternal life so bright and joyful that this life pales in comparison. We must all still go through the door of death, but Jesus' life and death and resurrection now assures us that there is something wonderful waiting for us on the other side of the door.

November 3

The Price of Heaven

The Lord said to the saved, "Come you blessed, take possession of the kingdom." What price did they pay for it? The Lord answers, "I was hungry and you fed me" (Matthew 25:34-35). What could be more insignificant than to break bread for a hungry person? Yet that is the price of the kingdom of heaven. But suppose you have no bread to break for them, or have no house into which you can invite them, or no garment to give to them? Well, Zacchaeus purchased heaven by giving away half his fortune but Peter purchased it by leaving his nets and a widow purchased it with two pennies. The conclusion is obvious: Heaven costs what you have to give.

Commentary on Psalm 49, 13

Jesus said that we need observe only two commandments to enter heaven: love God and love neighbor. But how we do this depends upon our individual circumstances. To love our neighbor does not mean that we need to sacrifice everything we have for their sake. We will not be asked to give more than we are able to give. Love of neighbor means that we are willing to give them what they need if we are able. The price of heaven is loving God more than ourselves and loving our neighbor at least as much as ourselves.

November 4

Christh: The Basis for Our Hope

Through his temptations, suffering, death and resurrection Jesus has become our hope. Now we can say to ourselves: "God surely won't condemn us since it was for us that he sent his Son to be tempted, to be crucified, to die, and to rise again. God cannot despise us since he delivered up his own Son for our sake." Christ gives an example of how we should live this life of labor, temptation, suffering, and death. Through his resurrection he is the proof for the life we will live after death. If Jesus had not come as a human being all we would know about human life is that we are born and we die. Jesus took upon himself the human condition we know and gave us a proof of the eternal life we do not know.

Commentary on Psalm 60, 4

The hope Christ gave us comes in many forms. In coming to redeem us he took away the despair we felt as a fallen race, a race incapable of ever getting to heaven. He gave us hope by demonstrating by his resurrection that death is not the end of life but the beginning of one that is eternal. Christ gives us hope in his example of how we can respond to the ups and downs of life. He experienced friendship, betrayal, the joy of weddings, and the sorrow of funerals. He even experienced times when his Father seemed far away. He gave us hope that we can endure this life because he is always by our side with his supporting grace.

November 5

Our Responsibility for Our Salvation

Your justification is from God but without your willingness to accept it, that justification could not exist in you. Justice exists in the universe without you willing it but it cannot be in you without you willing it. God made you to be a human being. If you were able on your own to make yourself just, you would have made something better than that which God made. God made you without your consent but he does not justify you without your consent. He made you without your even knowing it; he justifies you only with your willing consent.

Sermon 169, 13

One of the great mysteries of our salvation is how we manage to accomplish good, despite our flawed condition. Augustine explains this by showing how we choose good by the grace of God. Although we may freely choose to accept God's grace, it is because of that grace that we are able to freely choose. This raises the question of how then are we free? Does God "override" our freedom to influence our choice? Augustine answers that God works through the natural tendency of our will to choose what delights it. Just as we delight in a particular dessert, God brings it about that we delight in doing good and thus freely choose to do it.

November 6

A Pilgrim's Prayer

O God, even here in the midst of my darkness you speak to me of bright shiny places. You don't try to drive me crazy in the midst of my troubles and you forbid others to upset me as I live out my days. I know that some day I will go to you. Open up the door to my knock. Tell me how to get to where you are. I don't have anything now to help me get to you except my desire for you. I don't know anything beyond the passing things of this life. I want to know your eternal truths. Right now the only thing I know is that I must search out these truths but I don't know how. Help me find my way.

Soliloquies, 1.3 & 5

The prayer above appears in one of Augustine's earliest works written soon after his baptism. He had lived more than thirty years wandering around the intellectual worlds of Platonism and skepticism. Eventually he converted to Christianity, but he still did not know much about Christ nor what to do with his life. He desired to know the truths needed to make his way along the path of this life, and to know what awaited him at the end of the path. He had much to learn but he prayed for the patience to wait until the fullness of Christ's message was revealed to him.

November 7

Christ Must Be Our Foundation

Why is it said that Christ must be "our foundation"? The best way to explain this is to compare our spiritual life with a building. In a building nothing comes before the foundation. Those who have Christ as their foundation are those who have Christ in their heart in such a way that nothing comes before him, nothing earthly and temporal, not even those things which seem licit and allowed. Even though people may seem to believe in Christ, if they allow any such thing to come before Christ, then for them Christ is not their foundation. Still less do they have

Christ for their foundation if they despise and sin against
his saving law.

City of God, 21.26

To love God with our whole heart and mind does not mean
that we cannot relish the innocent joys of this life. It does not
mean that we must be thinking about Christ all the time. Our
lives are like an edifice that is made up of many parts—family,
work, citizenship—which we must attend to. But we must
direct such projects toward heaven, which can only happen if
Christ is the foundation of our lives. Like the foundation of a
building, he is not that evident day by day but if he is not supporting all that we do, eventually the edifice of our spiritual
life will not stand.

November 8

A Confident Prayer

O God, all the good things I have come from you and you
protect me from trouble. And so, I confidently make this
prayer to you. First of all I thank you for the ability to
make this prayer. If you ever left me, I would be lost but
I know that you are too good to let that happen. You are
too good to allow anyone to be lost who really tries to
find you. Indeed, you are so good that I know that you
will give me the power to try and find you. Keep me from
making any terrible mistake like attaching myself to some
false god or other. Wash out of me the fog of my earthly
desires so that I may be clear-eyed enough to see you.

Soliloquies, 1.6

Augustine wandered for thirty years before he was converted
to Christ. He knew from experience that no matter how far a
man wanders away from God, God can find a way to bring

him back. His prayer is thus a confident prayer that, just as God had brought him back from his roaming, God would certainly protect him from wandering away again. For God there is never anyone who is completely "missing"; it is just that some of us are occupied with other matters.

November 9

A Prayer of a Reformed Sinner

O Lord, light of my heart, don't let the dark places in my life speak to me. I know I slipped away from you down to a terrible place where my life was darkened. But even from these dark depths I fell in love with you. O sure, I have wandered, but I never lost the memory of you. I heard your whisper behind my back asking me to return, but I could scarcely make it out, what with the tumult of the enemies of my peace. But see, Lord, I am now returning to you gasping and perspiring as I reach for the fountain that is you. I shall drink of you and revive. On my own I lived a terrible life. On my own I brought death to my soul but in you I shall come back to life.

Confessions, 12.10

One of the saving graces for Augustine was that he had a saintly mother who, as a child, taught him about Christ and prayed for his eventual return to Christ. This impression never left him, and eventually played a part in his dramatic conversion. But to the end of his life he worried that he would fall back into his old habits. His life offers us an important lesson: no matter how good we think we are, no matter how much good we have accomplished, we need the grace of God to avoid falling away from him.

November 10

The Joy of Finding God

O Lord, you have already announced in a loud voice deep
inside me that you do exist and have always existed and
that you will exist forever always the same, never now
this way and then that. You have announced in a loud
voice deep inside me that you have made everything that
is. The only things that are not yours are those things that
simply are not, and (of course) the perversity of my will
which sometimes chooses to run away from you and to
latch onto something immeasurably lower. The perversity
is all mine. It does no damage to you. This I see clearly
now, because of the sight you have given me. Make my
vision ever more clear as I continue to be touched by the
wonders you reveal and live out my life quietly here
under your shielding wings.

Confessions, 12.11

The words above reflect Augustine's middle years, a time
of heartfelt closeness to God. The words are joyful because
Augustine remembered the years when God seemed distant.
Jesus had been with him in those years, speaking to him in a
quiet voice, but that voice was drowned out by his passion,
ambition, and confusion. It is indeed a great gift to finally hear
the voice of God proclaiming his presence in our lives, but it is
a gift that must be nourished by prayer and contemplation if it
is to remain vital.

November 11

A Prayer about Heaven

Lord you have announced in a loud voice deep inside me that the place where you live, the place that you brighten by just being there, is forever peaceful with no troublesome times. God how I love this place where my lovely and glorious Lord lives! What a bright and beautiful place it must be! As I continue my pilgrimage through this life, my spirit cries out: "O bright and beautiful place, I hope that the Lord who made you and also made me will someday bring me to you. I have wandered far like a lost sheep but perhaps someday I shall be carried through your gates by our Lord, that one who is both my shepherd and your architect."

Confessions, 12.12 & 15

Perfect peace is obviously not possible in this life. Even if we were able to enjoy moments of peace, it would not be perfect because we would know that it must end some day. Perhaps one of the greatest gifts from believing in Jesus is that he has proved to us that this life is not the end, but a beginning. He has promised that if we do our best to live decent lives now, he will bring us to a place where we finally and forever find the perfect peace that we so desperately desire.

November 12

Heavenly Peace

O Lord, give me final peace. You have given me the experience of the Sabbath rest after days of labor but, unlike Sabbaths now, the day of final peace will have no ending because you will have made it eternal. The fact that at creation you rested on the seventh day of your labors is a sign that we too shall rest in you through the unending day of eternal Sabbath once we have completed our own good works in this life, works we have been able to do only through your help. When that day comes you shall rest in us in the same fashion that you work in us now. Our rest then will come from you in the same way that our good works now come from you. How can any human being make another human understand what all this means! Only you, Lord, can make me understand all this. I must knock on your door. Only then will I receive enlightenment. Only then, there at your open door, will I understand what peace really means.

Confessions, 13.35–38

In heaven our essential condition will be one of peace. We know what peace means but in this life we have never experienced its perfection. Even on our best days there is a host of things that bother us: pain, fatigue, remorse, anxiety, or discomfort. All of this will be done away with in heaven. In the midst of our intense activity of loving, we will find perfect peace. Our heavenly Sabbath rest will be eternal.

November 13

Heavenly Happiness: I

How wonderful will be our happiness in heaven! Our undying body will be freed from the need to perform the ordinary tasks of this life. Who can describe the beauty of our bodies in that new life? Just imagine how they will act in that place where there is nothing ugly! Whatever our spirits decide will be accepted happily by our bodies. And our spirits will not be tempted to choose anything unbecoming either for themselves or for their friends, their bodies. We shall have perfect peace because there will be nothing inside or outside of us to cause upset. All of our parts will be drawn to praise the Lord. Our whole being will become one magnificent organ sounding striking melodies in praise of the wonderful artist who made us inside and out and placed us at the center of the overpowering structure of this universe, a universe that will ravish us with its beauty.

City of God, 22.30

Augustine did not know what heaven was like, only what it was not like. For example, we will not need to work but yet not be bored. All ugliness will disappear from our body and we will see it for what it is—a creation of the divine architect. It will have no discordant desires, no embarrassing temptations. Our spirit will not make untoward demands on it and it will happily obey all that it is asked to do. We will be drawn irresistibly to praise God and discover that it is the first job we ever really loved.

November 14

Heavenly Happiness: II

In heaven our reward will be our God, that same Lord who spoke about us to the prophet so long ago, saying, "I shall be their God and they shall be my people" (Leviticus 26:12). What the Lord is saying to us is something like this: "I shall be whatever you have thirsted for and hoped for as a human being. Be it life or health or food or respect or peace or any other good thing, I shall be all of these for you." This is what Paul meant when he wrote: "God shall be all in all" (1 Corinthians 15:28). Our God shall be the satisfaction of all our desires. We shall love him and cheer him without fatigue. All of us will share in this experience of overpowering love because all alike will have appropriate shares in this magnificent heavenly life.

City of God, 22.30

An analogy of this might be loving another human being from afar, only to later discover that they silently loved you with a greater intensity. Consumed by the joy of their union, all other desires fade away. If we magnified that feeling an infinite number of times, perhaps we would come close to the consuming happiness we will experience in heaven when finally we are united with the God whom our very nature longs to possess.

November 15

Christ Cures: I

Even after your sins are taken away you still bear a weak body. There still remain some carnal desires to tempt you, some suggestions of illicit delights. They come because you still walk around in a troublesome body. Death has not yet been absorbed in victory. This corruptible life has not yet put on incorruption (1 Corinthians 15:53-54). Moreover, your soul, even after its sins have been forgiven, continues to shake with confusion. It is still living in the midst of temptation, sometimes consenting to a delightful idea that is illicit. The soul (like the body) is still feeble. But don't be afraid. All your illnesses will be cured. You object: "But they are great!" The Divine Doctor is greater. There is no incurable illness for an all-powerful Doctor.

Commentary on Psalm 102, 5

Augustine's favorite image of our life—that we have been picked up and brought to the inn of the Samaritan—was a hopeful picture of our life now and our prospects for the future. It repeats the message of our faith: that Christ knows our continuing weakness and comes not as a condemning judge but as a good doctor. If we take the medicine he prescribes, we will be healed and be ready to go home with him to heaven when he comes to pick us up.

November 16

Christ Cures: II

Jesus knows what needs to be done to cure you but don't expect that he will always make you feel good. Put up with the pains of the medicine and think of the cure that is to come. Consider how much we endure to cure our bodily illnesses in order to live only a few more days. Many after putting up with great pains, after being cut open by the doctor, either die at his hands or (cured of this particular ailment) contract another infection and die from that. When Christ cures, you do not put up with the pain for an uncertain result. He who has promised to heal you is not able to fail because he knows how to remake what he created. Humans choose to be cut open by human doctors and put up with enormous pain for an uncertain cure and for this they are charged a huge fee. Jesus will cure you once and for all and this for free.

Commentary on Psalm 102, 5

Augustine obviously did not have too much faith in the doctors of his day but they did provide a metaphor for talking about the Divine Doctor, Jesus Christ, whom he trusted completely. He knew from the experience of his own difficult conversion that curing our spiritual ills is sometimes very painful, but he suggests that putting up with the pain of changing one's life is well worth the expense.

November 17

Christ Cures: III

Jesus-God will certainly cure our spiritual illnesses; after all, he has already redeemed us. The cure is not complete just now because the soul still lives in a corruptible body. How many obstacles there are to even thinking about God! Such a great pile of things are in the human heart, as though gushing from some internal worm of corruption! Will Jesus-God not cure you? The original plan was that human beings would never get sick. All they had to do was to follow God's instructions about what not to eat (Genesis 2:16-17). Scripture testifies that Adam and Eve did not pay attention to the instruction for preserving health. Now we need to listen to God's instructions for getting it back. Will God not cure someone whom he made in his own image?

Commentary on Psalm 102, 6

Unfortunately in our present "cracked" condition we are constantly distracted from the goal of happiness with God. Even at our best, we are distracted by a constant stream of images, dreams, and fantasies created by our imaginations. As Augustine says, this is not the world that God wanted for us. But, because of the sin of Adam and Eve, focusing on God was made difficult. Had it not been for the fall, like Adam we would have walked with God in paradise. However, we are still made in the image of God and he will certainly cure us of our confusion if we let him.

November 18

Christ Cures: IV

Who is not sick in this life? Who is not strung out with weariness? To be born in this mortal body is to begin to be sick. Our weakness is supported only by daily medication. Medication is the way we bear up under our feebleness. Would not hunger kill us if we did not offset it with some remedy? Would not thirst destroy us if we did not slake it? We only ease the malaise of our feebleness by the various potions we take. Whatever comes to the relief of one weariness begins another. Well, our eternal health will come only through Christ. We must take the cup of healing from him in order to heal all the illnesses of our spirit. If we wish to obtain this healing we shall. Jesus has already paid the price for our cure with his blood. If we only could be convinced of that, we would cry to the heavens: "Lift yourself up, O my soul, because you are of such great, great worth!"

Commentary on Psalm 102, 6

Augustine was no stranger to bodily ills. He almost died twice in his youth and complained of bodily ailments for the rest of his seventy-six years. There is nothing much we can do about the bodily and mental illnesses that afflict us in this life. As Augustine says, "We are born into illness." But it will not be that way for eternity. Christ has already paid the price for our eternal health. All we need do now is to follow our divine doctor's advice and take our medicine.

Christ's Prescription

The Lord has given us two rules to guide us while we are in the process of healing. We must love God and must love other human beings. We are really given three persons to love: God, our neighbor, and ourselves. We are not wrong in loving ourselves as long as we also love the Lord. We are obliged to love our neighbor at least as much as we love ourselves and we must help our neighbor to love God too. We should try not to add to their burden and help whomever we can along the way. We must start our loving at home where we find those whose needs we should know the best. As St. Paul wrote, "If you do not take care of your own, especially those of your own household, you have not lived up to your faith and have become worse than an unbeliever" (1 Timothy 5:8).

City of God, 19.14

As we live out our days in this place of healing, the doctor has left firm instructions on how to get better. There are only two, both of them instructing us on how to love. We must love God above all and our neighbor as ourselves. It is fitting that our medicine should be love because it was our perverse loving that made us sick in the first place. It is also fitting that our love of others begins with those closest to us. There is no merit in being an angel of mercy for the world if we are a devil in our own home. Our family needs our love even more than strangers.

November 20

A Prayer to Be Healed

Lord I want to know you as you have known me. You are my strength. Dive deep into my soul and wash it out. Make it a good place without spot or wrinkle, a fine place for you to live. I hope for this and when I am thinking straight the very hope gives me joy. As for the rest of the things in my life (other than knowing you) I have learned that those that receive the most tears deserve the least and those that have less tears shed for them deserve much more.

Confessions, 10.2

This is a good prayer for someone who wants God to visit them. Like Martha in the Gospel, when the Lord is coming we want to get our souls spotlessly clean. Of course, this is hopeless because only God can do that. That he would care enough to do so should give us joy. Once our soul is cleansed perhaps he will then sit down with us and teach us what is truly important in our lives. Just now we may not be sure that we know. But perhaps he will take that into account and have mercy on our confusion. But first he must come to us and we must invite him into our hearts, cleansed and shiny as best we can make them.

November 21

A Prayer for Renovation

O God, my soul is like a house too small for you to enter. I pray that you will enlarge it. It is in ruins, but I ask you to remake it. It contains much that you will not be pleased to see. This I know and I will not try to hide it. But who can rid it of these things? There is no one but you to whom I can say "If I have sinned unwittingly, do you absolve me. Keep me always as your servant" (Psalm 19, 13-14).

Confessions, 1.5

That God would come to live in a human soul seems impossible. How can something finite contain the infinite, especially when the finite is so cluttered with inconsequential things? There is need for renovation and the only one who can do this is God himself. He does this not by making himself smaller but by making us bigger. First of all he throws out all that is useless in our lives, that from which we must be dispossessed. Having done this God then enlarges our spirit, tearing down the walls of earthly passion so that our love can embrace the boundless God. Renovation is a painful task. While my home at Villanova is being renovated, I have been forced to live elsewhere. So far the renovation of the Villanova monastery has taken two years. I expect God's renovation of my soul will take a lifetime.

November 22

Signs of Our Woundedness

If you have any doubt that we humans have been wounded, just look at the trouble we cause in this life. How else to explain the fact that we are often so terribly dumb? It is this dumbness that is the source of so many of our mistakes. It is a stubborn dumbness which can't be overcome by me or by you without sweat, blood, and tears. And how about our crazy passion for vapid and vile things which, when we possess them, create in us anxiety, confusion, sadness, and fear? This is the madness that makes the human animal rejoice in fighting and war, in hating and plotting against others, in fraud and theft, in homicide and parricide, in savagery and cruelty, in fornication and adultery, in sacrilege and blasphemy, in calumny and lies and rash judgment. Indeed, the catalog of human sins is so long that it seems easier to commit them than to list them.

City of God, 22.22.1

All one has to do is look around the world and look into ourselves to discover how badly we need the help of the divine doctor. The list of the evils we commit, either out of stupidity or weakness, seems endless. Above and beyond these, there are all those wicked thoughts no one can see but ourselves. Truly, we need help. Luckily that help is available. The Divine Doctor is close by ready to protect us from ourselves if we would just ask for his healing grace.

November 23

The Battle against "Dumbness"

God in his goodness did not leave us mired in ignorance and passion. He did not abandon us to our woundedness. Rather he reached down and gave us laws and direction through which we are able to fight our wildness and our dumbness as long as we are willing to pay the price of work and woe that such a battle demands. And so it is that when we are little we begin to be "educated" by teachers with their rulers and straps and canes. We call upon the authority of the Scripture and "beat their sides lest they grow stubborn" (Sirach 30:12). The purpose of all this discipline is to overcome the dumbness and wild desires that every one of us is born with. Getting to know things is painful! Think how hard it is to remember anything and how easy it is to forget! It is easy to be dumb; so hard to be smart! It takes a lot of effort to get over being lazy because in our present situation, any kind of work is simply a huge pain!

City of God, 22.22

Augustine had experience both as an unruly student who had to be beaten to learn and as an incompetent teacher who could not control his classes. In his later years he admitted that most of the important truths he learned were through Jesus Christ teaching deep within his own soul. He learned that Jesus was the only one who can tell us what we are *really* like, what we *really* should do with our lives. He realized (as we should) that without that knowledge, all the rest is useless.

November 24

The Good Samaritan

There are some who don't think they really need the healing power of grace. At creation humans received great powers of free will but they lost a lot of these powers through sin. They became infected with a serious illness. They became weak. Their condition was like that of the man in the Gospel story left by robbers half-alive on the side of the road. A passing Samaritan lifted him up on his horse and took him to an inn. Why did the Samaritan lift up the poor man? So that he might be cured. Even though he had been saved from his wandering down dangerous paths, his weakness still had to be cured. We are in that place for healing now. Let us accept care cheerfully and don't boast that all of our weakness and woundedness is cured. By such presumption we actually get worse.

Sermon 131, 6

Augustine describes the difference between our power of free will in paradise and the way it is now. Before they sinned, unwounded humans had the full exercise of their freedom. Good and evil were in equal balance, making the choice of one as easy as the other. Now in our present wounded state the balance has shifted towards evil. Under the constant barrage of temptation it is difficult for us now to choose the right course of action. To say we need no further help would be just as foolish as the wounded man in the story above refusing the therapy he so desperately needed to continue his journey. He, like us, was saved, but he was not yet cured.

November 25

Listening to the Lord

O Lord of truth, you rule over everything and everyone including ourselves when we come to you for answers. You are ready and willing to answer any question asked and you always answer our questions clearly but not all of us can hear so clearly. Everybody asks you for answers they wish to hear but they do not always hear what they wish. Your best servant is the one who does not expect always to hear the answer he desires but always ends up desiring whatever he hears from you.

Confessions, 10.26.37

In the first years of our lives we are full of questions. A child will ask its parents, "Where are you going?" Or, when on a trip its refrain is "Are we there yet?" Likewise, we even ask God many questions which he answers from deep inside our souls. Of course we do not always like such answers as "You must give up this relationship," or "For a while longer you must endure your pain." God will always tell us the truth about ourselves, but sometimes we are not prepared to accept it. The sign of our closeness to God is our willingness to accept whatever he tells us. Admittedly sometimes this is very hard to do.

November 26

"Late Have I Loved You"

Late have I loved you, O Beauty so ancient and yet so new, late have I loved you. You were always there inside me and I was running around outside. I was looking for you out there, and confused as I was, I threw myself upon those beautiful things that you had made. You were always in me, but I was not always in you. Created things kept me apart from you even though they themselves could only exist in you. You called and shouted and finally broke through my deafness. You blazed forth and shone brightly and finally broke through my blindness. Your fragrance touched me. I inhaled and now cannot stop panting for you. I finally tasted you and now hunger and thirst for you. You touched me and now I am inflamed with desire for your peace.

Confessions, 10.27.38

Augustine's famous prayer above was written when he was a bishop after many years of serving Christ. He is reflecting on his early years when he was looking for something to believe in. His words of reflection were meant to be more a hymn of wonder for God's grace than a lament to "wasted" years. To the end of his life, he regarded his conversion as an act of divine intervention. It is a story with an important lesson for us: rather than moaning over our past mistakes, we should rejoice that by the grace of God we have survived.

November 27

Jesus Took Our Medicine First

The Lord put on our flesh because he wanted to experience first-hand the madness of being human. He wanted to show us his servants that it was not all that much to go through such fevers. Indeed, it is necessary sometimes for us to feel such unpleasant heat if we are ever to be cured of our sin-filled wounds and finally be made all better. Jesus our doctor first sipped the cup of bitter medicine himself so that we the sick might not fear to drink it.

Commentary on Psalm 98, 3

There are at least three great miracles in the history of the human race as revealed in Scripture. The first is that we were created out of nothing for no apparent reason other than that God loved us. The second is that, after we turned our backs on God, God chose to redeem us and open the gates of heaven for us once again. The third miracle is that he chose to save us by becoming a human being himself in the person of Jesus Christ. He came down and shared our life, with all its ups and downs. He was born as a poor man, lived as a wanderer, and executed as a criminal. He had loving parents, enjoyed deep friendships, and went to weddings and parties. Whatever good or bad things we experience in our lives, God was there before. His life is a proof that he understands the glory and travail of being human.

November 28

A Prayer of Thanksgiving

My merciful Lord, you made me. You did not forget me even when I forgot you. Come now into my heart, that heart which you prepared by giving it a thirst for you. Don't abandon me now, my Lord, when I finally have cried out for you. Remember that you came to help me even before I cried out. You called out to me in all sorts of ways so that even though I was still so very far away I could hesitate, listen for your voice and at last call out to you who had always been calling out to me.

Confessions, 13.1.1

Augustine always had a joy for living. Looking into his life in his later years, he could not resist offering a prayer of thanksgiving to the God who created him, never forgot him, pursued him in his wanderings, and continued to create in him a thirst for God even before he came to believe in him. It is a fine prayer expressing God's desire for his eternal life of happiness. He came to realize that every human being is not created simply to live now but to have a chance for eternal happiness. That thought made Augustine always thankful.

November 29

The Mystery of My Creation

Lord, you existed when I was still nothing. You had nothing to work with when you came to make me. Yet here I am, a product solely of your goodness. You certainly did not need me. Nor am I the kind of person who could ever be much help to you. When I try to do little things for you, I don't make you any less tired. And, when I don't do anything at all for you, still your great works are accomplished. You don't need me to take care of you at all. You are not like some untilled field, fallow without my labors to cultivate you. Indeed, the only excuse for my working for you is so that I can be happy. And you are the one who gives me that happiness, just as in the very beginning you

built me so that I would have the capability of being
happy.

Confessions, 13.1.1

"Why me?" was a question Augustine repeated all through
his life. It was not like our cry when things go badly (e.g.: "I
have lost my job. Why me?"). Augustine's question was rather,
"Considering all the people whom you could have created
who would have done a better job at living than me, why did
you choose to create me, O Lord?" The only answer he could
come up with was that God created him because he loved him,
just as he created you and me because he loved us.

November 30

Better to Be Small and Healthy

It is better to be a healthy finger than a diseased eye in the
Mystical Body of Christ. The finger is not much in the
body whereas the eye is a wonderful part, able to do tre-
mendous things. However it is better to be a finger and
healthy than to be a diseased or blinded eye. No one
should seek anything in the Body of Christ except health.
From health comes faith and by faith the heart is purified
and with a clear heart one is able to see that face which is
referred to in the passage: "Blessed are the clean of heart
for they shall see God" (Matthew 5:8). All the faithful who
love Jesus, . . . all of these will have their names written
in heaven. Though one may not be thought of very highly
in the world, if he believes in and loves Jesus, his name
will be written in heaven.

Commentary on Psalm 130, 8

It makes no difference what part we play in the Mystical
Body of Christ. If we are united to him in any way, we will be
saved. Doing great things, having positions of honor, means

nothing if we are diseased members of Christ's Body. Though we may be revered because of our oratorical powers or our ability to teach, it is not worth much if we speak blasphemy or teach hatred of Jesus. By our baptism we may still be members of his Mystical Body, but as diseased members we will eventually be discarded at the final judgment.

December 1

The Mystery of God's Providence

Some desire to have children and can't have them; others don't want children but can't seem to avoid them. Why is it that those of modest means are lavish in their gift-giving while misers horde their hidden treasure? Why is that some of the rich waste their ample inheritance on trifles while the weeping beggar hardly gets a coin all day? Why is it that the undeserving are honored while those who live blameless lives are ignored by the crowd? These and other things in human life cause some humans to believe that the world is not governed by Divine Providence. Others who cannot believe they have been abandoned by God are so confused by the chaos of the world that it is hard for them to see any order in it.

On Order, 2.5.14–15

On some days it is indeed difficult to believe that God is in control of things. Of course the fact that things are messed up is not his fault. He did not want humans to sin, but when they did, he respected their freedom. This does not mean that he has abandoned this world. He still works in the world to accomplish his most important task: the salvation of each person. There is much in this life we cannot get, but we can gain eternal happiness if we truly want it and live lives worthy of receiving it.

December 2

God Is Present in Creation

God guides his whole creation by a hidden power, and all
creatures are subject to this power. The angels carry out
his commands, the stars move in their courses, the winds
blow now this way and now that, deep pools seethe with
tumbling waterfalls forming mist above them, meadows
come to life as their seeds put forth the grass, animals are
born and live their lives according to their proper instincts.
It is thus that God guides the unfolding of the generations
that he created in the beginning. This would not happen
if the God who made the creatures had ceased to exercise
his provident rule over them.

A Literal Commentary on Genesis, 5.20.41

Looking at the non-human part of creation, everything seems
to go about its work, quietly performing its proper function.
Human beings are the only part of creation that is sometimes
disordered. Of course there are earthquakes, floods, hurri-
canes, but they are disasters, not because they are disordered,
but because we have put ourselves in their way. Even the unfortunate event of a child dying from a disease is a part of the
order of the universe, an order that allows the seriously dis-
abled or diseased to die. Of course sickness and death are a
result of the fall, which is now part of the order of things. However, even now, if we look at the world around us, we still can
come to see that a divine power guides every part.

December 3

God "Cultivates" Us

Just as man cultivates the earth to develop it and make it fruitful, so God in a much deeper sense cultivates man in order that he may become just. Just as man is said to cultivate the earth so that it may be adorned and fruitful, God also is said to cultivate man so that he may be devout and wise. He also guards him lest he delight too much in his own powers because when a person ignores the authority of God, he cannot be saved.

A Literal Commentary on Genesis, 8.10.23

God has not abandoned the human race since the fall. He is involved with his creatures the way a farmer is involved with his farm. While some of us are like stubborn animals, resisting the farmer's assistance, others of us are more like humble plants, allowing God to cultivate and guide our growth, fertilizing us sometimes in hard times, pruning away those parts of our lives that are dead or diseased, placing our new growth on the supporting trellis of his grace until we can stand straight and tall in the new heavenly paradise that he has prepared for us.

December 4

Why Do the Evil Prosper?

A great many people deny God's Providence when they observe how many things in this life occur apparently by chance. Some object, "If God really took care of our lives, he certainly would not allow the wicked and the impious to exist." To this St. Paul replied, "God will pay each one back according to his works" (Romans 2:6). How can you say that God does not take care of human affairs if he is going to "pay each one back according to their works?"

Sermon Dolbeau 29, 1 (a recently discovered sermon)

Perhaps the greatest reason why people doubt God's providence is the existence of evil acts by evil people. Not only this, but it seems that the evil prosper while the good suffer. How can a good and powerful God allow this to happen? The answer is of course that God's rule of the world is shown better when one takes the long view. This world, no matter how long it lasts, is but a dot on a line that lasts forever. God's justice may not seem to be served just now but, as Paul says, eternity is the true "pay back time," the time when the scales of justice will be balanced. Then the good people will join the Lord in heaven and those who never repented of their evil life will be excluded. Is this not sufficient "pay back" for what we do in this life?

December 5

Christ Is God!

Those who were estranged from God jeered at Christ as a poor human being but you must sing psalms to him because he is not only a human being; he is God! As a human being he was a descendent of David but as God he was David's Lord. Not only was he God before he took human flesh, he was God before the earth itself was created, before the sky came to be, before any angel began to exist, indeed before time. As Scripture testifies "In the beginning was the Word and the Word was with God; he was God. Everything was made through him; no part of created being was made without him" (John 1:1-3).

Commentary on Psalm 46, 8

The trappings of Christmas can easily make us overlook the fact that this Jesus who was born on Christmas was God! If Jesus was just another pious prophet, we might honor him, but there would be no cause to worship him. He would be someone to revere but not someone who had the power to redeem us from Adam's Original Sin. Sometimes we forget that the baby lying in the manger is God! Of course the angels knew it, the shepherds may have suspected it, but the rest of the world saw Jesus as just another poor child. But this human son of Mary, this foster child of the trusting Joseph, was from eternity God himself!

December 6

Believing Is Better than Seeing

Jesus said to Thomas "Because you have seen, you have believed; blessed are those who do not see, yet believe" (John 20:29). This was a prediction about ourselves. The divinity of Jesus was hidden from those who walked with him, who crucified him, who saw his risen body. We (who never saw him walk this earth) have come to believe that now he is enthroned in heaven. Even if we were to see him, would not what we saw be no more than what the Jews who crucified him saw? We have something better. We do not see Christ and yet we believe that he is God. Those who saw him thought him only a man. Thinking wrongly about him they put him to death; we by believing in his fullness are brought to life.

Commentary on Psalm 49, 5

Augustine firmly believed that those of us living after Christ's life, death, and resurrection are better situated to accept him than those who actually witnessed him. By being called to believe in him we are challenged to a greater trust and love than those who actually saw him. You cannot ignore the reality of someone you see but it is quite easy not to believe in something unseen. And more, if we have the gift of faith, we are able to believe more about Jesus than his compatriots ever saw. In believing in Jesus we can come to know that he still lives with us and in us. Those who saw him only as a man thought that, if they just executed him, he would be gone forever.

December 7

Sharing Christ's Divinity

Christ says "I have given human beings the power to behave well but they do so not on their own but only by being supported by my grace. When they do bad things they act like children of men; when they do good things they are my children." Thus it is that God brings it about that children of men can be transformed into children of God, just as the Son of God became a "Son of Man." Jesus promised us a share in his divinity, but he would be deceiving us if he had not first become a sharer in our mortality. The Son of God shared our humanity so that we might become sharers in his divinity.

Commentary on Psalm 52, 6

Augustine's reflection is startling: "We can share in the divinity of Jesus Christ!" Indeed, one of the reasons why he came to share our humanity was so we could do precisely that. What in the world can it mean? Certainly it does not mean that we will become God. That fantasy was what caused Adam's original sin. He thought he could be independent of God, on the same level as God, not subordinate to any God but himself. We are made in the image of God, and the goal of our lives is to make that image more and more perfect. If we do that, then when Jesus looks at us in heaven, he will see his own image perfectly reflected. In a sense we have become "like God" and thereby able to share in eternity with him.

December 8

Christ's Promises

Christ did not promise temporal riches nor earthly honors. He did not even promise bodily health or beauty or a long life. What he did promise was an eternal life where we would fear nothing, where we would be untroubled, from where we would never need to depart, where we would never die. It would be a place where we would neither need to mourn for ancestors nor hope for offspring. This is what he has promised to those who are ablaze with love for him.

Commentary on the Gospel of John, 32.9.2–3

Our life now is like the life of a young child waiting for Christmas. We live in a world of promises of the great things that wait for us, not when God comes to us, but when we go to God. It is hard to imagine what that untroubled life will be like, so immersed are we in the daily anxieties of this life. But we must believe that such a perfect life of happiness is possible. Christ has promised it and because he is God we know that what he has promised can come to be. The catch is that, for the promises to be fulfilled in the next life, we must love God and neighbor in this life. Though we may fail at this on occasion, like a child on Christmas we will not be denied our presents because we have been unable to be always good.

December 9

The Example of Jesus

Jesus came into this world so that he could give an example to those looking upward to God, an example to those looking downward at the wonder of being human, an example to the healthy to persevere, an example to the sick to be made whole, an example to those about to die that they might not fear, an example to the dead that they might look forward to rising again.

The Trinity, 7.3.5

One of the great benefits of God becoming a human being in the person of Jesus Christ was that as Jesus lived out his thirty-three years on earth he was an example of the greatness that could be part of human life. He was an example of the joy that comes from having a mother and father who truly loved you. He was an example of how one could add to the joy of weddings and be a support to the bereaved at funerals. He was an example of how one could die with hope. And, finally, he was an example of how we shall be on the day of our resurrection. Indeed, through the example of Jesus Christ we have learned much about God and about ourselves. For this lesson we should be eternally thankful.

December 10

Christ Was Born; We Are Reborn

We were mortal and weighed down by sins and their punishment. As a result, every human being begins this life with misery. Look at the child as it is born and see how it cries. The Lord Christ is forever God and yet on

Christmas he was born as a human being. Unless he had a human birth, we would never attain to divine rebirth. Jesus was born that we might be reborn. Let nobody hesitate to accept this gift of rebirth. His mother bore him in her womb; let us bear him in our hearts. The virgin was big with the body of Christ; let our hearts grow big with the faith of Christ. We must not be barren; now reborn, our souls must bear the fruit of God.

Sermon 189, 3

Augustine's words above are more than pious poetry. They point to an important fact about the coming of Christ. His being born allowed us to be reborn. When humans were first born into paradise they were innocent and pure. They lived with God and in God, but original sin undid this, causing death. Just as a dead person cannot give themselves life, so we on our own were unable to awaken the life of God within us. Thus the birth of Jesus brought with it the possibility of rebirth for us. Once again the gates of heaven were open to us, but to get there we must nourish our reborn life and let it enliven the world around us.

December 11

God Wanted Many Children

Many men in advanced age, when they have not had sons, adopt them. They do by choice what they could not do by nature. When a human being has an only son, he tends to rejoice all the more because he knows that this son alone will possess everything and will have no one who can demand a portion of the inheritance and thereby leave the natural son poorer. With God it is not so. Into this world he sent his Divine Son whom he had begotten from eternity and through whom he had created all things. He did this so that his Son would not be an only child but would gain many adopted brothers and sisters.

Commentary on the Gospel of John, 2.13.1

God created so as to bestow his love on beings other than himself, free beings who might possibly return that love. When those free beings (angels and humans) rejected that love, he sent his divine son to bring them back and even "adopt" them as brothers and sisters. Of course they could not be brothers and sisters by nature, only by adoption. They were not God but they could now choose to be like God by bringing God into their lives and hearts. Now God could look into their spirits and see his reflection there and say, "These indeed are part of my family."

December 12

Christ Has Become Our Neighbor

What is so far away from human beings as God, not by space but by unlikeness? But then this Immortal and Just One (who was so far away) came down to us sinful mortals and became our near neighbor. In order to be our near neighbor, he took on our punishment and by taking on our punishment (but not our sins) he canceled both sin and punishment. Now we can say with Paul, "The Lord is very near, do not be anxious about anything" (Philippians 4:5-6). Even though he has ascended to heaven in his body, he has not withdrawn his presence. He is present everywhere.

Sermon 171, 3

It is an amazing fact that God, by becoming human, has become our neighbor. He shared our human life and walked the same paths that we walk. It is an astonishing fact that he came so far to be our neighbor, especially because we are not always that neighborly to each other, even in the religious life. And yet God has chosen to come to us as a neighbor, an unobtrusive neighbor at that, one we can ignore if we want. At the same time he stays nearby and deep in our sometimes anxious hearts; it is comforting to know that he is near.

December 13

Unbelievable Births

The birth of Christ from his Divine Father was without mother; the birth of Christ from his earthly mother was without father. Each birth was wonderful. The first was eternal; the second took place in time. Why be astonished? He is God. Take divinity into consideration and any reason for astonishment disappears. When we say he was born of a virgin, you are again astonished. He is God and so, again, don't be astonished. Let astonishment give way to thanksgiving and praise. Let faith be present; believe that it happened.

Sermon 189, 4

The fact that Jesus Christ entered human history long ago is uncontested; how he arrived is hard to understand. Even more difficult is the question of what he was doing before he was conceived in the womb of the virgin Mary. Our faith gives us a direct answer: he existed from all eternity as the Son of God. Once we accept this, then his entrance into human history can also be accepted, though of course by faith. How can we be surprised by Jesus Christ being conceived by the power of the Holy Spirit in the womb of Mary when we believe that he is Almighty God? It is God who in the beginning determined how human beings would be generated. If he has the power to determine the general rule, certainly he has the power to go beyond that rule for good cause, and the cause in this case was to make clear that Jesus Christ was indeed God now existing as a human being.

December 14

The Humble Christ-Child

Jesus-God agreed to become a human being; what more do you want? Hasn't God humbled himself enough for you? The one who is God has become a human being. The inn for travelers was crowded and cramped, so he was wrapped in rags and placed in a manger. Who would not be astonished? Imagine, the one who fills the universe with his presence could not find any room in a Bethlehem inn. He chose to be placed in a manger for feeding animals, this God who was (on Holy Thursday) to become our food.

Sermon 189, 4

The greatest mystery of Christmas is not *how* God became a human being but *that* he became a human being. How low can a God get! We are told that he became human because he loved us, but could he not have shone his love in a more dignified way? Of course he could, but instead he chose to appear in this world as the child of a poor couple who apparently not only could not find space in the public inn but who could not even find a friend or relative to take them in, and this in a town where both of them had roots. Why did God choose to enter history as a homeless child? The answer is that he wanted to demonstrate a virtue needed for salvation—humility. If we don't go through life pretending in one way or another that we are God, then at the end of our time God himself will come to take us home.

December 15

The Animals at the Manger

Consider the two animals at the manger. The prophet wrote "The ox recognizes its owner and the donkey its master's manger" (Isaiah 1:3). The animals teach us that we should not be ashamed of being the Lord's beast of burden. Carrying Christ, you cannot go astray. Let the Lord sit upon us and take us wherever he wants. With him seated on us we are not weighed down but lifted up. With him guiding us, we can't go wrong.

Sermon 189, 4

Isaiah seems to suggest that the animals recognized who Christ was. What a paradox! Not even Mary and Joseph knew that. For certain the people of the town did not know. It was fitting that animals should be at Christ's birth because the coming of God to this world was reason for rejoicing for all of nature. I wonder if that donkey was the same one who later on carried Mary and the baby into Egypt and then brought them back to Nazareth when it was safe. If it was, and if it could somehow understand, the donkey must have felt that the burden was light. We know that carrying Jesus throughout this world does not crush us; rather, it lifts us up. In any case it was nice that animals were present at Christ's birth. Children love animals.

December 16

Christ Seeks His Image in Us

What vestiges of the image of God remained in humans after sin? They had worn down that image by their sinful lives. Just as a coin when rubbed with earth eventually loses the images on it, so too the human spirit constantly rubbed with earthly lusts eventually loses God's image. However, Christ, the master of the mint, came along to stamp the coins afresh. He did this by pardoning our sins.

Sermon 229W

In the beginning God imprinted a clear image of himself on the angels and human beings. Unfortunately it was not to last. Some of the angels rejected the image outright, preferring to gaze on their own self-created image in their darkened spirit. Humans walked away from paradise, to be sure, but their defection was not so radical. The image of God was still there, but it was gradually being rubbed away by the continuing friction of sin and despair. One of the reasons why God became human in the person of Jesus Christ was to restore that image. He did this by taking upon himself the burden of our sins so that they might be pardoned. Now, with a clean slate, he was able to begin again to imprint on each of us the brilliant image of God. It is up to us to make sure we do not dim it again by a sin-filled life. With the help of God's grace we can do that and become even more brilliant reflections of God.

December 17

Christ the Word

When I have an idea and want to communicate it to you, I use sound formed into words as an appropriate way to plant it in your mind. If I can speak my thoughts to you by my voice, could not the Word of God do the same through his flesh? That's why the Word of God, the Wisdom of God abiding unchanged with the Father but seeking to communicate with us, looked to flesh as a kind of sound and inserted himself into it and became a man.

Consider how great and wonderful this was and take care
to think even more grandly about God, that unchanging
God who surpasses all sound, all meaning, all understanding.

Sermon 28, 5

From the very beginning God tried to speak to the human
race through revelation, through prophets, through sacred
writers. Finally he decided to speak to humans directly through
Jesus Christ, the Word of God. In becoming a human being
God was able to speak to us face to face. If he spoke to us only
through books or through teachers, it would be easier for us to
ignore the message. With Christ, however, we could not ignore
him. That some came to follow him, while others executed
him, suggests that the message got through.

December 18

Listening Humbly to the Word

You ask what sort of God Jesus Christ is? Listen to me, or
rather listen with me. Listen to John telling us what sort
of God Christ is: "In the beginning was the Word and the
Word was with God" (John 1:1). Let nobody stop seeking
but let's all make progress. We can only make progress by
seeking seriously, not frivolously. We seek seriously by
believing; we seek frivolously by arguing. If you want to
argue with me saying, "What sort of God do you worship? Show me what you worship." I will answer, "Even
if there were something I could show you, you are not
ready to be shown."

Sermon 261, 2

The problem of human communication is illustrated by two
old codgers arguing passionately about something inconsequential. Finally one said: "I may have to listen to you but I

don't have to pay attention!" This is how we react sometimes to the Word of God telling us how to live. Sometimes we don't understand out of obstinacy. We say, "He can't be right because he disagrees with me!" At other times we do understand what the Lord is saying, but it is simply too difficult to bear. The coming of Jesus solved only part of the problem in God seeking to communicate with us. Now he needs to clear out our ears so we can hear, and cleanse our hearts so that we will want to understand.

December 19

Christmas Paradoxes

The Word of the Father who created all time, by becoming human created for himself a birthday in time. He with the Father existed before the vast extent of time; he through his mother Mary inserted himself into the passing procession of time. He the Creator of humans, he the Ruler of the Heavens, became human so he might become a baby at the breast, so that he the Divine bread might be hungry, so that he the Fountain of life might be thirsty, so that he the Eternal Light might fall asleep, so that he the Way might be weary from a journey. God became a human being so that the Truth might be accused by false witness and the Judge of the living and the dead be judged by a mortal judge. He became human so that strength might be shown as weak, that the author of life might die.

Sermon 191, 1

A paradox is a statement that appears contradictory, but in fact is not. Christianity is full of paradoxes. There is the first paradox that God, the infinite being, would reach down and create humans out of nothing. The second is that, after humans walked away from God, God would run after them, become one of them, and suffer for them in order that they might have a chance to return to paradise. Added to these are the string of paradoxes Augustine mentions above that flow from God becoming a human being. Our faith tells us that these seemingly contradictory facts not only may be true, but *are* true.

December 20

Christmas Honors Both Sexes

Since he created both sexes God wished to honor both sexes in his birth because he loved and came to save both. He wished to approve both sexes by honoring both because in Eden both had been tarnished by the stigma of sin. Creation is not denigrated by either sex and the birth of the Lord encouraged both to hope for salvation. The glory of the male sex was reflected in Christ being born a man; the glory of the female sex was reflected in his immaculate mother Mary.

Sermon 190, 2

Augustine in his many writings makes it very clear that men and women are equal by nature. Both sexes are called to serve God and both are destined for heaven. At the same time each sex has its own gifts and its own part to play especially in the generation, education, and protection of future generations. For example, it was a woman who nourished Christ in her womb, nurtured him as a child, and cherished him as an adult. Christ's gender bespeaks the dignity of men. Joseph's role in the upbringing of Jesus highlights the function of men as protectors of the weak. All in all, Christmas was a time of celebration for both man and woman because Christ had come to save them both.

December 21

Awake Mankind!

Awake mankind! God became a human being to save you
from death. If he had not been born in time, a happy eternal life would have been impossible for you. You never
would have escaped your sins if he had not taken on your
humanity. It was only through his mercy that you escaped
eternal unhappiness. You would have perished, had he
not come. And so, let us joyfully celebrate the coming of
our salvation and redemption. Let us celebrate the festive
day on which Jesus-God, he who is the great and Eternal
Day, came from the great and endless day of eternity into
our own short day of time.

Sermon 185, 1-2

After the loss of paradise the human race was in a sort of
stupor, so concerned about getting through this life that they
did not even dream of a happy life in heaven. Of course the
prophets spoke of a conquering Lord who would return as a
protector of his people, but most understood it to mean that he
would come as a great king to restore Israel to its dominance.
When Christ came even many of his disciples still expected an
earthly king, eager to restore Israel to the glory of her past.
Humans were not dreaming of a new life beyond death, but a
more peaceful life here. Thus, when God came as man his most
difficult task was to "wake up" human beings to their eternal
destiny. Some believed; for others it just seemed too good to be
true.

December 22

Strength Took on Weakness

Let us announce the coming of our Savior with joy! He lies in a manger but he holds the world in his hands; he is nourished at the breast of his mother but he feeds the angels; he is wrapped in swaddling clothes but he clothes us with immortality. He could not find room in the Bethlehem Inn but he now makes a temple for himself in the hearts of believers. We should not look down on his human birth but marvel that it occurred. On Christmas strength took on weakness that weakness might become strong. From his human birth let us come to understand how God emptied himself for our sake.

Sermon 190, 3

One of the many unbelievable aspects of Christmas was that a God of infinite power should take on the weakness of being a human—not the weakness of a powerful king, but the weakness of the poor. Why did God do this? If he had come as a powerful potentate, humans would not have executed him, thus frustrating the drama of our redemption. Perhaps it was also necessary to teach us an important lesson about our own lives, the lesson that having earthly power is not as important as the wealth we have in our souls. We will be saved not because of our successful lives but because in dying we did not turn away from God.

December 23

Growing Up with Christ

The one who regulates the movement of the stars is suckled at his mother's breasts. He is silent in his mother's womb but he is going to speak and create the gospel story for us when he reaches the right age. Look at the child lying in the manger. He made himself small but did not lose his divine identity. Choosing to become human, Jesus-God took on what he was not, but remained what he was. There you have it. On Christmas we see Christ as an infant. Let us grow up with him.

Sermon 196, 3

The first miracle of Christ's coming was that he was conceived and born. The second miracle was that he survived. Apart from the high mortality rate of children in that society, Jesus had the added threat of a king who was bound and determined to kill him before his second birthday. But he did survive and he grew to a point at which he was able to be taken seriously as a teacher. Augustine's message is that, just as the baby Jesus grew up, so too must we allow him to grow in us as a teacher, consoler, and savior. If we stifle his growth in our hearts, we will never come to hear what he wants us to do with our lives.

December 24

Light Shining in Darkness

Christmas is the day on which the Creator of the universe came into this world. This is the day on which the one who is always present through his power became present in the flesh. He came in the flesh with the intention of curing human blindness so that once we were healed we might be enlightened in the Lord (Ephesians 5:8). Then God's light would no longer be shining in darkness but would appear plainly to people who wanted to see it.

Sermon 195, 2

God was always present in the universe from its very beginning. Just as his power was the force that created it, that same power preserves it. Though many humans would come to realize God's existence as a God of power, no one could imagine that God existed in this world as a God of love, that he existed deep in the hearts of all those humans who were trying to live good lives. He came as a human being to show us his love. He wanted to convince us that he knew what it was to live as a human being and to promise us that he had a heavenly life prepared for us. The message of Christmas is not simply that God *is*, but that God *cares!*

December 25

Glory to God!

The angels sang "Glory to God in the highest, and on earth peace among men of good will." Let us reflect on these wonderful words and the event they celebrate, the birth of Jesus-God. To the extent that we believe and desire and hope in this life we give added glory to "God in the highest" and, after our resurrection, we shall be lifted up body and soul to meet Jesus. This will happen if we with good will work for peace while we are here on earth.

Sermon 193, 1

On Christmas day the angels sang of "peace on earth" to men of good will. It is a great song but on some days it seems unrealistic. Men and women of good will are often trampled upon by men and women of ill will. But it is important to remember that the angels were singing on the day when God almighty was born as a human being into this sometimes disordered world. His coming changed things. For those who believed in him, we are able to hope because God now lives with us. It was a hope based on his promise that if we are truly of good will in this life, we eventually will achieve the perfect peace of heaven. In the meantime we have our Christmas to celebrate, the feast that proves that God loves us even when our will is not so good.

December 26

Peace in the Family

> Greek mythology describes a man called Cacus. His kingdom was only the solitude of a horrifying cave. He had no wife to exchange soft words with him, no tiny children to play with, no older ones he could instruct. He had no friendly human whose company he could enjoy. All alone in his cave, he longed only for some peace, a peace which no force could take away, a restful peace free of fear.
>
> *City of God,* 19.12

Augustine's description of the monster Cacus's plight suggests that the peace he sought could not be found because he was without a family. It is easy to understand his sadness. It is hard to find peace without a family. Once Christmas is over, and the visitors have left, all we are left with is the family in which to find our peace. There is an important message in all of this: God gave us family to get through the ordinary days of our lives when nothing much is happening, and the bad days when we feel very much alone. The consoling message of Christmas is that God is part of our family now, that God who is calling us to heaven where finally and forever we will be at home with our flesh and blood, Jesus Christ the Lord.

December 27

Peace in Heaven

In heaven all the good things that God has given us as human beings will reach the peak of their goodness and will stay that way forever. In heaven every wound suffered in spirit will be healed by unending wisdom and every illness of body will be overpowered by resurrection. In heaven our good urges will have free reign. We shall no longer be at war with out passions. Our "wanting" to do good will have no opposition. We shall once and forever enjoy undisturbed unending rest. That is what is meant by final, perfect happiness. To be sure, we have some happiness now, but compared to the happiness that we shall find after death the very true happiness that we experience sometimes in this life will seem almost misery by comparison.

City of God, 19.10

Part of our joy at Christmas comes not only because God came to *our* home to share our humanity, but that one day we will share the eternal joy of being in *his* home. It is hard to imagine what that joy will be like. Certainly it is hard to conceive of such bliss when we have had little in this life. But even if we have had a life filled with joy, the joy of heaven is still beyond our comprehension. Just now our joy is dampened when we realize that the times of joy, like all our times, are passing. The joy of heaven will be different. Not only will it have a fullness never experienced in this life, it will also be unending.

December 28

The Joy of Friendship

In this life so full of confusion and discord there is no greater consolation than the trust and love of truly good friends. And yet the more friends we have spread throughout the world the more we fear for them. Not only are we worried that they may be hurt by hunger or war or sickness, we worry even more that we will do something to lose their love. There are some who say that we should not weep when we lose a friend. If they wish to forbid this, then they had better be ready to forbid all playful talk among lovers. While they are at it, let them also make a law against feeling good in the presence of a loved one and deny us permission to be bound in any way to friends. Or better, let them insist that all tenderness cease between humans. If this cannot be managed then neither is it possible for us to avoid the taste of bitterness upon the loss of a loved one who had brought sweetness to our lives.

City of God, 19.8

To have a truly good friend is a great source of happiness. The trouble is that the more we love them, the more we fear their loss. The wonder of heaven is that friendships will continue without any fear. We will know those who truly love us and know that their love is eternal. We will never lose their love. We know this because God himself has promised it.

December 29

Christ Became Weak for Us

By taking on our humanity Christ reduced himself to weakness so that he might gather us under his wings. In this he was like a hen weakened for the sake of her chicks. How does the hen reduce herself to weakness? We know how she makes her whole body a fluffy muddle. Her wings droop, the feathers are relaxed and she looks almost ill over her chicks. This is maternal love, expressing itself as weakness. It is for this reason that Christ compared himself to a mother-hen when he cried out, "Jerusalem, Jerusalem, how often I wanted to gather your children to myself, as a hen gathers her chicks under her wings, but you would have none of it!" (Matthew 23:37). Christ took on weakness for our sake by becoming human and thereafter being crucified, despised, slapped, scourged, and pierced with a lance as he hung on the cross.

Commentary on Psalm 58/1, 10

Augustine's analogy comparing Christ's sacrifice to that of a mother-hen protecting her chicks is a powerful image. By becoming a human being Jesus weakened himself in an infinite manner. While remaining the all-powerful God, he put his divinity in abeyance so that it might not compromise the trials of being human. Just as the mother-hen weakens herself so that her helpless brood might have a chance to be independent adults like her, so Christ became human so that we might become an image of himself and thereby be prepared to share his life in heaven. We should pray that we be worthy of such sacrifice.

December 30

Surviving the Times of Our Lives

"The times are bad! The times are troublesome!" This is what humans say. But we are our times. Let us live well and our times will be good. Such as we are, such are our times.

Sermon 80, 8

We are called to value our life in this world so that we might enjoy the unending future that is ahead of us. This does not mean that we ignore today for the sake of some promised tomorrow. Indeed, God wants us to be happy even in this life. But we must enjoy our present times without letting our pleasure stand in the way of our future. To do this means to endure our bad times with as much hope and joy as we can. The message of Christ's coming is that God does indeed reign in this world and, no matter how good or bad our times may be now, the most important fact is that we humans are on the move. We are no longer stuck in one place. We are on the move again towards that place where finally and forever we shall be at home with our flesh and blood, Jesus Christ the Lord.

December 31

Passing Time

It is unthinkable that the years of our life just now be considered eternal; they never stand still. How much of this year do we have in our grasp, except the current day? The earlier days of this year have passed already, and we cannot hold onto them. The days in our future have not yet come. Suppose we say, "This moment." But it is gone even while we pronounce its syllables! How, then, can we hold onto our years? We should rather focus our thoughts on eternity where our lives are not measured by a succession of days that arrive and pass away.

Commentary on Psalm 76, 8

Today is the end of the beginning. Tomorrow we begin a new year, a year in which we can come closer to Christ or push him farther away. The coming of Christ marked a true "end of the beginning," that first phase of human history in which humans, now expelled from paradise, wandered the earth with no chance for eternal happiness. God took matters into his own hands by sending his Son, Jesus Christ, to live with us and die for us and thereby redeem us. Then humanity began the second stage of its history which constitutes the beginning of the end. As our time flies by we should remember that this is where we are going. God willing, we will accept our salvation and move smoothly through our times into the eternal happiness that awaits us.

Appendix

January

February

Made in the USA
Middletown, DE
13 July 2024